THE CHEESE
CHRONICLES

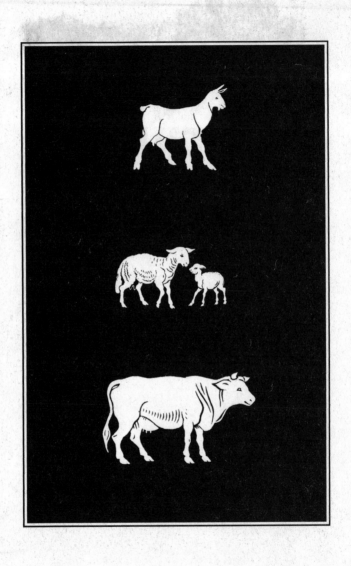

THE CHEESE CHRONICLES

A Journey Through the Making

and Selling of Cheese in America,

From Field to Farm to Table

Liz Thorpe

ecco

An Imprint of HarperCollinsPublishers

FIRST EDITION

Designed by Mary Austin Speaker

Library of Congress Cataloging-in-Publication Data
Thorpe, Liz, 1978-
The cheese chronicles : a journey through the making and selling of cheese in America, from field to farm to table / Liz Thorpe. — 1st ed.
    p. cm.
Includes bibliographical references.
ISBN 978-0-06-145116-4
1. Cheese—United States. 2. Cheesemaking—United States.
I. Title.
SF274.U6T52 2009
641.3'730973—dc22

2008053661

09 10 11 12 13 WB/RRD 10 9 8 7 6 5 4

For David
As the Big Bad Wolf said,
"All the better to see you with, my dear"

CONTENTS

LIST OF SIDEBARS

ACKNOWLEDGMENTS

There are so many folks to acknowledge, and it is with deep gratitude that I do so:

Captaining my team of advisers, Rob Kaufelt has given me every possible opportunity to make cheese my life, at Murray's and beyond. Plus he makes me laugh really hard, most of the time. Joe Moskowitz taught me everything about cheese behind the scenes. Dick Hecht has wisely and lovingly begun to shape my future.

I am blessed to work at a company with extraordinary people who love cheese and really take care of one another. The staff of Murray's Cheese backs me every day, and I am especially grateful to the management team taking this journey with me: Taylor Cocalis, Jason Donnelly, Christopher Fernando, Louise Geller, Frank Meilak, and Will Whitlow.

All the cheesemakers in this book and beyond who have taken time out of their exceedingly busy lives to talk to me, educate me, and show me their farms, with particular thanks to Mary Keehn, Mateo Kehler, Soyoung Scanlan, and Ig Vella.

My agent, Angela Miller; my editor, Emily Takoudes; my eleventh-hour editor, Ginny Smith; and my publisher, Dan Halpern, who have believed in and encouraged this project through its many evolving lives.

My dear friends: Clelia Peters, the sister I never had, who has kept the faith since freshman year in college; Angie Keefer; and Sister Goddesses Lisa and Mary.

And most important, my mother. I've got the best one out there and am tremendously blessed.

FOREWORD
by Steven Jenkins

I'm fifty-eight years old. I've lived in New York City for thirty-six years, since 1973, when I was just a twenty-two-year-old kid. In the late summer of 1975 I got a much-needed job in a cheese shop at 92nd Street and Madison Avenue. It could have been a pet shop in Greenwich Village, an East Side antique shop owned by some oddball, a kite store such as the one I had been working in not far away—I didn't care. Cheese had nothing to do with it. I decided I liked getting a regular paycheck and having something to do all day, so I resolved to do my very best to hold the job and pay the rent on my studio apartment, and not be a burden on my girlfriend (to whom I have now been married for twenty-seven years).

I became a maître fromager. In 1980, I became the first French-certified, practicing master cheesemonger in

North America. For all the years since then I've been up to my elbows and eyeballs in cheese and cheese-related substances. It is said I know whereof I speak. Last year I was given a lifetime achievement award by the American Cheese Society. I belabor my qualifications to state the following: Liz Thorpe has written a book about American cheese, and it is the best book about cheese you'll ever read. And I've read all of the books about cheese. My library is immense. Patrick Rance wrote a book about French cheese a number of years ago; he died recently after a long and fruitful life. Mr. Rance's book is magnificent and has been a huge influence on me for a long time. It's out of print, but it sells on eBay for many hundreds of dollars. Liz Thorpe's book has the same power and purpose that Rance's *The French Cheese Book* has. There are a number of new and newish books about cheese, among them Max McCalman's *Cheese*, that are excellent too. I have a raft of books about cheese written and published in Europe, and while clinical, they are very important. But to the reader who wishes to truly grasp and be exhilarated by the infinite connections between lyric beauty, the beast, the sky, the earth, and people, I cannot more fervently recommend these pages.

Liz's book tells you more about American cheese than my book ever did, that's for sure, and my book was the first to address the subject of artisanal American cheeses and cheesemakers. Liz's book goes way beyond the black-and-white static of my book. She makes the cheeses and the cheesemakers jump off the page. She teaches you how to look at a cheese, how to describe the flavors and fragrances of cheese, and what the nature and provenance and recipe of a cheese mean. I feel like I never even thought of these things until I read Liz's book, and that's flat-out amazing, because there is little else I have thought about for all these years, and I'm not exactly stupid. I'm not exactly without my own offices, so to speak.

What shames me most about this book is that I never appreciated how hard it is to do what these American cheesemakers do day in and day out, day after day, and how little they are remunerated for it. These folks have created an incomparable American heritage, and they have done so in an astonishingly short time. This fine book is a testament to that accomplishment, which is, or should be, what this country is all about.

FOREWORD
by Rob Kaufelt

For most Americans, the word "cheese" brings a smile to the face. Over time, the word itself has taken on a faintly humorous quality, as opposed to the French *fromage* or the Italian *formaggio*, which are proper food words and thus taken more seriously.

Which makes it all the more interesting—peculiar, in fact—that any intelligent young person coming out of one of our nation's leading centers of higher learning would ever consider seeking a career in cheese. Not law, not banking, not medicine, but cheese. Can a career in cheese truly be said to exist?

A decade ago, I would have said no. The business, such as it was, remained a last bastion of chauvinism, like the butcher shop, with old-timers manning the few service counters still left in New York. A few curmudgeons, like Steve Jenkins and myself, had been to college and wound up behind the counters like so many wheels of aged Parm. Although I'd purchased a small, old, dilapidated shop selling this comestible, I was without any pretension of calling it a career. No, I preferred the way Murray Greenberg, who named the shop after himself (Murray's, not Greenberg's), thought of it: "It's a living."

That was before Liz Thorpe came along. I date the modern cheese era from her arrival back in 2002. It began to seem possible, if not likely, that what we did was more than a job or a living, and certainly not a joke. Something worthy, something that one might take a little more seriously than had been the case up until now. Liz has led the way to a whole new career path for her generation, opened it up to women, too, and begun to professionalize our craft.

Yet even though I witnessed it, enabled it, and encouraged it, the whole thing still remains a mystery to me. As with my colleagues of a certain age, I am often compelled to political incorrectness, if only to feebly maintain my turf, having come of age in the time of women, yet having sought refuge in a man's world. How, I wonder, does an adorable blond Yalie with a nose ring take charge of a cheese revolution, write two books about it, arm-twist it into the modern age, introduce it into the nation's largest supermarket chain, and take over the daily operations of New York's premier cheese retailer, all before the age of thirty?

And having done so, she now pied-pipers a slew of even younger women (and a few men) who follow her, leaving me shaking my head in wonder and nodding in agreement over (most) of what she does. Learn from this, all you young investment bankers! Passion for your craft trumps money in any person with self-respect and true talent.

Truly, a mystery. But I am not one to look a gift horse in the mouth, preferring to see myself as mentor to this remarkable young woman whose words you will read in these pages. The chefs already know her—she sold them cheese for years when she was still a kid. The mongers know her—she was one of them once. The cheesemakers know her—she knows their work better than anyone else.

So read about it here, folks, I give you Liz Thorpe, who will be your very own cheese guide here in America for many years to come.

A NOTE ON METHODOLOGY

If I had to guess how many cheesemakers there are in America, I would put the number somewhere between five hundred and one thousand. The number of cheeses this entire group makes? Who knows? Into the thousands, for sure. Over the years, I've tasted cheese from hundreds of producers and have struggled to decide which to include here. Those I have selected are the clearest illustrations of the past, present, and future of American cheese. They're the people I know best, but also the people who define what matters most in cheesemaking (food making) in the United States: history, tradition, dedication to the local community, animal husbandry, grass feeding. But I couldn't just pick the virtuous cheesemakers. In the end, the final litmus test was my mouth. Above and beyond all things, good cheese must taste delicious. All the history and marketing in the world can't make a bad cheese taste good, which is why I've only included those I can say I would happily buy. For every farm and factory not listed here, I look forward to tasting soon.

THE CHEESE CHRONICLES

INTRODUCTION

When I was a little girl, I would come downstairs in the morning and look for evidence of my father. If I was lucky, I would find a tall glass, half full of water, and a small plate of cheese crumbs—tough edges of forgotten white cheddar. If the dog hadn't beaten me to it, I would snatch up the hard ends, in their peculiar combination of dry-yet-greasy from sitting out all night. That cheese was Cracker Barrel. Extra sharp. And always white. The yellow kind was somehow inferior in our house. When my parents had company, which happened maybe twice a year, I got the fancy stuff. Boursin, the garlic herb spread, which I could have (and probably did) eat by the containerful, and pristine white supermarket Brie, which I hated. It tasted like plastic.

Junior year of college, my friend Garrett came by, on

the eve of a semester abroad in Senegal. We were still too young to drink legally but old enough to desperately want to. Sharing a bottle of wine over lunch seemed profoundly sophisticated. That afternoon we'd gotten one somewhere, and I'd put together a spread from *The Moosewood Cookbook*. Living in an off-campus apartment, I'd taken up cooking and wanted to feed Garrett. She brought a small white lump of goat cheese. Chèvre, she called it, which only added to the glow of cosmopolitanism because she would spend her time in Africa speaking French. I don't remember what I made, but I do recall eating an obscene amount of the cheese, something I'd never had before. I marveled at each tangy, cream-cheesy smear, swiping it across hunks of baguette and laughing my head off as we sipped glasses of rough white and talked about culture and politics. It was heady stuff.

That is my history with cheese. My introduction to chèvre was a little more than a decade ago. I've always liked to eat, a lot, and I've always eaten everything, generally with great gusto. Cheese is no exception, nor had it ever been anything exceptional. I got into cheese because I thought it would make me cool. That's my big career confession. Some people choose their jobs because they want to make a lot of money, and other people go after gigs with great perks or because they want to save the world. Initially, I picked my job because it was odd and I generally enjoy being the person at a dinner party who has a good story to tell. It's much more satisfying to say, "I do cheese," than to say, "I am a corporate lawyer."

In addition to making me kooky and intriguing, "doing cheese" makes me likable because, it seems, everyone I meet really likes cheese. It's a food that moves people and engages them. It's much more compelling than, say, microgreens. No one cares if you know more about microgreens than anyone in the world. If you're an expert in heirloom tomatoes, that's more interesting, and if you make your own cured meats, you'll win fans with all but the vegetarians. But none of it is as compelling as cheese. Every person I have met in the past ten years wants to know more about cheese. Every dinner party I've attended, every class I have taught, every chat I've had through Match.com. They all want to talk about cheese. Everyone has a favorite, everyone has a story, everyone asks if I know that cheese, the-white-and-soft-and-really-good one that they had at their cousin's wedding last summer.

There is only one exception. One true exception, and even he is coming around. He's an exception simply because he hates cheese and that is a great anomaly. That's my friend Macky McCleary. When Macky first came to see me at work in 2002, behind the counter of Murray's Cheese on a hot, still, summer evening, he walked in the door, paused, turned, and walked out. I joined him on the old red bench we still have outside the shop, and he turned to me, stricken. Macky's intonation is a ringer for James Earl Jones's, and in his deep baritone he said, "Elizabeth, you have taken this job just to spite me." Macky eats cheese only on his pizza. He's crazy, but we've known that since college. But to his credit, when I brought a rank, funky French round to his apartment and lied and told him it tasted like mozzarella he gamely agreed to try it. I immediately felt guilty and told him he should start on something a little milder. Even Macky, who has lived thirty-plus years in intense food fear, is coming around to the idea that there just might be a cheese out there for him. It's a wondrous thing that cheese, made from three simple ingredients, manages to offer ten thousand faces, tastes, and even smells.

My point is, something about cheese speaks to people, the way it spoke to me when I was trying to get out of my fluorescent-lit cubicle in midtown Manhattan. At the end of the day, at the end of the year, I know I'm not ready to leave my job because I still love all those cheeses. When I take the time to look at them, lined up in the shiny glass case, they're like little people. There are the fat, runny ones, and I worry that no one will take them home and eat them in time. There are the austere, intellectual cheeses that require patient consideration to "get" and appreciate. There are the loud, flashy ones, like the Bentleys of cheese, that everyone, every time, is impressed by, and of which even the people who don't care about cars acknowledge the solid engineering.

They all look different, and down in the caves at Murray's each wheel contributes its mold spores and earthen reek to the walls and air, slowly seasoning the damp wood shelving. In the goat cave, dozens of small rounds and pyramids gradually grow fur, evolving into something minerally and hay-ey, with a milky creamline under their tricolor rinds. It's like watching the grass grow, only you can, because every day the cheeses change.

It's like that at the cheesemakers' as well. One room devoted to a single cheese, or maybe a handful of cheeses, each wheel struggling to become something really memorable. The young wheels are all white and crumbly, naked, with the beginnings of gray mold or red bacteria that look like some invasive virus taking over. Farther down the aisle are the teenagers, mature enough to play dress-up but tasting wobbly and shallow, with no depth or character. In the evening in any cheese cave, when the floors have been swept and the shelves scrubbed down, you can walk through and see the orderly rows, all labeled and resting on their racks, like children put to bed.

I love to drink, and I buy wine and cellar it, but there's something so sterile about all those glass bottles. They're not alive like cheese, and I like them best when they're held in the worst condition, high humidity, so the labels begin to mold and peel. Then, beneath the sticky cobwebs of my mother's basement, they begin to develop personality. Perhaps that's why I'm such a sucker for a good label. Looking at one's elegant and refined cursive letters next to another's blocky font with a big red wagon, you catch a glimpse of the bottles' souls.

I was lured into cheese by a glass case with all its lactic oddities. The case in question still exists, in a store that's been a Brooklyn staple for longer than I've been alive. It was on Court Street, at Staubitz Meat Market, that I met my first cheese case. I still live in the neighborhood, and I still shop at Staubitz, but it was in the beginning that my heart went atwitter when I examined the cheese. Back then I was shopping for Easter dinner, the first I cooked in New York, for company, and I wanted a real New York spread of cheese for my guests. The idea that Staubitz cut each cheese to order, that all I had do was point and indicate with my thumb and forefinger how slender a wedge I'd like . . . it was so European and exquisite. As I am wont to do when food shopping, I bought four times as many cheeses as I needed—such excessive overkill that only two were consumed in their entirety.

That cheese case was one small lesson in my education of how food used to be before Stop & Shop, where my culinary adventures had hithertofore been conducted. That Easter I also bought my first raw ham. I did not know that deli ham is cooked and "ham" itself is simply a pig's thigh. When I unwrapped my "ham," it turned out to be a huge roll of pinkish meat covered with a very thick slab of skin, which looked just like, well, skin. With some hairs still on it. In my horror and paranoia I briefly thought the butcher had played a mean joke on me and given me an animal head. In Stop & Shop the ham does not have hair. I had no idea. Though I still shop at that butcher, Esposito & Sons, who, by the way, make the rosiest, porkiest soppressata I have ever eaten, liberally laced with big chunks of creamy white fat, I did not fall in love with meat. I did, however, develop a little crush on cheese.

Enter a no-bullshit guy named Steve Jenkins. Steve is an incredibly ornery, semideaf and therefore loud, often filthy-mouthed, always sarcastic guy with a wicked sense of humor, who happens to be primarily responsible for the introduction of great imported cheese into New York City, and therefore the United States. He ran the cheese counter at Dean & DeLuca in the 1980s, when the rest of the country was congratulating itself on rotisserie chicken. Steve, meanwhile, was running around Europe buying from all these farms and cooperatives, many of which remain the definitive producers of the best European cheese today. Once, at a swanky awards reception, Steve lit a cigarette, carefully cupping it in his hand when he wasn't taking efficient, furtive drags. Some organizer ran around the room trying to bust the wiseass upstart chef who was smoking inside, and Steve just smiled at me. He may have started great cheese in America, but he's also like your cool bad big brother. And he wrote a book called the *Cheese Primer*, which is still, more than a decade after its publication, a classic and one of the best cheese books on the market.

Being a good student with a growing fondness for cheese, I bought Steve's book and decided that what I would do was go work for him. By that point he was running Fairway on the Upper West Side, so I resolved to go to Fairway, where Steve would hire me, and then I could really taste all these cheeses and learn them, because it's so hard to learn food from only reading a book. I called Steve, and damn if he didn't call me back and invite me to come up and interview for a job. My head already knew where this was going. I was going to impress Steve with my acumen, and he was going to hire me to be his assistant/cheese apprentice, and we were going to travel together (or sometimes he was going to send me because he was too busy) and my job would consist of roaming small Provençal roads and doing research, and making serious, thoughtful consideration of the virtues of cheese. It's a pretty long subway ride from Brooklyn to the Upper West Side.

When I got to Fairway I was nervous, because this was such a huge job for such a young person and I really wanted to nail the whole thing down. Fairway is my nightmare store because it's absolutely stuffed with good things to buy, big displays, shelves of glass jars with goose rillettes and pickled vegetables and rosewater jellies, so I'm constantly looking everywhere, except in front of me, and dozens of pushy ladies are elbowing their way past me to the pyramid of parsnips just over there.

Steve walked me around, showed me the cheese corner, with its warm and pungent cloak, and then took me up to his desk, where he made The Offer. The Offer was that I could come work part-time on the cheese counter with the middle-aged men who'd been there for years. I could earn minimum wage and fumble to cut exact pieces of crumbly blue cheese while those same pushy ladies glowered and warned me against pawning off old cheese or too much cheese or the wrong cheese. And if I was good, Steve said, we could see where things went. I was twenty-one. I took six seconds to look around before I thanked him and got the hell out of there. Clearly, I was going to go work for a dot-com.

Having no idea what to do with your life is one of the worst feelings in the world. I used to think hating your job was the worst, and it's true, that's also pretty bad. But direction-lessness trumps that. It causes inaction, which means you remain in the (fill in the blank): awful job, unfulfilling relationship, cramped apartment that looks out on an air shaft, town you grew up in . . . because those things are familiar and the alternatives seem at best clear but impossible and at worst elusive and foggy. Just being miserable isn't enough. You have to get miserable enough to take action, because no one can come along and make the change happen for you. After meeting Steve Jenkins I found a "real" job, but not before I spent the Christmas season working at the East Side uptown food mecca Eli's Manhattan. In a noble effort at networking, I'd called my best friend's mother, the only New Yorker I knew, and praise be if she didn't sit on the board at a prestigious elementary school attended by the children of Eli Zabar. From there it was a short hop to meeting the mother of Eli Zabar's children: his wife, Devon. A tiny sprite of a woman who worked her butt off behind closed doors at Eli's, Devon ran the holiday mail order business, conducting the traffic of tens of thousands of dollars of food baskets sent to every dog walker, manicurist, hair salon, housecleaner, doorman, personal shopper, Hamptons gardener, and interior decorator who keeps the people of the Upper East Side afloat.

Devon's a wry lady, and though Eli scared me (and I think just about everyone else) with his preternaturally ice blue eyes and perennially pissed-off voice, Devon just sat on a stool with a long copper braid hanging down her back and a little knitted elf cap that kept her warm in the drafty back room. I spent a sum total of four weeks there, beginning each day with an escalator descent through the warm, humid flower room, down into the crowded basement overflowing with smoked fish, cheeses, and twelve-foot-high shelves of grainy, snappy flatbreads. Winding through to the back corner, there was a little staircase that took me up to my table, where I hunched in front of a computer and handwrote cards to the invisible forces that organize, beautify, and spoil Manhattanites. The job was nothing special, and I would be shocked if Devon even remembers who I am. But that walk in, and my lunchtime wanderings, made those days deeply satisfying.

The thing about Eli's, Fairway, the stalls down in Chinatown, and every other cramped, crowded, overstuffed grocery shop in New York is that people get fed there. The sheer enormity of choice is thrilling, the moist clouds of meaty, garlic-laden air that hang over pork haunches, the clear, golden juices that drip off golden-skinned chickens, the little tastes that are stolen, fruits that are fondled, meals that are carefully planned. All these shops are so intimate in their exchange of sustenance and knowledge, verdant olive oils dribbled onto bread so you can really understand the flavor profile of "green banana" or the way a well-made Camembert, even one of pasteurized milk, squashes around your tongue and releases its milky goodness, redolent of porcini mushrooms (uncooked) and mushy broccoli (overcooked).

Every job puts you on the inside of something, behind the scenes, where you know and tacitly understand all the tricks that form and power an enormously complex machine, when all the visitors see is a car. During the last December of the twentieth century I got to step behind the curtain of a glorious food machine, and I fell deeply in love. I also developed an addiction to Eli's Parmesan Crisps, which magnify all that is good about Parmigiano-Reggiano: its essential cheesiness, the perfect balance of salt, the almondine crunch, a bit of toastiness, a whiff of caramelized milk, and a general harmony that hovers on sweetness but maintains its essential savory identity. All this baked atop a thin, brittle, crunchy bread slice that is the greatest cracker thing I've ever had. I would never bastardize it by eating it with anything. Its perfection should be marred by nothing (except maybe a drink).

Being on the inside of the machine that builds Web sites for television and movie studios is of passing intrigue, mainly because you get to do things like see the first three episodes of *Six Feet Under* before they air on HBO, but the intrigue of the dot-com was not enough to sustain me for the year and a half I worked behind the scenes of that world. The intrigue lasted about four months, and the people who worked there took me through another few quarters. But mainly I stayed because I didn't know where else to go. I spent a few months harboring very deep resentment toward my mother who did not (the gall of her) offer to bankroll my entire life so I could just stop working because work really sucked. I talked about food sometimes but more often whined about not being able to do it. Finding a great job, the right job, was supposed to be obvious. But there was no cheese help-wanted posting on Monster.com. I tried Martha Stewart and thought about food magazines, but no one called back, and those jobs weren't the right fit for me anyway. How did one work in cheese? What did that even mean? With no clear path, no cheese alumnus to turn to, and only moderate commitment to get creative, it took fourteen months before I resumed my search, in earnest, for a job in cheese.

By then I knew New York a little better, so I knew to call Murray's Cheese. I had never been to Murray's Cheese, mind you, but I knew people who had been. It's amazing to me how much more focused kids are today then I ever was. People call me, and they've been to gastronomic university in Italy, they've interned with cheesemakers, they've gone to culinary school to become well rounded. I didn't even know who Murray was, but I did know how to use the Internet, and so I found my way to a guy named Rob Kaufelt. I called to ask if he could find half an hour to meet with me on an impeccable early-spring day and tell me how one gets into cheese. I met him at his tiny, overflowing shop on the corner of Bleecker and Cornelia in the West Village. My purpose was to get information: what it would be like to really understand the differences between the fetid, squidgy cheeses and the firm, noble ones? How did one learn cheese? I was prepared for a deeply important meeting of the minds.

A few words about Rob: Rob is a good-looking guy with a modernized D.A. (my mom's charming fifties-ism "duck's ass," where the tousled hair feathers along the back of the head). In Rob's case, the D.A. comprises the crest of his head, more like a rooster's comb. With his jeans, it fits right into the messy charm of the Village. Rob used to have one of the shortest attention spans of anyone I knew, which meant he asked ten million questions to keep himself engaged in the conversation. He seems to have mellowed with age, but talking to Rob used to feel like a double espresso at 3 P.M.: the initial rush, accelerated heartbeat, and dilated pupils quickly followed by the crash, where I wished I hadn't gotten into the thing in the first place. Rob interrogated me on the bench out front, barked at me for not bringing a résumé (I wasn't looking for a job, just information!), asked me where I was born, what my parents did, what I studied in college, did I like Bob Dylan, had I been to the Grey Dog for coffee, did I know Dave Van Ronk, the local folkie who gave him guitar lessons, did I know Dave Van Ronk used to play with Bob Dylan, did I know that his friend Fred Plotkin had just finished a new book, where was his PR girl (she should be here, she lives just around the corner!), had I tried that new smoked ricotta they'd just imported, reminded me that I should have brought a résumé, and generally avoided or otherwise did not answer every carefully crafted question I posed to learn more about working in food. Finally, he hit his limit (I think I lasted seventeen minutes) and told me that if I really wanted to work in cheese I should go work an event for him, that afternoon, in celebration of his friend Fred Plotkin's new book, giving people tastes of that new smoked ricotta he'd just imported.

Now, the knowing cynic in me recognizes that Rob is no dummy, and on a gorgeous, gently warm Saturday the last thing he wanted to do was stand in some Union Square wine shop and pass out cheese samples to people. The optimist in me fondly recalls that he saw I had potential. The truth lies somewhere in between. Regardless, he told me I could work an event that very day featuring the cheeses from "Free-ooo-lee-ah Julia" (turns out it was cheese from Friulia Venezia Giulia, Italy). I was high as a kite. I was also, on that fateful Saturday, roundly rejected from the one Ph.D. program I had applied to in my blind groping for professional direction. The event went well. The decision, it seemed, was made. The way one gets into cheese, like everything in life, is to get into it. Rob offered me a job at Murray's Cheese, working behind the counter, for minimum wage, with a bunch of middle-aged men. This time, I said yes.

The first tasting notes I ever wrote on cheese were from that event, hosted at a now-nonexistent place called Vino, on 122 East Twenty-second Street, Saturday, March 9, 2002. I carried a leatherbound journal with me, and jotted down reminders to get me through the afternoon:

1. *Smoked ricotta: for cooking (salads, pasta).*
2. *Montasio (type of cheese; popular; government-controlled name): "toffee flavor." Grassy edge, liked better over time.*
3. *Cividale (town).*

The next night, thrilled that I was slated to join the exclusive ranks of true cheesemongers, I went to my local gourmet store, a little shop called Tuller's, which is also now defunct. Alone in my house, I was on a roll:

1. *Reblochon: hard rind; slightly nutty, barn smell; milder taste than 2; pleasantly smelly.*

2. *Taleggio: total funk smell—barnyard—meaty—mellower taste; soft, not runny; eewy gooey and yum.*
3. *Roquefort: very salty—TOO salty; a bit crumbly; sharp mold strain.*

The mystique of the Murray's machine began with the cheesy fog that shrouded every truckle, wedge, and wheel crammed in that tiny, eight-hundred-square-foot shop, and, like the sparkle of all new things, it devolved into the carnal funk that permeated every pair of jeans and beat-up top I wore to work. It was mere weeks before I reeked of work. The delicious and delightful nuances I had cherished as a sometime cheese consumer gathered beneath my fingernails. My prized Prada sneakers, purchased at my first New York City sample sale, became caked with an unidentifiable black scum that left me slipping on the ancient tile floor. The cheese pride I had thrown my arms wide open to shriveled under the dismissive comments of chic young women who swept through the store, loudly announcing that they were in a rush and couldn't someone else help them, as I labored to slice through crumblingly uncooperative slabs of cold butter-blue Roquefort. I felt awkward, unskilled, grimy, and uncouth.

The men of Murray's were surprisingly tender. Cielo, who nowadays sports a Day-Glo goatee and has been known to dye leopard spots on his head, quickly taught me his shrieking routine: "You want cheese? Ah, sorry. We only have fromage today [or queso, or formaggio]." "You see this goat cheese? It's very special, it comes from all the way across the river in a little place called Brooklyn."

Tony was gay and British, with bulging green eyes and a sharply hooked nose. He greeted everyone the same way: "Hello, darling," which drove the women crazy (in a good way) and drove their swarthy, hulking boyfriends crazy (in a crazy way). The pinnacle of Tony's flirtations came one Sunday in July when he pointed out a wedge of Brie that had been cut and stacked atop a larger, three-kilo wheel. It was languishing in the heat, its golden insides bulging against their plasti-wrapped restraints. Lying limp, its pointed tip slowly melting over the edge of the counter, the Brie was ripe for the taking. Or, as Tony knowingly pointed out to the next tourist from New Jersey who walked in the door, "Darling, take this one. It looks just like an old man on the [nude] beach at Fire Island." Mmmmmmm. Now that's the way to sell cheese.

Willie came to my rescue when the bitchy girl demanded I hurry up and cut the Roquefort, and Frankie taught me how to do everything: cut it, wrap it, and ring it up. But it was Francis whom I loathed and admired. He knew everything about cheese and could answer every customer's question. He was the guy you called when someone came in wanting to pair cheese with a legitimately priceless bottle of Bordeaux; he hustled over to help the Mafia guys buying only the best and most expensive Italian cheeses, and he was then tipped a careless twenty in thanks. Francis was covered with neon tattoos and could rattle off the dates that all the cheeses of France received name protection, he could perfectly imitate everyone on staff until you couldn't breathe for laughing so hard, and he had what I perceived to be the greatest honor of all. He wrote Murray's famous cheese signs:

Durrus: smelling like a sailor on shore leave
Tetilla (Spanish for "tit"): breast-shaped, albeit a
     robotic breast
Roquefort: sheep's milk transmogrified . . . into soothing
     milky lozenges

It was all so effortless for Francis. I wanted to *be* him, yet I feared and somewhat hated him. Francis was pure poison, and just when I thought we were buddies he would bite me in the ass so hard I'd slink to the other end of the counter and meekly slice salami and scoop feta for several days. The guy was bitter and pissed off, and with him, the ground was always shaky. Couple this with the fact that retail is hard. You stand on your feet all day, watching the rest of New York slurp ice cream cones on a glorious Sunday morning while you press panini and bag cheese sticks. Your two days off don't come together, and no one else is around on the odd Monday and Thursday you find yourself free. The "offices" of Murray's required one to shimmy down stairs that were tantamount to a ladder into a windowless subterranean pit that I refused to show my mother for a year and that caused her to tersely point out (several times), when I did finally show her, that if there was a fire she had no question I would die in it. The money was crap, and the motley crew that had seemed novel and bizarre in the beginning grew to seem merely bizarre. I was hyperaware that I didn't fit in.

And then there was the true wild card. Rob. I remember four distinct moments with Rob my first summer at Murray's:

1. *Week one:* Francis told me, with narrowed eyes behind
    thick black glasses: whatever I do, never, never, never

stand against the counter with hands in pockets when Rob comes in. Find something, immediately, to be busy with. I washed many knives while throwing furtive glances over my shoulder at the narrow shop door.

2. *Week three:* After being pulled in to perform administrative tasks for Rob (clearly because I was the only girl. Clearly!), I made Rob wait when he wanted me to fax something. I was furious at being told what to do, furious that he pushed me around, furious that I had left a comfortable job with people who liked and respected me to work for some nutter who treated me like an imbecilic secretary. When I finally shimmied down the "stairs" to speak to Rob, I would like to say I was icy and razor-tongued, spitting a composed but deadly monologue his way. In fact, I think I was nearly in tears and yelled that I would send his faxes if he asked me nicely and said "Please" and "Thank you." Then came the glint in his eye. Rob respected my efforts. Our fight turned into one of those hourlong sessions in his office talking about a thousand things to which I nodded affirmatively, not really understanding the point. We parted, if not friends, then with a tacit understanding. Seven years later Rob reminds me that I was the first person who told him to fuck off that he didn't fire. Our bond had begun.

3. *Week sixteen:* I waited until Rob was out of the country, in Spain, to tell Frank I didn't want to work full-time. I wanted to learn the cheese, but not for fifty

hours a week. I had landed another part-time job working for a restaurant consultant. Rob's return to find me working for, if not his nemesis, then a blowhard he didn't respect, perfectly timed with my bubble bursting. My job for said consultant consisted of unwrapping his lunchtime tuna sandwiches. Rob asked me back, offering to split my time between the counter and an assistantship with him. Murray's was in the midst of opening its second store, and he suggested I could work on that project. Everyone, most especially Francis, told me I was certifiably insane to say yes. For some reason, I said yes anyway.

4. *Weeks twelve through nineteen:* Rob was asked to speak at the American Cheese Society conference, discussing the naming conventions of cheese. I think I found out only because Francis was complaining that he didn't want to do the background research. There seemed a great opportunity. On my Saturday shift, when it was slow in the oppressive afternoon heat and the store was dead, I would stand at the back computer and write about American cheese names.

American cheese is complicated, because there's no way to tell what you're getting based on the name. Certain styles have become familiar, cheeses like "cheddar," "Havarti," and "Jack." But a new breed of American cheese was developing—unique products from individual producers, many given to romantic monikers that gave no indication of flavor, texture, or milk type. How would consumers know which to buy? With European cheeses, the focus is on the cheese first, the region second, and the producer third, if at all. For the little farmhouse guys, middlemen fight tooth and nail to ensure that overseas buyers never know where a cheese is coming from, lest their competitive edge be lost. Over time, the Greatest Hits of France, Spain, Italy, and England can be comfortably understood. There are Brie and Camembert, Roquefort for the newbies, and the more advanced offerings like Ossau-Iraty, Comté, Selles-sur-Cher, and Époisses. From Spain, the eponymous Manchego, the misunderstood blue Cabrales, and newer, populist inventions like Drunken Goat. Bella Italia boasts the granddaddy of cheese: Parmigiano-Reggiano, which has been watered down and bastardized under the names Parmigiano, Parmesan, and Reggianito. There are also Gorgonzola, pecorinos of a zillion sorts, Provolone, and Asiago. England gives us two of the vaguest cheeses of all: Cheddar and Stilton (which is not always blue cheese but sometimes a gruesome white cheese studded with icky treats such as chocolate chips and dried blueberries). There are literally thousands of others, and within each of these comfortably familiar types exist good versions and bad, traditional and mass-produced, a huge range of variety. Still, once you see and taste a Brie, you have a place-holder in your mind, and when you see Brie again you can reasonably expect to know what you're eating. Taleggio is always pungent and creamy, Provolone generally firm, somewhat spicy, though sometimes soft and floppy as in the American slicing kind. I'd be crazy to suggest there isn't a whopping spectrum of nuance, but European points of reference remain fairly reliable. Many producers make cheeses under the same name, and that name signals a type, a shared group of flavor or aroma characteristics, some tenuous string that tethers all the options together.

American cheeses don't toss the same bone. Do you want to guess what Cato Corner Hooligan is? Or Rogue Creamery Echo Lake? There's a small clue in the latter name, if you happen to know where in the country Echo Lake is. How 'bout Old Chatham Camembert? You've likely had Camembert. Soft, runny, cow cheese from northern France? Generally buttery, mushroomy, earthy? Okay, so a guess can be made there. But then there are Coupole, Green Hill, Grayson, Vermont Shepherd (that is likely from Vermont and may involve sheep), Pleasant Ridge Reserve, Hoja Santa (if you speak Spanish or hang out in Mexico, you might know that's a kind of leaf, so you might guess that the cheese somehow involves or incorporates the leaf), and so on.

My self-imposed research project breaking down American cheese names during that first summer at Murray's made me feel like some kind of detective. It was fun to consider that a hooligan is a snot-nosed little punk, and Cato Corner's Hooligan was a sticky, raunchy little wheel that didn't care if it stank up the room. I began to notice that, unlike European cheeses, American artisan and handmade cheeses took the name of a single farm, marking that producer's unique contribution to the boggling breadth of cheeses in the world at large. It felt important to observe the choices of these fledgling cheesemakers as they took on the oft-mocked assumption of what "American cheese" was all about. Perhaps the owners of Old Chatham, as they drove into Manhattan each week from their farm in New York's Hudson Valley, chose to call their most popular cheese "Camembert" because they were among the first to make a soft French style and were dependent on the recognizability of the famous French cheese name to garner the attention of chefs and small retailers. But then again, the unavoidable comparison with the granddaddy of oozing French goodness was a risk, as well as an opportunity for buyers to point out that this new American effort was commendable, but still inferior to "real" Camembert.

The challenge of these new American cheeses, still unknown to the larger market in the summer of 2002, was that they offered little guide for consumers to know what they were getting. Cheesemakers needed to break free of the public's limited cheese knowledge and distinguish themselves from flaccid slices of prewrapped "American" cheese like Kraft singles. But in their struggle for a new identity, these cheesemakers placed a very heavy burden on those of us trying to educate consumers that American cheese had begun to mean something new, perhaps something inconsistent, but something with real potential for good eating. I don't know if Rob ever used my notes for his presentation. What I recall is that he called me out for being too hokey, cramming my observations into an essay claiming to be inspired by the famous Romeo and Juliet soliloquy "What's in a name." Rob was right. My premise was forced. But I had caught the bug. I had started to think about these countless cheeses as unique foods, coming from real people, and from the get-go my eye was trained on the renegades of American dairying. A cheese revolution was under way.

That first opportunity to talk with producers and ferret out fledgling American cheeses left me hungry—and bored— as I accidentally slipped into full-fledged retail, working at our new store in Grand Central Terminal. Opening time was 7 A.M., and even then the air was warm, smelling of Indian food from the downstairs food court and day-old crustaceans from the Pescatore fish stall. Scads of Scarsdale-bound businessmen didn't care what I knew about raw milk cheese, and there was no flirty Tony, no barking Cielo, no Dylan on a busted boom box. If this was retail innovation, I was done. I made it through the entire Christmas season, my first as an actual employee and not just a mail-order interloper who got to run home on December 20. It was a shock to be in an industry where everyone works while the rest of the city decorates, celebrates, feasts, and commingles. More than anything, I itched with assuredness: I did not want to be a store manager. I wanted to be a cheese expert. But to be an expert I needed the proper audience.

And so it was that another young woman's misery led to my salvation. Downtown, in the windowless cell known as the Murray's office, the woman who had begun our wholesale business decided she wanted to return home. To France. Hallelujah! Valérie had come to Murray's with a big idea: to offer good cheese to New York's best restaurants. In the late 1990s the cheese course was new, and a few forward-thinking restaurants—Alain Ducasse, Chanterelle, Daniel, Jean-Georges, Le Bernardin, and Picholine—had begun to offer a selection to their high-rolling clientele. In those early days it was primarily the French chefs who understood the importance of a cheese plate, and a young Frenchwoman who understood the value of getting in on the ground floor. Valérie saw them come in to buy at the downtown counter and realized the business potential if Murray's could send the cheese out. But post-9/11 she was ready to leave New

York and I was ready to take over. In January 2003, Rob and I wandered the halls of Grand Central. After some good-natured haggling and my veiled threats of departure, we agreed: I would return to Greenwich Village and take on the chefs. After nine months in cheese, life began to get interesting.

My gig as the "girl who works with the chefs" took me through countless seasons of openings and closings, Wednesdays waiting for *The New York Times* to dole out stars or snatch them away, James Beard Awards, a couple of notable restaurant scandals involving strippers and orgies, a lot of pavement pounding, hundreds of staff trainings, menu writing, wine pairing, and, through it all, every day, often several times a day, cheese tasting. Tasting alone in the refrigerated storage room of the old Murray's, fancy formal tasting in the classroom of the new Murray's, farm visits, gatherings with friends to hone my tasting notes for *The Murray's Cheese Handbook*, research for magazine articles, blind comparative tastings for our new venture with Kroger supermarkets, cheese festivals abroad, cheese festivals at home, and always, always looking for the next great cheesemaker or a local butter for a chef or the perfect cheese that would round out our ever-shifting selection of several hundred.

Murray's used to buy American because we wanted to support emerging cheesemakers. And it used to be easy, because there were so many bad American cheeses that the good ones became self-selecting. Now, after seven years, I have notebooks and paper scraps and Excel documents so stuffed with tasting notes that I think I might go crazy keeping them all straight, and yet . . . every day now I hear of five cheesemakers that are brand new to me. It's like mushrooms after a rainstorm, sprouting from every nook and cranny, and each year, as they get more prolific, they get better, more refined, harder to eliminate. On some days, after tasting forty new choices, I feel as if I might drown in cheese.

Through all this tasting, dozens of visits, thousands of conversations, what seems like millions of e-mails, the soul of my job has distilled into the simplest, most obvious point: all this cheese is the product of a very tenuous, delicate, and incredibly important web of people, land, and animals. American cheese is about cheese in America. It's about food in America, about the way we produce, the way we consume, the way we transport, and the economic, social, and nutritional value we place on the food we put into our lives and into our bodies. I see so much that's wrong, scary, overwhelming, and dangerous about the way we make and eat food in this country. In cheese, because it's what I know, I see limitless opportunity to produce good food on many scales. Tiny and local, yes, but also regional and even national. Delicious, beautiful, stinky, heartening, melting, comforting, nourishing cheese that can support the land, support families, feed people, and generally make life better.

The number of cheesemakers in America is well into the hundreds now, and there is no small amount of pressure in my industry to know each one, to pull them out like baseball cards and compare notes, swap cheeses, and build a whole collection. For every farm I know intimately, there are ten I've only heard of. For every tiny stall at a farmer's market, there are fifty others, and for every indiscernible supermarket private label, there are supermarkets in states I've never visited. My years in cheese, American or otherwise, have included some glorious finds, but they've also included plenty of atrocious mouthfuls I wouldn't wish on my worst enemy. There's plenty of bad cheese out there. I'm less interested in cataloguing every cheesemaker in America than I am in considering the best of the producers I know and the ones who articulate the most critical aspects of cheesemaking—food making—in America.

Every time I'm asked if I still like cheese, after all this time, I have to say, yes. I really do. And I think it's really important. American cheese is one of the cornerstones of preserving responsible agriculture, respectful animal husbandry, and all-around good eating in this big country of ours. From the farm next door (while there still is one) to the megamarket next door (there are probably many), I see a dozen important reasons to get out there and get a wedge.

MECCA

IN FOOD CIRCLES THERE ARE TWO RESTAURANTS FOR WHICH the highest reverence and shiveriest awe are reserved, and both happen to be located in the San Francisco Bay area. The first is the womb from which truly seasonal and fiercely local cooking sprang, Alice Waters's famed Chez Panisse in Berkeley. I've never actually eaten there, but the dozens of tales from friends and colleagues, waxing poetic about its worn floors, fraying rugs, down-home service, and pristinely fresh ingredients give me a picture. It is said to be the perfect marriage of simple, unpretentious fare and impeccable ingredients: tiny, pulpy beets, spider-thin carrots, and bristly boughs of rosemary, all plucked from nearby gardens in the heavy, moist predawn fog for which the area is known.

The counterpart of this suburban landmark is the Napa Valley, Michelin-three-starred temple presided over by Chef Thomas Keller: the French Laundry, my most prestigious wholesale client. I had flown out one February weekend after several years of weekly phone calls and countless shipments of our best cheeses from around the globe. I was there to teach a cheese class for the entire staff, both front and back of the house, and my reward was dinner in one of the restaurant's precious few seats. Teaching is de rigueur for clients in New York, where a staff training requires a few nubbins of cheese and my handout on the major styles into which they are categorized.

But this was the French Laundry, and as with all things Keller, the stakes were considerably higher. A year earlier, New York had seen the opening of the French Laundry East, officially called Per Se, because the philosophies, practices, and even the famous blue front door were inspired by Napa, though it wasn't exactly the French Laundry per se. And so my frame of reference was built on the things I saw in the restaurant at the Time Warner Center. Per Se was opened, to much gossip and disbelief, with a $10 million kitchen so vast and spotless that nearly every New Yorker I know would happily have lived there and enjoyed seven times the space they had ever known in an apartment. When, a mere month into service, a kitchen fire caused Per Se to close down, its legions of chefs were shuttled off to stage at the city's best kitchens: Daniel, Jean-Georges, Le Bernardin, while Per Se continued to pay their salaries and reportedly invested an additional $2 million to fix up its smoke- and water-damaged back of the house.

Despite the cavernous rooms, it is the quietest kitchen I've ever been in, mountains of shrimp efficiently peeled, lobes of foie gras silently deveined, dozens and dozens of cooks in immaculate starched whites who look up only to say hello when you enter or assent, "Yes, Chef, coming right up, Chef" when a superior requests anything. In the main kitchen there is a wall-mounted television screen with a satellite link to the kitchen at the French Laundry, where, even at 10 A.M. EST, a few bodies can be glimpsed, moving around the Yountville, California, home base. Per Se's chef de cuisine, Jonathan Benno, has always reminded me of a monk with his shining bald head, but there's more than a whiff of army general about him. The place runs like a machine. Famously, every carton and container, every mise en place, is neatly labeled in black marker on white masking tape. And the tape must not be ripped by hand. It is always cut with scissors, so the ends are even, the tags orderly.

Driving the meandering roads to Napa, I was all disorderly glee. I was alone! In Napa for the first time! My good friend James, who has been known to play around in his Chinatown apartment turning out wild duck dinners (watch the buckshot) and handmade ravioli bulging around a wobbly, liquid egg center, was due in that night to join me for a weekend of wine tasting, long boozy lunches, and, of course, The Dinner. The class I was there to conduct was a tiny dollop of crème fraîche on the sheer, glorious indulgence of the whole visit. I love teaching and was looking forward to meeting Cory, Adam, Devon, all these polite young men who talked cheese with me every week. That first day, though, my only task was a drive down windy streets alongside knobbly black grapevines tightly laced, like lumpy licorice, to vineyard trellises. In February, Napa is mild and moist, and the head of each vine row sports chamomile that flowers in effervescent sprays of yellow sunshine. Shoving my arm out the window, I snapped photos on my cell phone. They're all blurry mist, sharp vines and lemony clouds, which is how I always think of Napa.

I wasn't due in the kitchen until the following afternoon, but I drove down the main street of Yountville, past Bistro

Jeanty, with its recommended rabbit patés and gluey pigs' feet, to Keller's Bouchon Bakery and Bouchon, where I planned the next day to get warm, buttery croissants and coffee with hot milk for breakfast, followed by oysters and steak frites for lunch. Farther down, Washington Street dead-ends at a playground. Somehow I had missed the illustrious French Laundry. When I doubled back, at the corner was an ordinary brown stone building, partially hidden behind a porch and deck supporting climbing, leafy vines. The bronze sign announcing the restaurant is embedded in stone, making it nearly impossible to read through spitty mid-winter drizzle. This was it! The French Laundry! It looked, well, like a Swiss chalet mated with a French roadhouse.

The kitchen can be accessed in three ways. The easiest is through the back door, which opens onto a driveway like the one you might have had growing up. It's shared, in fact, with the house that Thomas Keller lives in, so his commute averages about twenty seconds. The kitchen is small but bright, with windows that open onto a patio where diners have been known to take a few lurching laps halfway through the infamous ten-course tasting menus. On sunny mornings the whole room is puddled in golden light, and though the satellite screen is there, it lacks the Big Brotherness of New York. Chefs aren't exactly bumping into one another, but there's efficiency as in a ship's galley, with everything at arm's reach, the briny steam of lobster stock happily commingling with roasting pork belly. A few steps out the kitchen door is a miraculously tiny dining room with low ceilings and stone walls, the simple sconces casting a warm, flattering glow. The stairs are creaky, the furniture simple, the tables close enough for the intimacy of shared experience without the unpleasantries of hearing about your neighbors' sex life. It's incredibly cozy.

As I was slicing cheese for the forty-person tasting, a body brushed against my back. I was shocked to see bare legs, white elasticized socks, trainers. Who was this guy? Portly belly, meaty hands with wristbands grasping an iPod, T-shirt, and sweatband. "My dear, are you new here?" he asked, grabbing a perfect triangle of cheese. I stammered something genius like "Uh, I'm here to do the cheese class," and then he wandered off through the kitchen, poking into various saucepans as he went. The cook chopping away beside me gave a grin, remarking that the old guy was probably disappointed I wasn't new, because he had a particular fondness for the young ladies. "You'll see him again. He always shows up for staff meal. That's T. K.'s father, Ed."

T. K. That's Chef Thomas Keller to you. And his former military drill instructor father, Edward, who, once upon a time had quite the temper, as T. K. was reputed to have in his early days. The chef who insists on perfectly trimmed labels in his kitchens has a sweatband-wearing father who grazes in the kitchen at the French Laundry. Despite its incredibly prestigious leanings, the French Laundry was already starting to feel like family.

After class I went back to my tiny B&B on a remote horse ranch and changed for dinner. The restaurant sent a car to pick me up, reasoning that enough wine would be served during my meal that I'd best not consider driving. James and I were nestled in a corner, paper-thin flutes of champagne appeared with so fine a bubble it barely broke the surface, and a dish of hot dough puffs was served, the golden crust emitting breaths of cheesy steam as we tore into the restaurant's signature gougères. Dinner had begun, and according to my handwritten notes, the damage went like this:

Dinner at the French Laundry, 21 February 2006

Gougères, made with cave-aged Swiss Gruyère

Sesame tuilles, snappy thin and toasty, formed into cones and
    stuffed with salmon tartare and crème fraîche

Puree of parsnip soup with Périgord truffles

"Peas and carrots": puréed pea shoots and pickled carrots
    carved into tiny rounds like peas

"Oysters and pearls": Sevruga caviar, Nova Scotia oyster,
    and pearly beads of viscous tapioca/Sevruga and avocado
    purée

Poached shrimp with orange and matsui/Dungeness crab
    with Granny Smith apple gelée/Cured steelhead roe
    doused in melted, grass-fed Animal Farm butter,
    house-cured bonito, a sprinkling of dehydrated lime peel

Pig's trotter braised and recombined with bits of forehead and
    sweetbreads, wrapped in caul fat and pan-roasted, atop
    lentils *[My notes read, "soft, moist, piggy wonderfulness"]*

Egg custard with veal stock, white truffle, and a potato chive
    chip/Thomas's English muffin topped with a poached egg,
    hollandaise, and a smattering of white truffle *[My notes
    read, "heady, rich, dense fluff"/"goosebumps. crunchy, buttery,
    yolky, thick"/"Oh shit. We're still at canapés."]*

Endive, radicchio, apple, parsley shoot with cider reduction/
    hearts of palm from the Big Island, blood orange confit,
    see-through thin radish, arugula sprouts, ginger gastric,
    powdered orange rind

Bouchon Bakery butter-based bread with coarse salt crust and
    Animal Farm hand-churned butter with *fleur de sel*

Egg pasta with black truffle/Risotto with black truffle and

Castelmagno cheese *[My notes read, "and more black truffle, shaved, a lot"]*

Salt-crusted Branzino atop melted leeks with diced melted leek and black truffle

Lobster! Lobster! Lobster! Sous vide lobster with roasted romaine lettuce and grated bottarga/Sous vide lobster with artichoke and spicy lobster broth *[My notes read, quoting our server, "You have many, many more courses. Notice, you are still on white wine."]*

Seared mallard duck, foie gras, and sous vide vegetables/Frisee with black truffle foie gras tourchon and black truffle paste

Pierogi with deep-fried hen of the woods mushrooms/Fillet of beef with bordelaise *[My notes read, "rare, juicy, pinky"]*

Cheese!

Jasper Hill Farm Winnimere with chervil and oyster mushrooms

Mandarin orange sorbet with frozen sections of mandarin orange/Ruby red grapefruit granita with blood orange coulée

"Coffee and doughnuts": warm, deep fried, airy, cinnamony, sugary doughnuts and coffee semifreddo topped with foam

Chocolate mousse with crème fraîche and dark cherry/Valrhona chocolate something with butterscotch-candied peanuts *[Note: At this point I was so tipply and stuffed that my notes dissolve into ingredient lists, and I couldn't accurately say what the Valrhona chocolate was doing, though I'm sure it was not just served as a block on a plate.]*

Crème brûlée, puff pastry with chocolate macademia nuts/Tahitian vanilla pot de crème

The Origin of the Composed
Cheese Plate

Both the French Laundry and Per Se serve what is called a composed cheese plate, a concept T. K. is largely credited with inventing in the United States. I tend to be a cheese purist, opting for crusty baguette and little else, but a well-executed composed plate is like an excellent wine pairing, elevating the cheese and teasing out nuances of flavor that would not otherwise have been present. The French Laundry's compositions use cheese as the focal ingredient that may involve the creation of a cheese custard, a cheddar-apple pie, or just a wedge of cheese accented by fleeting, seasonal accoutrements.

One of the more ambitious projects I've undertaken for a restaurant client was the creation of a custom cheese. In this case, Jasper Hill Farm took its seasonal washed-rind Winnimere and had a crazy Vermonter brew a singular wheat beer with which the cheese was washed. The Laundry and Per Se then served the cheese with a small shot glass of the beer. One of the more cumbersome undertakings of our arrangement was the lengthy process of bubble-wrapping cases of beer to FedEx from Murray's to Yountville.

Somewhere around the block of Valrhona that had been transformed into a glorious indulgence I cannot remember, the table of Hollywood producer types sitting across from us knocked over one of several very expensive bottles of Burgundy in the center of their table. The most coherent of the bunch scolded his neighbor, lamenting that he couldn't stand to see such precious stuff wasted, poured the rest of the bottle into two gaping glasses, and brought them over to our table. With the teeniest bit of regret, he bade us enjoy. I didn't think to write down what it was, but I remember the dusty rusted liquid and that incredible poopy, earthy Pinot delicacy. The guy just stood there as if we were guests in his house and watched us enjoy.

For all the lavish complexity of that meal, the French Laundry remains utterly human to me. The staff training was just a bunch of kids in a room wanting to learn a bit more about cheese, and their curiosity was my ticket into this intimate, sacred, creaky house on the corner of a tiny town in California.

NOTES ON CHEESE, PREPARED FOR THE STAFF OF THE FRENCH LAUNDRY

When customers look at a selection of six, ten, or fifteen cheeses, how do they know which to choose? How can they guess the texture? The flavor? Ultimately, how will they know if they *like* it? Chances are, they'll ask you to tell them. And so the question becomes, when you look at a cheese selection of six, ten, or fifteen cheeses, how do you know which to recommend? Or when you have a single composition in front of you, how do you talk about the soul of the thing, the cheese itself, before you get to the wizardry of its pairing and preparation?

The best approach for getting to know cheese is to have a basic understanding of the styles in which it is made. The families of cheese share aromas (hay, woody), flavors (mushroomy, truffly), and textures (semisoft, melting, crunchy). If you know the family, you can accurately estimate what it might smell, taste, and feel like, and that's the first step to guiding a diner.

STEP ONE: MILK

Cheese is made from milk, usually from one of three animals: cows, goats, or sheep. Some generalizations can be made about milk, but the truth is, when people say they "hate goat cheese," they hate that white crumbly stuff omnipresent on winter beet salads. They hate that tangy, milky flavor with its soft yet chalky residue in the mouth. That's one face of the goat, but there are dozens of others.

Here are the milk generalizations I am comfortable with:

- Cow -

- Most versatile: made into the greatest range of styles
- When the cows are grass-fed, the color is deep buttercup yellow
- Least prone to seasonal shortage

- Goat -

- Lower in fat (but only marginally); tastes "lighter"
- In fresh styles, tangier with lemon/citrus flavors
- Color is discernibly whiter, especially in fresher styles

I'll See Your Piquancy and Raise
You Peppery

Citrusy. Spicy. Piquant. Peppery. Zingy. Sharp. Goaty. Bucky. Bitey. Sheepy. Woolly. Lanoliny. Mouth-watery. Tangy. Hot. Intense. Bracing. Zippy. Prickly. I have used all those words, at one time or another, to try to describe the uniquely sharp/animal intensity of certain goat and sheep cheeses. Even the sharpest cow milk Cheddars don't have it. It's a peculiar high note of flavor (and aroma) that's almost vibrational. And there's a reason: short-chain free fatty acids.

Milk fat is made of glycerol molecules bonded to chains of fatty acids. Fatty acids themselves are chains of carbon atoms. More than ten carbon atoms qualifies as a long-chain fatty acid. Less than ten, and it's a short-chain fatty acid. Goat and sheep milk have more short-chain fatty acids than cow milk does, and these are responsible for piquant flavor when their bond to glycerol is broken by lipase enzymes as the cheese ages. Separate them, and they become free. Short-chain free fatties are desirable in the proper proportion for zip. Too many or in the wrong proportions, and you get rancid cheese. I've found that some people do not like the intensity of flavor of goat and sheep cheese because it tastes sour, or "off." The aroma and flavor should always be balanced, but these cheeses may not be immediately pleasing to folks used to cheese from cows.

- More prone to "barny" flavors (makes you think of the animal)

- Sheep -

- Highest in fat, even when aged (dry) it feels richer, rounder, heavy in the mouth
- More prone to "barny" flavors (gamy, like lamb chops), with an aroma of lanolin (sheep wool)

STEP TWO: HOW TO TASTE

We consume all day, mindlessly or even deeply appreciatively popping food into our mouths, chewing, and swallowing. That's eating, and it's not the same as tasting. When you're trying to learn a cheese, detect its animal origins, determine its style, you need to taste carefully. If you've participated in formal wine tastings, you'll notice the similarities of approach.

First: Taste with your eyes. What color is the outside (rind) versus the inside (paste)? Is the texture uniform? Are there holes ("eyes"), cracks, fissures, salt crystals, white patches, color variation? Is it weepy and wet? Crumbly? Sweaty? Many styles or families of cheese can be identified just by the color of the rind or the interior paste.

Second: Taste with your nose. A lot of the "tastes" of food—and cheese is no exception—are determined not by your tongue but by your nose. Your sense of smell kicks in while you are chewing but continues to direct your impression of flavor long after you've swallowed.

Third: Taste with your mouth. Your tongue is actually a limited tool. It can detect sweet, salty, sour/acidic (mouth-

Tasting with Your Nose

led a blind cheese tasting during Murray's weekend-long classroom-intensive Cheese U. Boot Camp. It was our third, but I found this one particularly challenging because there were interns and employees sitting in on the class—people who work with cheese every day—and I was concerned that they were intimidating the students who had taken a gamble on this (long and expensive) course simply because they wanted to learn more.

We had just sampled a rare French goat cheese, and I was describing what I tasted in the hope of getting some students to pipe up and read their tasting notes aloud. For me, this cheese is all about minerality—it's got a lot of chalk and reminds me of a damp stone cave. Limestone. A tentative hand went up. It was one of the quieter students, a middle-aged man who just the previous night had introduced himself as taking this class because "It was something I felt I should do." I was so pleased and wanted him to enjoy and to learn. He asked, very quietly, earnestly, and with the slightest bit of bewilderment, "But limestone is a building material. It doesn't have a taste. Right?"

Right indeed. I don't do a lot of building licking. I realized my total oversight in not discussing the importance of retronasal tasting, or, as it's better understood, tasting with your nose. When you eat cheese (or drink wine), there are very specific physical sensations associated with taste: sweet, salty, sour/acidic, bitter. But your mouth is actually quite limited. Most of the romance of food comes after it's been swallowed. You exhale. A breath of air rushes up the back of your nasal passages and out

your nostrils, and suddenly there are a million sensory impressions, most of which have to do with smell: grass, hay, stone, soil,
leather, soap, perfume, swimming pool, lead, pencil eraser, and
on and on.

   Tasting is experiential—cheeses recall certain places I've
visited and experiences I've had, because the retronasal
impression is about dozens of ancient and far-distant smells,
instantly, magically recalled by a cheese. That's a big part of the
challenge in communicating flavor—you may not share my frame
of reference, or, even tougher, you may not know my frame of
reference. So taste with an open mind, but more important, taste
with your nose. Taste after you've swallowed. And enjoy
whatever summer camp, root cellar, or horse barn an innocent
bite of cheese can return you to.

watery), and bitter flavors. These impressions are focused on
specific areas of the tongue, so look for sweetness (or the absence of sweetness, a kind of puckery tannic feeling) on the tip
of the tongue. Sourness comes in the form of astringency on
the sides and back of the tongue, usually accompanied by an
instant mouthful of saliva. Bitterness catches you where your
tongue meets your throat, way in the back, as if you're trying to
swallow a prickly little pill. Salt is concentrated on the front
sides of the tongue. Also, trust your mouth to suss out the texture of a cheese. Many cheeses look great on the plate only to
feel like rubbery eraser or mealy, greasy particles once you
chew them. Well-made cheese may have many different textures: airy whipped cream that dissolves in the mouth, or heavy

and moist like a lump of cheesecake, or packed clay that smears on the roof of the mouth. There isn't a "right" texture, but some cheeses are exceptionally pleasing.

STEP THREE: CHEESE FAMILIES

- *Fresh* -

A high-moisture style usually eaten within days of its production. Fresh cheeses aren't typically included in formal tastings because they're regarded as simple and straightforward; they are more often used as an ingredient than as a stand-alone. Expect a creamy texture, no rind, and a milky, neutral aroma. The flavor can be sweet and mild (when made from cow milk) or tangy and lemony (when made from goat or sheep milk). Some of the better-known fresh cheeses are fresh goat cheese (chèvre) and cream cheese. The proximity of a local American producer can be tasted in cheeses such as Westfield Farm's Capri.

APPEARANCE: Smooth, snowy white, rindless
AROMA: Very little; milk
FLAVOR: Milky, lactic, tangy (if goat or sheep), sweet (cow)
TEXTURE: Wet, curdy, crumbling, milky

- *Bloomy* -

The classic examples are Brie and Camembert, but the bloomy family includes all exterior-mold-ripened cheeses. From a layman's perspective, what might that look like? The best-known bloomies sport a soft, furry white skin encasing a soft, squashy, or runny interior. That mold is *Penicillium candidum.* It is added by the cheesemaker, and its spores actually bloom like microscopic dandelions on the outside of the cheese. Many small-format goat cheeses also fall into the bloomy family and tend to be ripened by an onslaught of the curious-looking mold *Geotrichum candidum* (which I love, because it makes the cheese look like a brain), followed by ambient molds that turn the exterior gray, white, and even blue or green. Whatever the mold(s), bloomies ripen the same way. Over the course of several weeks, the blooming coat is patted down and the cheese is turned and flipped to encourage a thin, even skin. The molded rind breaks down the fat and protein of the interior paste, creating a texture that ranges from creamy but resistant to warm-buttery to nearly drippy. The flavor of the cheese also intensifies with the textural breakdown. American cheese-makers have taken the traditional French model and run riot with it, playing with unusual shapes and milk types, as in the *P. candidum* bloomies Jasper Hill Farm Constant Bliss and Cypress Grove Humboldt Fog, and the *Geotrichum* bloomy Andante Farm Trio.

A subsection of the bloomy family are the cheeses known as triple crème: these all sport the bloomy rind (there is one exception in the world that I know of, where a triple crème is not bloomy, but washed-rind; see below for more on that), but during cheesemaking the milk is enriched with cream, making the butterfat content 75 percent or higher. The texture tends to be stiffer than that of a regular bloomy, like cool butter, and the flavors milder, richer, and saltier.

APPEARANCE: (Edible) fluffy/furry white, almond-
colored, or ashed rind; white or blue mold spots;
brainy texture; brown mottling; white to straw-
colored paste

AROMA: Slight ammonia, hay, mushroom, mown grass

FLAVOR: Mushroomy, truffly, cooked broccoli/cabbage,
  buttery, milky, cream; lemony tang for goat cheeses
TEXTURE: Ranging from dry, dense clay to cream-
  cheesey with liquid under rind

- *Washed-Rind* -

Aaahhh, the great specimens of stinkdom. The washed-rind cheeses have got the funk, thanks to regular washings in brine (salt water) that may be fortified with booze, yeasts, or butter-milk, intended to cultivate and foster the growth of bacteria called *Brevibacterium linens* (*B. linens* for short). What's groovy about the *B. linens* is that they make these cheeses very easily identifiable in two ways:

- They impart a light pink to dark orange hue to the outside of the cheese.
- They smell. Often pretty bad. Like used diapers and sweaty feet. Touch one if you don't believe me. The pungency of the washed-rinds belies a flavor profile that may be relatively milky and mild, with a good brininess, or can veer off in the leathery/petrol/corky direction.

Like the bloomy cheeses, the ripened exterior of washed-rinds breaks down fats and proteins, so expect a relatively plush, creamy texture that can be so runny the cheese is bound with bark or contained in a little wooden box.

Not to further complicate things, but there are many aged cheeses (especially cooked pressed, see below) that are brine-washed in the beginning of their life span and do sport *B. linens* on their rind. This contributes a lot to flavor and aroma, but the cheesemaking technique places them in the style described below.

The only nonbloomy triple crème I know of is the California stinker Cowgirl Creamery Red Hawk. I also reserve particular affinity for Cato Corner Hooligan, Meadow Creek Grayson, and Twig Farm Soft Wheel.

> APPEARANCE: (Edible) pink to orange rind, shiny, sticky, tacky, Vaseline-y
>
> AROMA: Stinky! Barnyardy, pungent, fermented fruit
>
> FLAVOR: Bacony, fruity, meaty, peat mossy, salty
>
> TEXTURE: From runny to pliable, bulging, buttery

RIND LINE

Crossing the rind line, you'll find families of cheese whose exterior rind tends to be thicker, chewier, or downright hard due to extended aging. Generally, I consider these rinds inedible, and though they will never hurt you, they tend to taste like the aging cellar. In other words, like dirt.

In addition to crossing the rind line, we've crossed the line into boring categorizations taken directly from cheesemaking practices that determine style. Fun words like "fresh," "bloomy," and "washed" give way to technical words about cooking and pressing. I've yet to come up with a catchy but accurate way to encapsulate these differences, so for now, we're sticking to the technicalities. Up to this point in the cheese styles, we've considered relatively young, relatively high moisture examples that are made, roughly speaking, in the same way. The milk is coagulated (the proteins knit together through a combination of time, acidification, and coagulant), and the liquid is drained off. The resulting curd is minimally handled, scooped up, formed into a shape, and salted, and then the magic of molds, bacteria, and time impacts the texture and flavor of the cheese from the outside in. See "Cheesemaking: The Summer of 2002 at Major Farm" on page 56 for more on the technicalities of cheesemaking.

The age-ability of a cheese is determined by steps taken during cheesemaking to rid the curd of as much moisture as possible. Take a Brie and "age" it for ten months, and you will not have a sophisticated and complex result. You will have an old, desiccated, and spoiled piece of cheese. The pressed cheeses (uncooked and cooked) are designed from their inception to be ageable. The more water that is removed, the firmer the cheese and, generally, the more lingering the flavor.

- Uncooked Pressed -

These tend to be aged for two to eight months, with an interior texture anywhere from semisoft to firm. The rind is developed, thick, and crusty and not usually eaten. The first two steps of moisture removal are present here: first, the curd is cut down during cheesemaking. While the curd of bloomies is like thick, strained yogurt, the curd of uncooked pressed cheese is a firmer, rubbery mat that is cut into pieces ranging in size from handheld eraser to olive pit. Once cut, the liquid is drained and the curds are scooped into a form and pressed. The pressing may be brief and gentle, and in fact many washed-rind cheeses are, technically, uncooked pressed. Once formed and pressed, if the cheese is not washed, natural molds, yeasts, and bacteria in the milk, the air, and the aging environment take hold and flourish in various stages of technicolor fur. Over time, these are patted and brushed, the cheese loses additional moisture, and the outside firms into a drier, chewy-looking crust. The European greats range from French tommes and Pyrénées sheep wheels to Spanish Manchego to Italian pecorinos to the classic English Cheddar. Here at home, cheeses made in those styles will follow suit, from Vermont Shepherd to Bellwether San Andreas to Cabot Clothbound Cheddar.

APPEARANCE: (Less edible) thick, rough, earth-colored rind, often with white or yellow mold

AROMA: Wet dirt, straw, rye, bark, horses

FLAVOR: Grass, clover, herbs, earthy, leathery, some sweetness

TEXTURE: Semisoft to firm, pliable, potentially mealy or chunky, as in Cheddar

- Cooked Pressed -

The difference between this family and the former is simply the cooking. While it is being stirred, the curd is cut to a small size, often as tiny as a rice grain, and the cheesemaking vat is heated, cooking the curd and causing contractions that expel water and ultimately produce a smooth, elastic texture that can (and must!) age for the long haul. Traditionally, cooked pressed wheels were larger in size: 50 pounds and up to as much as 150, and the cheese was aged for nine, ten, up to thirty months. The cooking of Alpine-style cheeses like Gruyère, Comté, and Swiss cheese results in a bendy, chewy texture with sweet flavor. There's very little acid in the cheese. Longer acidification, higher cooking temperatures, and extensive brining of wheels such as Parmigiano-Reggiano produces a drier, flakier paste that is crystalline and butterscotchy, but also considerably sharper than the mellow, roasted notes of the Alpine behemoths. We have both approaches in the United States, as in Uplands Cheese Company's beloved Pleasant Ridge Reserve, and though I hate the co-opting of European names, the easily identifiable and addictively good Sartori Parmesan.

APPEARANCE: (less edible) firm, smooth, hard natural rind, sometimes clothbound in the case of Alpine types; hard, craggy, glossy, hard rinds, often waxed, in the case of Parmigiano-Reggiano (Grana) types

AROMA: Not a lot, often because the rind encases the paste; cave and fruit notes ranging to toasted nuts and burnt sugar

FLAVOR: Cooked milk, butter, dates, hazelnuts, ranging to butterscotch, caramel, and burnt toast

TEXTURE: Smooth and elastic for Alpine types to firm-curdy to dry and flaky for Parmigiano types; breaks apart when chewed

- Blue -

It's not a kind of cheese, it's an entire family of cheese. I always get a little nervous at the grocery store when I see a wedge of something called "blue cheese." Or worse, the fancy, Frenchified "bleu cheese." Nowhere in the world is there such a thing as "blue cheese" without a unique name. There are dozens, even hundreds, of different blue cheeses. They share one thing in common, and that is the presence of the blue mold *Penicillium roquefortii* (or sometimes the milder *Penicillium glaucum*). Like the bloomies, this family has mold introduced in powder form during cheesemaking, and like the *Penicillium candidum* in bloomies, the mold needs oxygen to grow. It is only after the cheese is pierced and air can get

American Blue

I've tasted a lot of blue cheese. I was wondering what the differences were in the "classic" American blue cheese: they're all five to six pounds, wrapped in foil, rindless, sheathed in a nonblue perimeter of crumbling white paste that can be mellow, bitter, or bland, depending on the cheese.

The American standard is Maytag Blue. I'm not sure how Maytag became the poster child for American blues, though the family name and the eponymous washing machines may have something to do with it. Like many wealthy families in the early twentieth century, the Maytags had a herd of show cattle. E. H. Maytag began showing those cattle in the 1920s, and his son, Fred Maytag II, began milking the winners to make the now-famed blue, Maytag. Maytag Blue has never moved me in any great way, but I appreciate the story and the fact that it's one of the few cheeses, even today, from the state of Iowa.

There are so many choices of blue cheese, all suited up in tight wraps of green, black, and silver foil. The perception most people still have is that these guys are going to be sharp, slatey, unforgivably bitter, acerbic, and biting. They may be fantastic crumbled on a salad and drowned in oil, but many American blues lack the range, nuance, and complexity of Europe's proud-chested offerings, from moist, smushy Fourme d'Ambert to austere, minerally Stilton.

What I've found, tasting four, six, or ten American blues at a time, is that rind makes a difference. The foil-wrapped style, unless it's enhanced with smoke or wine or other flavorings, has a smaller range of flavor. Once you get into a rinded wheel, with its generally drier, denser texture, there is a world of cocoa, nutty, earthy tastes that are simply remarkable. I know foil-wrapped is the classic, but that doesn't necessarily mean it's the tastiest.

into the paste that the blue mold develops and these guys become something unique. They run the gamut from creamy to crumbly, mild and sweet to fiercely metallic and salty. Like goat cheese, blue cheese is an oft-maligned style, because people have had bad experiences with searingly spicy, cheaply produced French Roquefort. U.S. producers play in all styles, from moist, crumbly Point Reyes Original Blue to the limited-edition Rogue Creamery Rogue River Blue, wrapped in pear-brandy-macerated grape leaves.

APPEARANCE: Blue veining

AROMA: Wet stone, mold, cave, mushroom

FLAVOR: Salty, peppery, metallic, spicy, mushroom

TEXTURE: Anywhere from soft and oozing to dense and dry to high moisture and crumbly

RAW VERSUS PASTEURIZED

The most oft asked question comes with narrowed eyes, when patrons inquire, "This is raw milk cheese? So it's illegal, right?"

Whispers. Head nods. Hand rubbing. "Contraband?"
No! Not right!

Raw-milk cheese may be perfectly legal in the United States. It must be aged, however, as the FDA has determined that beyond sixty days potentially harmful pathogens such as *Listeria*, *E. coli*, staphylococcus, tuberculosis, and brucellosis cannot survive. The International Dairy Foods Association provides the minimum time and temperature requirements for all types of pasteurization. The two most commonly used by cheesemakers are vat pasteurization, which requires a minimum of 145 degrees Fahrenheit for at least thirty minutes, and high temperature short time pasteurization, which requires a minimum of 161 degrees Fahrenheit for at least fifteen seconds.

The fear of raw milk is as profound as the fascination with it, and I wonder why our laws mandate that sterilized, heat-treated milk is preferable to clean, raw milk (the obvious answer—lobbying—notwithstanding). Making milk "clean" by pasteurizing it is what really scares me. Milk should be clean and healthy before it's cartoned for drinking or made into cheese. Producers who pool thousands of gallons of milk, truck it across state lines, and let it sit around in silos for days are breeding bacteria, especially if that raw milk comes from confined cows fed an unnatural diet of corn, antibiotics, and growth hormones. Those producers are asking for trouble, and unfortunately those producers generate most of the milk we drink in this country.

While I prefer my milk from healthy, unstressed, ideally grass-fed cows, I can't begrudge those American cheesemakers who pasteurize theirs in order to make creamy, damp, oozing cheeses that are aged for less than sixty days. Cheese made from pasteurized milk is by no means inferior, even if much of our drinking milk may be. The point for me is: Know where your food is coming from. Strive for cheese made from milk you'd be thrilled to drink. At the end of the day, you'll enjoy tastier, more complex, more nuanced cheese. As with all food, it is the building blocks that matter.

SEASONALITY

The seasonality of food, as in the first spring ramps, summer heirloom tomatoes with awesome names like Green Zebra, and tiny, briny winter shrimp from coastal Maine, is both a blessing and a curse. What makes food in season special is, first, that you can find it! Second, when it's around, it's uniquely stupendous. I'll eat six or seven peaches a day in August and in September avoid the clumpy, sticky-thread mess they have become. Sure, I can find hothouse tomatoes in January, but their listless flesh bears no resemblance to that of a sun-swollen summer fruit. Such is the case with cheese.

The logic is simple: left to their natural proclivities, animals don't make milk all the time. First of all, they have to birth something. The gestation can take anywhere from five months (in the case of goats and sheep) to nine months (in the case of cows). Then the milk flows, but without the addition of hormones animals' lactation is finite. And it cycles, increasing steadily, plateauing, and naturally diminishing as the wee ones mature. For goats and cows that's about ten months of milk and for sheep only five months. Then there's the additional complication of breeding seasons, as an animal is predisposed to mate at a certain time of a year (in the case of goats and sheep, that time is autumn, generally between September and November). Cows, meanwhile, are the most like people (at least in the breeding regard) and are primed to go every month. Together, there are three sets of variables that make naturally occurring milk a precious and limited resource. To further complicate seasonality, milk can be turned into cheese intended to age for as brief a time as a day or two or as long as two or more years.

The end result is an infinitely moving target, a fleeting bite of lactic immortality available for a few short months before it's gone for another year. These are the general guidelines to the seasonality of cheese:

Goats tend to mate in the fall, producing little or no milk into the winter months as they prepare for early-spring kids (little goats). Goat milk tends to be made into fresher styles, a few weeks to a few months in age. If you think back to the more durable families, produced in larger wheels and aged for many months, it makes sense that these are typically made of cow milk. You'd need the milk of several hundred goats to pool enough raw material to make a single fifty-pound wheel.

Sheep follow a birthing pattern similar to goats', producing milk in early spring that can be made into creamy, oozing cheeses but is traditionally pressed or even cooked and so has a much longer shelf life. Therefore the season seems longer. Sheep are bigger than goats but relative to their body weight give a limited amount of milk. The stuff is considerably higher in fat and protein, but there isn't a lot of it. Plus, sheep are naturally inclined to produce milk for half the time of goats. Between the richer milk and shorter lactation time, sheep milk is the most limited, the most expensive, and the quickest to run out.

The natural cycles of goats and sheep mean they tend to birth just as the new spring grasses push through the thawing earth, so the milk that becomes cheese is powered by the most complex and varied fuel of all: herbs, flowers, weeds, and leaves. Fresher, younger cheeses that appear in winter may be made of frozen curd, or animals (especially goats) may be coaxed to mate during the winter, meaning there's milk all year, albeit in more limited quantity.

These days, *cows* are universally impregnated by that most reliable of sources: the local vet, wielding a syringe of portable bull semen. That means calves all year round, milk all year round, and the cheese that naturally follows. Here, the seasonality of cheese is more clearly tied to what the cows are eating during their milking time. Some producers, such as Mike Gingrich of Uplands Cheese Company, will tell you that cheese from cows eating anything other than grass is not worth eating yourself; that the complexity, the variability, and the bounty of unique, seasonal pasture are captured and become the soul of the cheese. Others have told me that the milk is inconsequential to cheese and that the flavor and quality of the final wedge lie exclusively in the province of the cheesemaker. What can't be disputed is that feed affects flavor, and it also affects the content of fat and protein. Hay- and grain-fueled milk may be more consistent in flavor, but it is also produced by still cows, often indoors, who get plump as they pump out fattier, creamier milk. And so the cheese changes.

Don't fall into the trap of thinking winter equals inferior cheese. Instead, ask yourself: When was this cheese made?

Freeze Your Way to
Year-Round Cheese

The greatest challenge for cheesemakers working with goat and sheep milk is seasonality. If you can't get the milk all year round, you can't make the cheese, right? Wrong. The most common way of extending the limited milking seasons of both animals is to freeze milk or cheese curd when there's a glut in the summertime. Not all producers do this—goats and sheep can be tricked into thinking it's summer if they're kept in a barn with very bright light for twelve to fourteen hours a day. But short of the light trick, salvation's in the freezer. *If* you freeze the right thing.

You cannot freeze goat milk intended for cheesemaking in its liquid form. Instead, the milk must be made into fresh curd and then frozen. Here's why: remember the lipase enzymes breaking the bonds between glycerol and short-chain fatty acids? Each snip from the enzyme and a short-chain fatty acid is freed, intensifying the peppery flavor these molecules are known for. This can be fine in cheese. In milk, however, you wind up with spicy, rancid, goaty-tasting milk.

So why is this a problem for goat milk but not for sheep milk? It has to do with the amount of naturally present lipase. Goat milk (and cow milk) has a lot of lipase, and the bond-snipping process will happen prematurely, in the milk instead of the cheese, if the membrane of the short-chain fatty acid is compromised or weakened. Freezing milk weakens the membrane. It weakens the fat membrane in sheep milk, too, but there just isn't the same amount of lipase to go attacking those short-chain fatty acids. In order to maximize the summertime yield, goat milk must be made into basic fresh curd (milk plus starter culture plus rennet) and then frozen. Sheep milk, on the other hand, can be frozen in its fluid state.

Ideally, cheese is made from fresh milk. But a talented cheesemaker, with carefully preserved milk, can make such good cheese that you'd be hard pressed to tell the difference. Many small cheesemakers use a blend of fresh and frozen during the lean, late-winter months, while larger producers may have entire weeks or months of production using predominantly frozen curd or milk.

You'll need an approximate age to ballpark the answer. From there, consider what the animal was likely to have eaten and if it should have been making milk at all. It's a more roundabout path to the question of seasonality but a major part of what makes cheese so neat in the first place.

CHEESEMAKING: THE SUMMER OF 2002 AT MAJOR FARM

DAVID AND CINDY MAJOR WERE PIONEERS. THEY WERE AMONG the first farmstead cheesemakers, meaning they owned animals and made cheese on their own farm. Along with Tom and Nancy Clark at Old Chatham Sheepherding Company, the Majors introduced American cheese shops to domestic sheep milk cheese. They're no longer married, though David continues to make the eponymous Vermont Shepherd in Putney, Vermont, and the name Major still equates to the finest American sheep milk cheese.

Like every cheesemaker I've ever spoken to, David welcomed my visit. In August 2002, I took a long weekend trip to my friend Rebecca's house in Chester, Vermont, bound for cheesemaking on Saturday morning. When I teach, folks always ask about cheesemaking. It's the subject I'm least comfortable with because it is essentially chemistry, plus brutally hard work, patience, and detail. One degree too high, and the curd is shot. Seven minutes of stirring instead five, and you wind up with a vat of paste instead of anything remotely edible. To cap off the experience, the floor, cheesemaking vat, drainer, stirrers, cheese forms, tables, and sometimes even walls must be scrubbed, cleaned, and sanitized before and after cheesemaking. And when you're finished, you can look forward to one of two things:

- Repeating this process exactly the same way, every day, in a valiant effort to deliver consistent results

or

- Repeating this process exactly the same way every day in a valiant effort to deliver consistent results, only to produce some lumpy deformed thing that tastes like poison because: the barometric pressure is up; the cows started eating spring grass (instead of winter hay) and are suddenly producing liquid protein masquerading as milk; an intern came through and "cleaned" the cheese-aging cave without your realizing it, killing the indigenous yeasts you've carefully cultivated for two years

Cheesemaking makes me squirmy because all the cheese in the world is adapted from a portfolio of about twenty basic recipes, but infinitesimal tweaks can be made.

1. Begin with fresh milk.
2. Add starter bacteria to acidify (milk sugar is converted to lactic acid).

   [You can experiment at home with the traditional method. Leave a carton of milk out on the counter. Come back in three days. The natural bacteria in the carton will acidify the milk if given enough time and helped along by warm temperatures. You will wind up with thick, clotty, sour milk. As you can imagine, trusting ambient temperatures and naturally existing bacteria to acidify milk in a consistent manner, to make consistent cheese, is lunacy. Today, cheesemakers can choose from hundreds of strains of starter bacteria, sold powdered or frozen, each designed to tease out specific flavors as the milk makes its miraculous journey into cheese.]
3. Acidified milk gets chunky/solid/gelatinous/thick.
4. Add coagulant (aka rennet) to solidify. This is an enzyme traditionally of animal origin, though microbial rennet is of mold or yeast origin (coagulation results in anything from Jell-O to yoga mat in texture).
5. Stir and cut if you want to get rid of moisture and make a firm cheese.
6. Heat/cook if you want to make a really firm cheese.
7. Press (this can be done with the hands or mechanically under weighted or even hydraulic presses).
8. Salt.
9. Age.
10. Enjoy.

At any stage, you can play with time, encourage or subdue the development of acid, manipulate texture, add or kill enzymes (they make most of the flavor happen), introduce molds, or cultivate bacteria that will determine smell, taste, even appearance. The variables are crazy.

Making cheese was essential to my understanding of how milk becomes a solid and infinitely variable food. For me, the lesson began on a Friday night with a bottle of the great southern Rhône red Châteauneuf-du-Pape made by the Perrin family. The wine is Beaucastel, and Rebecca's family cellars the stuff by the truckload. Her father is a pioneer in his own right and began importing the wines of the Rhône back in the 1950s. The Perrins are his close friends and business associates, and his nineteenth-century farmhouse sits atop a root cellar–cum–wine cellar that would make the sommelier at any four-star restaurant curse or cry or dance. Perhaps a combination of all three.

I knew enough to know I was drinking very special, very old, very delicious wine. It's like drinking the earth, but so delicate and unfolding that each sip is a tiny, perfect meal. It doesn't make you drunk but extraordinarily grateful to be alive to taste such an exquisite thing over and over again. So happy to be alive, in fact, that you want to keep sucking in life, and in rural Vermont that means heading out to the shuttered ski resort town of Killington to explore. In my particular case, however, the only exploration to be done was at the local pool hall, with a drink selection limited to pitchers of beer, albeit solid local microbrew. We lived life a little too long that evening, and it was nearing dawn by the time we made it back to bed. Beaucastel may not make you drunk, but five pitchers of Long Trail Ale will.

Driving through densely shaded woods, I could easily convince myself that a delightful adventure awaited. I arrived at David Major's place and followed him up the dirt path into his yard, up to the cheesemaking room, where I slipped on a pair of knee-high white rubber boots. Like most cheesemaking rooms, his is a very simple, relatively small shed of twenty by twenty feet, with windows on each wall to take in the picturesque, rolling green hills.

I threw open the screen door, chatting about cheese, and the smell hit me. It was worse than that, really. The smell embraced and enrobed me. In late August the temperature in Vermont is 80 degrees by 8 A.M., and the humidity is high—high enough that the air clots the little hairs of your nostrils and warm enough that you're not quite sweating but glazed in a skim of moisture. Cheesemaking rooms smell like milk. They don't smell like cheese, which, for me, is a wondrous and changing amalgam of hay bales and toasted nuts and leather and warm animals. Cheesemaking smells like warm milk and the immediacy of the source of that milk. At Vermont Shepherd, that meant warm milk plus a decided sheepiness. You hear that word in cheese descriptions, and I can best describe it as clean but damp wool sweaters mixed together with chewed, or maybe mown, grass. It smells like lanolin, the oil in sheep wool. It's a heavy smell, and the close, warm air was viscous.

For me, in my compromised state, it was horrendous.

I apparently managed to make some semblance of conversation with David for several hours, but what I remember is the feeling of making cheese. My late-night carousing meant that I'd arrived at what seemed a painfully early hour but was in fact a quarter of the way into David's daily morning routine. The sheep had been milked at their parlor down the road, obediently running up a little gangplank to stand in two rows, their bodies held in place by a drop-down gate around the neck so their udder bags were free and clear for a vacuum-powered sucking machine and their heads could dip into buckets of waiting grain. With a flock of 175, the first of two milkings began at 5:30 in the morning, with David finishing around eight o'clock and transporting the milk an eighth of a mile up the road to the cheesemaking room. Careful transportation is always key with fresh milk, but particularly so for sheep milk. The larger fat molecules are particularly susceptible to bursting from rough handling—sloshing, sloppy pouring, and jiggling truck transport can all damage the delicate globules and imbue an unpleasantly strong, sheepy, oily wool flavor to the cheese, even after months of aging.

David had gently tipped the previous evening's milk, kept cold overnight, into the open stainless-steel vat and begun warming it to 90 degrees, while the still-warm morning milk was acidified. Starter culture was added—the liquid bacteria that dive and swim, breed and multiply in the raw sheep milk while David waited for the milk to thicken. He cleaned the plastic forms that would later shape wheels of cheese curd while the bacteria colonized the milk, eating its natural sugars called lactose and converting them into lactic acid. Within an hour, the yellow, fatty sheep milk had begun to acidify into something gelatinous. Slowly, deftly, David added the freshly acidified morning milk to the now-warm evening milk, dribbled in a few droplets of rennet to really seal the deal and solidify the jiggly mass, retrieved me from the driveway, and in half an hour was ready to start cheesemaking in earnest. The beginning of my visit was observation, so I stood there in the hot, damp, milky closeness, a cheap hairnet cutting into my forehead, and watched the milk curdle. Thick liquid knitted together, and as David stirred this enormous witches' cauldron, masses of clumpy islands began to form. This was the formation of curds from liquid. This was milk's great leap into immortality! I watched his elbow go round and round, stirring the buttercup yellow liquid, and felt the uncomfortable fullness of my belly holding only old beer and fresh coffee.

David was eager in his encouragement, excitedly showing me, with the slice of the knife, how the vat was suddenly, magically full not of liquid but of stuff that resembled pastry cream. I could slip my finger into the knife wound and it did not break apart, simply parted like a stiff pudding or custard.

Warm. Hot. Milky. Woolly. Steamy. Slippery. Slick against my skin. My head pounded.

David began to stir the brew with a wire harp, cutting in figure eights, his forearms taut against the ever-congealing mass, little bits and flecks of cottage-cheesy stuff sticking to his freshly scrubbed wrists. As he sliced and swerved, the glistening, perfectly smooth surface parted again and again, breaking into blocks, into chunks, into smaller and smaller bits. With each cut, the uniform mass released liquid whey trapped within. The tightly bound matrix, the proteins of milk microscopically twisted together to form this perfect Jell-O, was pried apart by David's wires, and with each swish it bled watery blond whey. The cutting of curd is so important for cheeses destined to age, because it delivers a smaller, drier particle that will evolve with time rather than rot in its internal juices. But there with David on that dank morning, the curd was a sloshy, stewy mess of chunks and fluid, swirling around that metal vat, running in milky streams, steaming and burbling as he stirred and carved with his gleaming wire paddle.

My stomach dropped in waves, and I began breathing through open lips so I didn't catch the smell of woolly milk, damp hiking socks, scalded butter, and sheep oil, now heated to 100 degrees over twenty-seven long, slow minutes and rolling in invisible swells from the open vat.

When the curd was ready, about the size of whole corn or peas, David tipped the vat, opening valves at the bottom to empty out the liquid whey. In one momentous shift, hot yellow rivers poured down, splashing untended feet and coursing toward drains that peppered the floor. Then the work began. I hope I looked excited. Rivulets of salty water and cheesy stuff stuck in the creases of my neck and the soft, lined place where my arm bent. Cheesemaking vats aren't small, and unless you're gifted beyond the five-foot-five I'm sporting on my best day, you have to pitch yourself over the edge to get inside. My first task was to divide the mat of curd, still in the vat, into piles: the number of wheels we'd make that day. On David's biggest production day, midseason in June, the curd is heaped into thirty-five little piles. On an average day, eighteen piles. By season's end in mid-October, when he's down to a single milking a day, there are a scant six piles. For us it was twenty-five or so. My job: to bend over, the sharp steely edge of the vat hitting me right in the tender lower abdomen, and divide the curd as quickly as possible. And you have to be quick, because the warm, sticky stuff is just sitting there, waiting for the cheesemaker to be slow and careless so it can solidify into a gluey mass that fast approaches spackle if given the opportunity. Cheese curd, even cut and drained of whey, is heavy and wet. There's still whey everywhere, which is really acidic, so it starts to itch and burn between your fingers and on that perfect, soft expanse of lower inner arm that otherwise never touches anything except your sleeves.

Swoop. Push. Heave. Pat, pat, scrabble, pile, pat, move along. Somewhere between building a sand castle and constructing a gerbil bed, I dipped and dove and pushed the piles of curd around. David armed me with a plastic colander, more familiarly known in the comforts of my home anticipating a sloshing load of al dente pasta. But here I was equipped like a butterfly catcher. Time to get the curd out.

Bend. Scoop. Once your basket is piled high with squeaky bits of curd, the remnants of the now-drained vat, you scurry over to the stainless-steel table, but scurry carefully, lest you slip on the oily slick of whey and fall on your tail. The making of cheese wheels ensues. The trick is to take the form (in this case, colander) of popcorn curd bits and pack it down, even the surfaces, press out air with darting fingertips, standing on tiptoe for better leverage before shifting forward and down and pressing with fingers spread wide. Tentative, oozy, yellow streams of whey seeped out of the colander holes. I became painfully aware that the pressing of cheese is often done by machine, and as the webbing between my fingers started to itch and burn insistently, I wished more and more fervently that I hadn't picked such an authentic operation to visit.

Fiddle, even, pack, smooth, press until the curd is evenly

distributed, the whey exuded, and the newly formed wheel shaped as carefully as a kid's mud pie. The pressing, like the cutting, is essential for a cheese intended to age. The objective is to remove moisture. The smaller the curd, the less the moisture; the firmer the curd, the less the moisture; the more tightly packed and pressed the curd, the less the moisture. Sickly trickles of my sweat joined the driblets of whey that slid across the table, my palms, the floor. My stomach had not improved.

After that initial press, David handed me a bunch of wooden numbers, like kiddie blocks, arranged around a carving of a cute, fluffy sheep. I carefully positioned one block at the dead center of the freshly packed wheel. Then, with confidence and speed, I raised the colander, flipped it upside down, and smacked it onto the tabletop. When you look at **Vermont Shepherd**, the cheese I was helping to make, in its fully formed, properly aged shape, there's a ridge that runs around the perimeter of the wheel, making it look rather like a flying saucer and less like a perfect round. I could see the seam on each plastic colander that was responsible for this distinctive rim. I could see it, and I kept jamming the packed, pressed curd against it as I tried to flip the naked wheels over. Every time I dug the plastic seam into the pristinely mounded curd, a hunk would crumble off and I'd shove it back into place, pissed off and frustrated, sure that David found me a moron who was going to ruin one of the twenty-five precious wheels turned out that day. When the seam wasn't foiling me, the effort of keeping the number block in place was plenty cause for concern. If I flipped unevenly, with anything less than total authority, the number block would shift, wedging into the colander and digging into the delicate, crumbly chunks of almost-cheese.

After pressing and flipping, the wheels were salted, that ever-important step in beginning the formation of a crust, which, when joined by ambient molds in the air of the Majors' underground aging cave, would form the hard, dusty-colored shell I know as the rind of Vermont Shepherd. The number blocks, I later realized, were the farm's insignia and its way of marking and tracing each individual wheel. Months later, you could look at a wheel and see the impression of the wooden sheep I'd so carefully placed at bull's-eye and know you had wheel number 13. If you were to call people at the farm, they'd be able to look up your wheel in their daily log and tell you that wheel 13 was made on a Saturday morning in August, when the sun was high and bright, the sheep were munching rag-weed, and a slightly green, uncharacteristically silent visitor had helped make the cheese.

After "the make" (cheesemaking plus obligatory cleanup), David offered to take me into the caves so I could see where the wheels would age. I followed, light-headed, tripping along and gulping fresh, clean, unmilky air that benefited from an occasional gust of breeze, as we headed for a wooden door that opened into the flowery hillside, like something straight out of *Little House on the Prairie*. To escape from that close, moist, hot cheesemaking room seemed like the stairway to heaven—until I walked into the cave. People often ask if a cheese cave is like it sounds. A cave? Really? The answer is, not always. Often the cave is a temperature- and humidity-controlled room, rather like a rec room or an airplane hangar, only stuffed full of moldering cheese. Many American producers, however, the Majors among the first, have constructed true caves, built into the earthen mounds of their land. The cave is naturally cool

(45 to 50 degrees Fahrenheit) and naturally moist (80 to 95 percent humidity), containing neatly organized, usually wooden shelves that hold maturing cheese.

When they're young, straight from the make room from which I had only recently escaped, they look like naked wheels of cheese curd. Yellowish white, packed together to maintain a shape, but composed, on closer inspection, of firm, springy bits the size of rice grains or cherry pits. Imagine tall popcorn pies. The older wheels (a week or three or ten) have a brackish coat, the beginnings of mold from the air that will take root over the ensuing months and grow into fur that is patted down as the wheels are turned and brushed, the whole thing eventually drying into an impenetrable crust that consumers know as a cheese's rind.

Having grown up in a house that was built in the 1830s with a basement that I used to claim held prisoners, I am all too familiar with the earthen dampness of root cellars. The smell of a cheese cave is like that, plus mold plus pleasant ambient farmy smells (hay, grass, etc.) plus ammonia (a natural by-product of aging cheese) plus clinging, moist dirt plus slightly sour milk. You can smell milk transforming into something more permanent, but in that evolution is the whiff of decay.

I tried. I really did. I tried to be cheerful. I tried to make cheese. I spent three hours in a room that was like swimming, lolling, floating in a cloud of thick, burbling milk. I scooped and pushed, packed and pressed, flipped, salted, tried to ask questions. I wanted to learn and to love the caves. But that day I did not. My body revolted. I ducked outside, gulped benign summer air, and threw up behind the hill. Then I threw up a second and a third time for good measure. I'd like to think that, along with my humility, five partially digested pitchers of beer were my small contribution to life on the farm. I don't know if he had any idea what was going on, but David firmly cemented himself as a thoughtful and generous man when he invited me on a run to the tractor store and then bought me a cheeseburger, fries, and a Coke for lunch. Grease and caffeine. Salvation at last.

NOTES ON SHEEP CHEESE

Not all American sheep cheeses are made like Vermont Shepherd, though the Majors' early success led many aspiring cheesemakers to study their approach and recipe. There are far fewer sheep dairies in America than cow or goat dairies, fewer than one hundred nationwide, with the highest concentration (eight producers) located in Vermont. My inaugural cheesemaking experience and the questions I clarified with David Major in the ensuing days solidified the key points about sheep cheese in America:

1. Sheep give less milk, for less time, than do cows and goats. They lactate for five to seven months, and though their milk has nearly twice the fat and protein

content of cows', their yield is one tenth to one twenty-fifth that of cows. A sheep gives an average of 4 pounds of milk each day, while a dairy cow might give 40 to 50 pounds, though an industrial operation can push a cow to yield as much as 130 pounds (this is accomplished with bovine growth hormones and is not representative of responsible farming or cheesemaking). Sheep's short, limited milk yield makes it difficult to run a profitable (or even sustainable) sheep cheese business. Lots of American producers augment their income with cow milk blends, meat and wool sales, or outside income from another job.

2. Although sheep milk can be made into younger, fresher styles, the Majors' early success, and their willingness to teach and share recipes, led many others to make firm cheese, aged for three to six months. Most American offerings hit the market at the same time, generally in early to mid-September. It's definitely a feast-or-famine challenge. Chefs and retailers wait all year for the cheeses to be available, and then, suddenly, there are half a dozen choices that arrive (and disappear) around the same time.

3. Vermont Shepherd was one of the first American producers to build a natural cave for aging cheese. Quite literally dug into the hillside, these subterranean rooms are critical for the development of a "natural rind," the hard, crusty shell that you see as a cheese rind, but which began its life as a coat (several coats, really) of

naturally occurring molds and yeasts that live in the air of a certain region, a specific cheese cave. These molds grow and harden over time into an earthen shell that encases a cheese, and are crucial to the anaerobic breakdown of these cheeses. They don't ripen from the outside in, like bloomy or washed-rind cheeses. All the magic happens, free from oxygen, in the interior paste. Cave aging of this sort is incredibly labor-intensive, requiring a cheesemaker to regulate and monitor each wheel, flipping, turning, and brushing them to ensure proper rind development. Building a cave basically means that a cheesemaker has created an entirely new and separate chapter of production, one that must continue alongside—and long after—the cheesemaking part concludes. It's a tricky proposition for a small cheesemaker, who is likely overextended just getting animals milked and cheese made. See "The Rogue Cheesemakers and the Future of American Cheese" on page 346 for more on the future of cheese aging in America.

> **VERMONT SHEPHERD**
PUTNEY, VERMONT

The farm that put American sheep milk cheese (particularly aged sheep milk cheese) on the map began making cheese in 1990. Its first attempts were apparently so bad that Steve Jenkins at Fairway made Cindy Major cry when she brought a sample for him to taste. I seriously doubt that was his intention, but he likely told her exactly what he thought of the cheese (not much good) and she held it together until she got out the door. Along with her husband, David, Cindy had begun experimenting with cheesemaking on the farm where he grew up in southern Vermont.

With absolutely nowhere to turn for help in the United States, the Majors went to the French Pyrénées to study Basque sheep milk cheese. When they returned, their cheese was remarkably better, and by 1993 they were producing exceptional cheese, not just by fledgling American standards but by any standards. They made one cheese in 1993, and the farm still produces that one cheese today. Although Cindy has left the farm, David continues to produce the eponymous Vermont Shepherd with his current wife and partner, Yesenia Ielpi.

For several years in the mid-1990s, the Majors' relative success with sheep made them a hot destination for aspiring cheesemakers. Their idea was to teach the Vermont Shepherd recipe to neighboring producers, who would then bring the wheels to Putney for aging in the subterranean cave the Majors had built, one of the first in the country. The problem with this approach was twofold: On the one hand, aging cheese is, in fact, a proactive and incredibly laborious undertaking, and there was a real shortage of hands to flip, turn, and brush the wheels as they developed. On the other hand, developing markets like New York City had discovered Vermont Shepherd and loved it. The problem was that no one wanted a Vermont Shepherd–style cheese. They wanted the real thing. And the real thing was often better than the imitators. The upside of this education was a slew of new producers committed to sheep who now live and make cheese across Vermont.

What's so great about this aged style with its sandy brown rind, and what Vermont Shepherd manages to capture every time I eat it, is a heady balance between elegance and edibility. This is the mark of a well-made, aged sheep cheese. The raw material is tricky: stuffed full o' fat (twice as much as cow or goat milk), it's volatile. Fat molecules can burst when handled roughly, and in the case of sheep milk, busted molecules give a decidedly "sheepy" impression—something between the taste of pinky-rare lamb chops and lamb fat. It's that ambiguous zone between the smell and taste of something, in this case, lanolin, the oil in sheep wool. A funny Spanish colleague of mine describes it this way: "You should taste the milk, not the animal."

So in mediocre sheep cheese, you taste the animal. The other potential shortcoming of fat is the greasy scum it can leave on the roof of your mouth. Great cheeses manage to capture the rich density of fat without the oiliness. The textural impression (especially impressive when the cheese itself is firm rather than creamy) is one of tender chewiness. Each bite breaks apart delicately, with a satisfying smush. The flavor, too, is understated. The adjective that is tossed around most often is "grassy." Grassy can be aromatic, but in the case of Vermont Shepherd it's more about the clean heartiness of raw, grass-fed sheep milk. After you swallow, the flavor that's left is informed as much by your nose as by your tongue. It's little whiffs of clover, perhaps some thyme or mint if the sheep have gotten into the stuff. The flavor is quite mild, and the overall cheese makes for easy eating. The flavor of the pale blond interior deepens and intensifies as you move from early-spring wheels to late-summer offerings, my favorite for their acorny toastiness.

In general, Americans are least familiar with sheep milk and sheep cheese, but I find it's often the most approachable choice available.

One of my grossly overgeneralized but consistently reliable wine and cheese tips is to look for an aged sheep cheese when you're drinking an austere, earthy red wine. Those are hard to find harmony with, and though I can drink them by the bottleful, the smoke/earth/puckery finish will run roughshod over most cheeses. Vermont Shepherd, and the other aged sheep, are stoic little soldiers. They're not flashy, not supersharp, *über*-stinky, or loudly beefy. They're subtle and approachable, with a gradual unfolding of nut skin and home-dried herbs. Most of all, there's a sweet, fatty chew that balances their tannic acidity. I'm not necessarily discouraging white wine, but the red/sheep is a go-to. It's not failed me yet.

> **BELLWETHER FARM**
PETALUMA, CALIFORNIA

Knowing you're twenty miles from the Pacific Ocean and smelling brine in the air, it's peculiar to look around at verdant, rolling green hills and see wiggly, round, woolly sheep bodies. But so it is, and nestled in Petaluma is Bellwether Farm: this is Cindy Callahan's house, a field of slow-blinking sheep and a cheesemaking-aging compound out back. I met Cindy after a brief year in cheese, at some unfortunate convention in Washington, D.C., and our dinner together is the only fond thing I recall from that southeasterly visit. Like so many people, she got into cheese by accident, having bought some sheep to eat the thirty-four rolling acres she and her husband purchased as a country home. But sheep make more sheep. And when the babies started coming, Cindy found herself in the lamb business. There was no shortage of interest from the Bay Area's better restaurants—milk-fed lamb is not to be taken lightly—but with sheep and lamb, and milk, comes . . . cheese?

After Cindy's family went to Italy, her son Liam started crafting recipes inspired by the cheeses they'd eaten, particularly the ubiquitous semifirm pecorinos of Tuscany. This led to the farm's **San Andreas** (the farm is located just about where California's San Andreas fault lies, slightly northwest of Petaluma). I love its firm, waxy yellow rind, smattered with white mold and smelling of cool, wet rocks and damp wool socks. Though Tuscan pecorino can be many different things, San Andreas is more akin to the younger Italian styles, and though a rind develops, the crumbling, raw-milk interior smacks of acidity. It's a funny combo, because the bright flavor is one I associate with goat cheeses, but in this case, there's a lanoliny undercurrent and the distinctive, fatty chew of sheep milk cheese, married to a lean, high tartness. Bellwether built new caves in 2008, and at Murray's the first of the new-cave batches were abnormal wheels that looked like weathered yellow brains. The airborne molds seem to have regulated themselves, and the better wheels I've tasted positively sing with lemony pucker. They also make a solid **Pepato**, generously flecked with pepper. I'm used to the cheap, aggressively salty varieties, but Bellwether's has that brilliant balance of dense, sheepy hunk and racy, spicy, aromatic whole black peppercorn, the kind where a bite makes your nose prickle. Also, if you're out West, for God's sake get some sheep milk **ricotta**. It is nearly impossible to find stateside, and most of what's imported is two gasps away from rancidity. The fresh, whole, coddled, curdled sheep ricotta from this farm is extraordinary. It's so unbelievably rich and jiggly, smelling of fresh grass and totally lacking the oily impression left by aged sheep cheese. The barest drizzling of black buckwheat honey, astringent like molasses, makes me shivery with happiness.

Bellwether combats the seasonality of sheep milk by buying local Jersey cow milk and turning it into similarly Italian-inspired table cheeses. **Carmody Reserve**, which I prefer to their **Carmody** because it's unpasteurized, could be the poster child for the Italian concept of "table cheese." Table cheeses are generally semifirm to firm in texture, intended to be lopped off in big chunks and put on a table for everyone to pick and dig at. I managed to squirrel my way into the VIP section of a barrel tasting last time I visited Sonoma wine country, and there were wood boards of Carmody on offer. It tasted exactly right. Dense, smooth, intensely buttery in hue and character, with the barest, faintest edge of toffee, it was supremely approachable and especially well received alongside a giant California Cab intended to spend another five years in cask. I probably ate half a pound in the early-spring sunlight, deeply appreciating its straightforward, toothy crumble.

> **HOPE FARM**
EAST CHARLESTON, VERMONT

Hope Farm is one of the few sheep milk cheese producers in the United States, and one of even fewer that produce a style that is not directly inspired by Vermont Shepherd. Hope Farm's cheese was particularly phenomenal in the fall of 2008, when it came back to market after the summer hiatus of milking, making, and aging. Additionally, Barbara Levin, who owns the farm with her husband, Harvey, sends really funny e-mails.

The Levins began farming in New Hampshire in 1979 and got their first sheep in 1981. They developed a meat business with other producers for the Portsmouth Farmers' Market and eventually pursued cheese as a way to make profit beyond meat. Plus, "sheep are cute." Hope Farm makes cheese from the milk of thirty-five to forty sheep a year, and when I asked Barbara about economies of scale and why there aren't more sheep dairies in America, she said, first, "The business is only twenty years old. Give us time." And then, even more practically, "There are economies of scale. If our land base was larger, we could have fifty sheep and that production would be mostly profit. Sixty sheep and we would have to hire help; then you need one hundred sheep to pay the help." In an operation that's so small (and many of the sheep dairies in America are, as mom-and-pop operations), expansion may be desirable to a point, but then it becomes a necessity to fund the investments one has made in help and equipment to support the expansion in the first place. And then there's the reality of land. David Major is very careful to identify his flock in terms not just of the number of sheep but also of the number of sheep his land can support. Without more space to graze, the farm can only be as large as it is.

The Levins relocated to Vermont, where they have thirty-seven acres ("not enough," says Barbara) and milk their sheep from May through the end of September. Their aged cheese first hits the market about three months later, at the beginning of the autumnal windfall of American sheep cheese. The sheep graze the Levins' land, lured to milking with just enough grain to get them into the parlor, and are dried off (no longer milked) during the winter. When I asked Barbara what the sheep ate, her swift answer was "Pizza." Proving there's humor even in sheep farming. In fact, the flock eats hay.

Hope Farm produces several cheeses, but the one I know best is **Tomme de Brebis**. Like Vermont Shepherd, it is an uncooked, pressed cheese with a natural rind, but it's a mere two inches tall, with a considerably knobbier, lumpier exterior, built of layers of mold that grow and firm over time. If you know the French tommes like Tomme de Savoie, it's more like that. The paste, too, is moister than Vermont Shepherd's, more semisoft and yielding than the dense, butterfat firm of the Pyrénées style. Mostly, though, it's the taste that's different. The 2008, particularly the end-of-season cheese, which we were buying around February 2009, made an incredibly deep chestnut impression, both aromatically and in the mouth, that reminded me of coarse black Italian chestnut honey without the sweetness. As I cut into a fresh wheel, pushing through rind the color of potato skins, this incredible waft of steamy, roasted chestnut would open around me. It was uncanny, this next to the incredibly reserved, grassy, almond-skin austerity of Vermont Shepherd and others like it. Tomme de Brebis is husky, substantial, and lush with all the excess fat of good raw sheep milk. With a hardly massive annual production of 2,300 pounds, Hope Farm's distribution, like that of many sheep cheese producers, is limited to the East Coast.

➤ LOVETREE FARMSTEAD CHEESE
GRANTSBURG, WISCONSIN

Mary Falk's low, gravelly voice reminds me of Marge Simpson and her sisters. You wouldn't know it, but it's a daily reminder of how she wound up in cheese in the first place. In 1986, she bought eighty acres and a house ten miles away from her mother's in Wisconsin. She'd hurt herself working in a California cannery, and while she was on workman's comp it was suggested that she return to school. She studied broadcasting and began working in radio news. Then she met her now-husband, Dave, and they decided to revive the soil of her land, which had been stripped of all nutritive value after years of corn harvests. Dave was building silos and Mary was running the airwaves, but she'd always loved sheep. And when her asthma got so bad she needed to quit radio, Dave picked her up some sheep from a farm where he was working in 1989.

Their part of Wisconsin is the beginning of the Ice Age trail, extremely steep, with rocky, sandy soil. Mary describes it as a "hardscrabble" existence (oddly enough, so does Willow Smart, of Willow Hill Farm). She also said that when she first arrived in 1986, she took a look around and thought, "This is sheep country. What the hell are they doing with cows out here?" The answer is, having a hard go of it, though the land is well suited to sheep. Mary's intention was to raise sheep for meat, and as she sold off lambs, she found herself with the maternal breeds, those that are hardier and thriftier (and give milk). The basis of a solid dairy flock developed unintentionally as Mary and Dave cultivated the animals that were best equipped to survive organically in a pretty intense climate. The sheep spend one day a year indoors—the day they birth their lambs. Mary spent some time working as a dairy herd innovation technician, tracking productive cows around the state of Wisconsin, and what she saw was that pastured cows flourished, living longer and milking more than their confined counterparts.

By 1994, the Falks had created their own breed of Trade Lake sheep, twenty generations that began with four maternal breeds: the Dorset Horn (a docile, milky, maternal breed), the Romney Marsh (hardy sheep well suited to humid environments), the Clun Forest (somewhat wild and crazy, but very hardy and excellent converters of grass to milk), and the Finn (prolific and milky). Each of the original four was selected for its ability to thrive on a pastured diet. For three years, East Friesians were bred into the mix, but they struggled on grass and were found to lower the butterfat content of the milk, and so they were bred out. Mary sold the milk to the Wisconsin Sheep Dairy Cooperative, where Dave sat on the board of directors. Meanwhile, Mary decided to learn cheesemaking. Licensing in the state of Wisconsin requires a year's work to learn the craft, and in her excitement Mary imagined there would be a line of aspiring cheesemakers out the door of her local factory. For $6.55 an hour, there was no line, so for one year she worked for the third largest Muenster producer in the country. She got licensed and began experimenting with milk from her herd of goats. The cheeses were aged in bamboo steamers in the fireplace.

One night in 1997, Dave came home and asked if Mary could make cheese from sheep milk. Their aging cave was under way, it would be ready in two months, and he'd abruptly left the Dairy Sheep Cooperative. They needed a new outlet for their sheep milk, and so cheesemaking began. Mary's first sale was to a restaurant owner whose daughter wanted cheese at her wedding reception. Eleven years later, Mary recalls her terror at sending the raw-milk cheese out at fifty-seven days instead of the requisite sixty. Afraid that everyone at the wedding reception would drop dead, she didn't answer the phone for several days. Needless to say, no one dropped dead, everyone loved it, and LoveTree Farmstead Cheese was off and running. A year later, its **Trade Lake Cedar** took Best in Show at the American Cheese Society conference.

Although LoveTree did wholesale its cheese for a time, many of its restaurant clients were hit hard after 9/11 and business dried up. Happily, the Falks found they could survive more comfortably on the higher-margin sales of cheese direct to consumers. These days, the St. Paul Farmers' Market gets nearly all of their production. The sheep are milked from May until the end of September or beginning of October, and the cheeses age in the Falks' open-air cave. There are eight lakes within two miles of the farm, and the unusually high atmospheric moisture creates a phenomenon known as "toolie fog." From the marshes with their abundant cattails comes a low fog that hangs just above your feet. It's ground fog, slow and creeping, and though the pastures are clear through hot days and cold nights, the toolie fog seeps off the ponds and lakes, permeating LoveTree's caves and carrying the aromatics of the region. Mary accentuates this terroir by layering her cheeses with cedar boughs and sumac, nestling and wrapping the various cheeses in leaves that stew in the cool, damp wafts of toolie fog.

The terroir doesn't end in her cheese caves. A recent shipment I received arrived in a Styrofoam cooler, within which the cheeses were packed in balls and wads of dry grass. The whole thing smelled like pipe tobacco. And that continued on into the cheeses. My favorite is the raw-milk **Tavern Cedar**, with its insanely thick, coarse, pockmarked rind resembling moon rock. My whole chunk was draped in cedar greens, and the interior was scarred with nearly as many pocks as the rind. It looked like Swiss cheese, and I feared the flavor would smack of unplanned fermentation, a little bit sweet, a little bit feety. I lifted and sniffed, and there was a whiff of the Swiss. Beside that whiff was the enduring intensity of tobacco, but close to the cheese it was more aggressive, like a cigar or even an ashtray. I had been so excited to taste, and my heart sank the smallest bit, so sure was I that the cheese would be awful. So I took a small slice from the dense, toothy wedge. It was . . . floral?! I could see from the craterous holes and dusty residue that there was some serious cheese mite action (see "Cloth Binding and Cheese Mites and Crystals, Oh My!" on page 318 for more), but what I didn't count on was the honeyed flavor those little guys would impart. There was salt, for sure. It was present and affirmative, but in such a way as to heighten the flavor of the cheese, rather than to overwhelm or confuse it. It was like eating a solid chunk of unprocessed peanut butter. Smooth and creamy, the slightest bit oily, a whiff of toasty, and somewhere in the background was the fruitiness of cave-aged Swiss cheese, without the gassy finish I hate. It was bizarre and completely delicious.

LoveTree's trademark raw-milk Trade Lake Cedar sat

nearby, smelling equally cigarlike, bundled in its own swath of cedar boughs. It looked very similar but shorter, not quite as tall or wide a wedge and clearly cut from a slightly smaller wheel. There was that rich chew, but this one tasted more of the sheep, with a lanoliny finish and a tangy high note my colleague described as "whey-tainted." It had a sharper taste, a tad prickly and lacking the incredibly elusive floral flavor of Tavern Cedar. I enjoyed it, to be sure, but had by that point been so bowled over by Tavern that it was hard to make a lateral move.

➤ NORTHLAND SHEEP DAIRY
MARATHON, NEW YORK

How can you not buy a three-inch-thick sheepskin rug from a woman named Maryrose? I couldn't resist, though I picked a classic parchment yellow color over the beasty brown option. That was a bright, perfect Saturday at the Steamboat Landing farmers' market in Ithaca.

Maryrose Livingston fell in love with a cow in the Irish countryside and went to Michigan State to learn dairying so she could practice her love for a living. With no sustainable operations in the Midwest (she worked at a conventional dairy that set national fat and production records and milked its cows to death) and the realization that cheese (not milk) was the ticket to financial stability, Maryrose and her husband bought land in New York State in 1999. Unfortunately, they picked a plot that just didn't sit right. It didn't feel good. But they also found Jane and Karl North, who owned Northland Sheep Dairy and were looking for partners. Maryrose and her husband sold their original plot, joined the Norths in 2000, and bought the operation in 2007.

I visited the farm where Jane and Karl still live. I enjoyed their open-air outdoor toilet, which they use in upstate New York all year long (even winter). They're hard-core. Northland Sheep Dairy is too. To give a more useful example, Northland was certified organic until USDA regulations were established, which the Norths decided were too lax. There was no requirement that animals eat grass, which was the soul of their operation. So they stopped being organic but kept being seasonal. Their summary? Grass season equals lactation cycle (of sheep) equals milking season; hay in winter equals self-sufficiency.

Maryrose's take on self-sufficiency, when I asked her about the challenge of having sheep and their limited production and short milking season, was that in order for a sheep operation to succeed, you must use all the parts: the wool for rugs and yarn, the meat, and the milk for cheese. In the summer of 2007 at the farmers' market, the cheeses were all pretty similar to one another, and they were all okay. Firm, with dusty natural rinds, they were akin to Italian pecorinos of various sorts. Their faults ran to the mealy end of things, the finish a little greasy. Maryrose stood next to me in overalls, finishing my tentative attempts at gentle criticism. She knew what the problems were. But Northland's new cave for aging and recipe tweaks are now turning out some cheeses that are far more delicious.

At a recent tasting, the rind of my **Bergerino** looked gnawed, as if some lumpy, crusty, mushroom brown fungus had eaten into the paste. I was on guard. Happily, the cheese didn't taste bad, even though it looked as if it might. After a brief fifteen minutes on my plate, it exuded a delicate skim of cheese sweat (aka butterfat), and I worried it was going to taste like dirty sheep wool, that flavor so fondly known as "lanolin." It didn't. In fact, it was earthy and hearty, with a pleasantly mushy, brown-banana-skin fruitiness. It's a perfect nosher and would be even better alongside one of the farm's sheepskin rugs. They're at the Ithaca market, too, for $100 apiece.

➤ WILLOW HILL
MILTON, VERMONT

Vermont has more sheep cheese producers than any other state in the Union, topping the charts at a whopping eight farms. There was something of a 1990s sheep farm craze in these parts, with dozens of folks apprenticing with the Majors, learning to make Vermont Shepherd, and then breaking off on their own.

Willow Smart wasn't one of those. She already had a farm, 478 acres, primarily wooded, and completely abandoned when she and her husband, Dave Phinney, bought it in 1991 (in the same town that Dave had grown up in, much to his chagrin). It was an enormous and beautiful plot but pretty busted, from the way Willow describes it. I believe her words were "We're still building fences."

Growing up around cattle ranches in Hawaii (her grandfather was eighth generation), Willow decided that she hated cows. But sheep, for meat and wool, she had always liked. When she mentioned all the forest on her property, I immediately thought of goats. They could've helped clear the land for free. But Willow hates goats. No, wait. She corrected herself. She thinks goats are too damn smart, and keeping them contained would present a pretty serious challenge. Plus she didn't want to make goat cheese. Plus she wasn't thinking about cheese at all. She was thinking about meat and wool, and goats aren't much help there. So Willow and Dave started with blackberries, raspberries, blueberries, orchards, and a small but diverse crop of vegetables to sell at the Burlington Farmers' Market along with grass-fed beef.

By 1996, they were ready to go, and then there was a grass fire that burned down the entire barn. They lost everything and had to rebuild, but still bought Dorset sheep, a breed known for meat, and two llamas, which are big enough and screechy enough under coyote pressure to function as successfully as guard dogs. Did you know that llamas can scratch their ears with their back legs?

So where did the cheese come from? This meat- and wool-focused woman can't really remember, to tell the truth. There was no "Aha!" moment. She just decided to go for cheese, too. That's when she ran into the Majors, but not to learn cheese-making. Willow wanted their breeding stock, to take her flock of Dorsets and introduce genetics that would make them more milkable. In response to her letter requesting sheep sperm, Willow received an apprenticeship application. The Majors had a state grant to teach Vermont Shepherd making to aspiring cheesemakers and then age the cheese in their caves. Willow figured, "What the heck? I might as well apply." She did and was accepted. While other apprentices spent four to six months with the Majors, Willow made five Friday drives, three hours each way, from Milton to Putney. She still had her own farm to run.

As for the breeding, she and Dave took a different route: embryo transfers, much like in vitro fertilization, actually. Two purebred Canadian East Friesian sheep (dairy sheep) got together and fertilized an egg; Willow bought these and had them implanted in her surrogate Dorsets, which, at the end of gestation, gave birth to purebred, milkready East Friesians. Since then, she and Dave have grown their herd from the inside up, keeping rams around to do the dirty work.

Willow Hill did in fact make Vermont Shepherd for three seasons (1997–1999), as the smallest satellite producer in the state, while developing its own recipes. In 1999 the first Willow Hill original, **Autumn Oak**, won second place at the American Cheese Society conference, second only to Vermont Shepherd. Then there were a subterranean cheese aging cave that went up in 1999, more cheeses, and one essential realization.

Willow Hill is unique not only because it milks sheep but even more so because of the styles it produces. Soft, fresh, melting, bloomy-rinded styles. Those are *impossible* to find in the United States. The investment in pasteurization equipment was huge, but the payoff (and market distinction) was perhaps irreplaceable. Soft cheese production means a few weeks of aging and faster cash flow, rather than the necessary two-month waiting period for raw-milk styles to become legal. It also means a tricky insider secret: soft cheese has lots of water. Sheep give small amounts of very rich milk. The production of soft cheeses allows a producer to sell more water and less milk. Please don't think I'm suggesting that Willow is watering down her cheese. There's a reason why so many cheesemakers start out with fresh styles: you get more cash, faster. You also, in Willow's case, get something very few American cheesemakers have: lush, mild, grassy cheeses that come to market in the summer, when the guys making aged cheese are tied up in the caves.

As the first Willow Hill original and one of its most balanced offerings, Autumn Oak deserves first crack. Despite its name, the raw-milk Autumn Oak pops up in late summer, smaller, denser, and moister than Vermont Shepherd and its ilk. All the glorious fat of Willow's sheep milk is transformed into cheese with a velveteen texture that sits heavy on the tongue. It's soft like kitten fur, and though the cheese is pressed, the roundness of little curd bits is retained. Though the thin, sandy rind is lovely, I avoid the paste just beneath it, where the salt seems to concentrate and subterranean musty roots dominate my mouth. Sticking to the interior paste, I can enjoy something akin to pan-toasted pine nuts or the butter-roasted almonds my mother made every Thanksgiving of my childhood. Autumn Oak is richer in its rusticity than America's French Pyrénées interpretations.

Before even Autumn Oak comes to market, there is the soft, oozing, and bloomy group, which includes **Vermont Brebis** (a small pasteurized sheep patty), **Alderbrook** (a six-ounce truncated pyramid of pasteurized sheep milk), and **La Fleurie** (a slightly larger ten-ounce pasteurized round made from the milk of Brown Swiss cows). The difference between Vermont Brebis and Alderbrook has everything to do with shape; the former is a thin disc that breaks down rapidly into a mushroomy slick, tempered by the weight of good fatty milk. But I prefer Alderbrook for its balance and austerity. It hasn't a whiff of the ammonia that can so quickly dominate Brebis and tastes richer and even more buttery. Then there's the melting **Summertomme**, made with the peak of July and

August's rampant herbs, which are carefully dried and dusted across the exterior of the cheese. As with the French Brin d'Amour, a weighty, drooping crust forms around each piece, ambient molds take hold, and the entire cheese begins to cave under its own weight. When you slice into a round, a veritable river of delicate, lanoliny cream is released amid the heady aroma of Provençal herbs. Though the sheep milk is pasteurized, the finish of this cheese is nearly floral. It rocks.

And then sometimes, occasionally, thanks to the particular forage of late-summer/early-fall grasses, when the sheep milk is especially rich and complex, only then, once in a blue moon, is Willow Hill's signature blue produced. **Blue Moon** is hard to come by but worth seeking out. The veining is tentative, the cheese covered in a thin, dappled rind, like creeping lichen covering flat mountain rocks. The salt can pack a punch, but Blue Moon boasts a horsey, toasty quality that is far more engaging than the typical foil-wrapped American blue. Well-made natural-rinded blues take me back to the horse barn, in all the best ways. There's a lingering impression, long after the cheese has been swallowed, of leather and saddles, fresh hay, warm animal perspiration, dusty particles, and saddle soap. It's an incredibly comforting and welcome memory to me, and there are a few blues that take me back. The raw-milk Blue Moon is one of them.

Even with this range of soft-ripened and aged styles, Willow Hill's cheeses are gone by early winter. Depending on the short milking season of sheep is grueling and means no income for half the year. So why would anyone do this? Willow snorted when I asked her and said, "It's called Hardscrabble Road for a reason." The farm is, in fact, located on Hardscrabble Road, a rocky area with shallow soil and bedrock. It's not good cow country. More sheep are milked worldwide than any other animal, because they are so adept at managing marginal land like Willow's. But in 2000, the pressure of subsistence by sheep proved too much, and the farm began buying organic cow milk from a neighbor. The intention was to make a cheese that could be sold during the fallow winter months. Then people wanted the cheese all year round. As demand grew, it got too hard to pick up milk. So Willow and Dave bought two cows of their own (there are ten now, Brown Swiss and Dutch Belted), which meant another enormous investment in equipment: two milking parlors, two bulk tanks for holding milk, two of everything. But ultimately, cheese year-round. The other crops are gone now, except blueberries for six weeks of the year, grass-fed lamb, and whey-fed pork, which bring in cash at various points in the year.

Although Willow has been at the Burlington Farmers' Market for sixteen years, she sells only 12 to 15 percent of her cheese there. Even in Burlington, the land of Phish and granola, sheep cheese is a little weird. She's actually finding that more people go for the cow milk varieties. Her flock of sheep holds steady at ninety, and there's no plan (or room) to grow beyond that. Although the farm runs organically, she and Dave chose to decertify so there would be more opportunities to buy sheep milk from other farmers, given the shortage of organic in their area. It's likely that we'll see more cow cheeses from Willow Hill in the future. The remaining 85 percent of her 15,000 pounds is sold to distributors and shipped across the country.

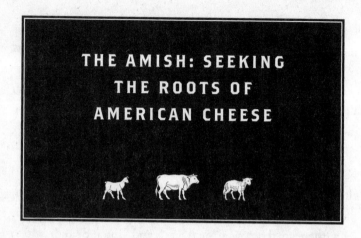

THE AMISH: SEEKING THE ROOTS OF AMERICAN CHEESE

CORRESPONDENCE WITH JOHN ESH IS FRUSTRATINGLY SLOW. Is he going to start making raw-milk cheddar? May I come visit again? I want to make cheese with them, now that I've seen the farm and the animals. Does he know anyone who can make me a new dining room table?

I always feel as if I have no soul when I write to him, because I do it in Microsoft Word, printing out the letters, the only human flourish when I scrawl my signature at the bottom of the page. I write by hand so infrequently that I'm slow, and my old writing callus from elementary school gets pink and irritated.

Five, seven, twelve days later comes his answer. Yes, they are testing a few raw-milk batches. He thinks it will be fine for me to come make cheese, but it will be several weeks until he can ask his cheesemaker, who is 180 miles from his farm. He knows many woodworkers who would be happy to make my dining room table. One has a brochure of fat pine "country" tables and chairs that bear zero resemblance to the photos I sent. John is surprisingly quick to acknowledge me as the gatekeeper to opportunities that abound for his cheese, and though he is patient, in each letter he sends there is an inquiry about expansion, private label, broader national distribution.

I know that cheese swiftly followed cows to colonial America, but the American cheese that dominated the twentieth century, with its proud heritage of industrial revolution, bore less and less connection to people, animals, and land. Blocks of cheese cranked out en masse couldn't be the only tradition left. Where could one begin, in 2007, to discover authentic cheese like the ones Americans once made? I decided to start my search in Pennsylvania, whose Lancaster and Harrisburg regions are known for rolling, wooded hillsides and the largest Amish community in the United States (the second largest is in Ohio).

I know very little about the Amish and their neighbors the Mennonites. My exposure was limited to a handful of visits to urban Philadelphia's Reading Terminal Market, a massive indoor food court with stalls of greasy meats and limpid doughnuts staffed almost exclusively by somber, earnest-looking Amish teenagers. I'm always thrown when I head to the train station, ready to come home, and the McDonald's is crammed with Amish kids buying Cokes and Big Macs.

What I knew of the Amish was this: they don't drive cars, they have no telephones or electricity in their homes, and they live in remarkably contained communities centered around dairy farming and woodworking. On a clear, hot Saturday in June I drove four hours west of Philadelphia to visit some farms and learn how cheesemaking in America once looked.

I am lucky in my professional connections, and as a face of Murray's I was permitted inside, guided by the "English" office manager of a cooperative from which we buy block white cheddar. To begin with, you must understand that non-Amish are "English." Not only was I English, but as a woman, I was concerned about the reception I could expect. Carolyn the office manager prepped me by e-mail:

> *As for appropriate clothes, just regular clothes are fine, but keep to the conservative side. T-shirts and shorts are fine, but not suggestive or have questionable writing on them. The longer the shorts, the better, but you don't have to wear a dress or pants. You may want sweatshirts for the cooler evening times. As to the recorder and camera, sure you can bring them, just do not take any pictures of the Amish people, as they are not supposed to be filmed in any way. You can take pictures of their stuff, animals, etc., but not people. Most of the people we will be talking to will understand and answer any questions you have about their way of life. At the auction, please take care not to ask questions of anyone not directly introduced to you, as some will not be receptive. Most are very friendly, but women especially will be shy.*

The day begins at noon, at an auction in a field with open-air tents, babies, skittering horses, Whoopie Pies, cabinetry, quilt fronts, and rabbit cages all strung out in the still, hot air. Along the road we passed carriages pulled by teams of flashing, trotting horses, driven by young men in suspenders, black pants, and the ubiquitous straw hats, banded with strips of cloth. Women young and old wear long, solid blue and gray skirts and thin cotton bonnets, straight pins holding the folds of cloth together, because buttons are not used. Throughout the crowds are odd accessories of modernity: mirrored wraparound sunglasses, standard-issue car seats, required by law despite the use of carriages, icy buckets of Pepsi and Mountain Dew. I make a beeline for doughy homemade pretzels, slippery with butter. There are Heinz ketchup and French's mustard at the concession table. Everywhere are small glimpses of the present. The women gossip amicably about buying and reselling furniture in their shops along the main road; young guys show off on horses up for stud fees. It's not so unlike the town fair that came to North Haven, Connecticut, every September of my childhood.

It's clear that this foray into the past is a lot more complicated than I had hoped and expected. The thing about any community or any industry is this: there are always the innovators, the traditionalists, the leaders, the rabble-rousers. It's been true of all the cheesemakers I've met, European and American, in the past six years. People mark progress, efficiency, and quality in different ways, and rarely, if ever, is there harmony.

The first cheesemaker to visit is Raymond Fisher. I meet his oldest son first, toting the youngest, a girl, on his narrow hip. Everyone, but especially the children, speaks in a lovely, soft lilt, the result of early years speaking Dutch German dialect rather than English. His wife comes next, carrying the last of the spring strawberries in an enormous bowl, pleasant but distant, to reclaim her baby and quickly move inside, leaving me kicking dirt clods in the driveway and waiting for Raymond to appear. When he does, driving a team of sturdy field horses fresh from setting the irrigation system, he is young and friendly, covered with the dusty soil of this rainless early summer.

We go into the cheese house, a small shed with a room and self-serve case for yogurt, cheese, milk, and cream. I noticed in earlier, unsupervised pokings that Raymond also sells kombucha, the fermented black tea that is gripping New York, Whole Foods, and the like as the latest get-healthy trend. As we talk in the cheeseroom, he suits up with a beard net, latex gloves, and plastic apron, all of which seem bizarrely out of place next to the rusty, paint-flaky cylinder used for cottage cheese making. Raymond is well schooled in the teachings of the Weston A. Price Foundation, a group I know from the farmers' market entrepreneur Nina Planck for its education about, and resources for sourcing, raw milk. In his study I see a copy of *The Milkweed*, a lefty newspaper about world dairy markets, one of the few resources I trust to learn what's really going on in the world of milk futures and FDA approval of cloned dairy cows. Raymond reminds me so poignantly of dozens of young cheesemakers I've met who are deeply concerned with their animals, their industry, the food they make every day to feed visitors to their farms. And yet, when September 11 comes up, he pauses, remembering that day in, what was it? 2003? When the terrorists flew planes into the World Trade Center. Raymond remembers that day because so many people in his community were late to finish their work, crowded around contraband radios to hear the details of the historic attack. The whole meeting is an odd collision of curiosity and accessibility. His interest in cheese, dairy, and food is palpable, but his access is almost unbelievably limited. I offer to send him a copy of Paul Kindstedt's *Artisan Cheesemaking in America*, my favorite and best resource for understanding where cheese comes from and how it is made today. Raymond is amenable, and I realize that I've come looking for the history of cheesemaking in America, only to offer a key to its far-distant present.

From Raymond's I'm off to pick up John Esh, the Amish renegade who brought me to Pennsylvania in the first place. Within every community there are the boundary pushers and the traditionalists, and the Amish, I find, are no different. That John will ride in a car at all might be considered questionable by more traditional members of the community. That he will ride in a car with a strange girl from New York City and take her around to farms is definitely questionable. That he is, in fact, an incredibly shrewd businessman looking to expand the reach of his cheese, interested in learning what faraway urban markets like Philadelphia and Washington, D.C., will buy, and how much they will pay makes him something of an upstart. John is an Amish badass. Make no mistake, however; John may be a boundary pusher, but he's not a rule breaker. He doesn't have electricity, he won't drive, he has no telephone on his property, nor does he insist, like some of his woodworker neighbors, that a cell phone is necessary to conduct business. John is solidly, unequivocally Amish. But as a partner in the Goot Essa cheese company, he's willing to interface just enough with the outside world to sell more of his product. Not just willing but curious. He's a sharp guy, quick to recognize opportunity. Apparently, he considers my visit such an opportunity and suggests we visit another neighbor and friend, Mark Stoltzfus.

Like Raymond, Mark has a small shed with a self-serve, honor-system fridge packed with raw milk, raw butter, cottage cheese, and Baby Swiss. John wants me to taste Mark's cheese. What's interesting is that John doesn't make his **Goot Essa Cheddar**; instead he sends his milk off to Isreal Kinsinger, the preeminent cheesemaker in the area. In fact, Isreal rules the cheesemaking roost in these parts. Those farmers who don't send milk directly to him (there are five besides John) make cheese at home, following his recipes. This came up at Raymond's, when I tasted his Colby and, though I wished otherwise, found it just wasn't that good. I asked how he had learned cheesemaking and everyone looked at me as if I were nuts. Obviously, he learned from Isreal. Everyone does. Isreal's been making cheese for twenty-five years. As a small child he learned from his father, and now is training his two boys in the craft.

Most American cheesemakers I know have studied. The best ones have gone abroad or brought in European cheesemakers to help establish their operations. The early pioneers have taught their neighbors, who have augmented this study with classes, lectures, endless nights on the Internet, and limitless tasting of everything they can get their hands on. But here, everyone learns from Isreal.

Undoubtedly, Mark Stoltzfus did as well. But Mark has been doing a lot of tinkering. He's making the cheese himself, in a room off his barn, and has come up with products John is eyeing. We sit down to taste, starting with a fat lump of yellow butter. I've had a lot of raw-milk butter, especially from Amish producers, and it often tastes cheesy, which isn't a good thing for butter. It's not typically light and delicate but gamy, as if you know there was manure nearby when the animal was milked. Mark's, though, is sweet and clean, like milk and clover, all smooth and fatty. His cottage cheese, a food I've never had a particular fondness for, is how I imagine the ecstatic union of ricotta and fresh cheese to be, though it has little to do with either one. Little curdy bits bound together with yellow cream, it's insanely rich, thick, and spreadable, singing with sweet, milky intensity. I gobble down several heaping spoonfuls while Mark watches me shyly. The stuff is delicious. Before we even get to the cheese, I ask if Mark has a pasteurizer. Raw-milk butter and cottage cheese, mere hours old, is completely illegal for sale in most markets, though by Pennsylvania law, folks can buy raw dairy that's sold at the farm of production. If Mark could duplicate this in pasteurized form . . . I could think of three dozen restaurants that would buy it by the tub, not to mention the farmers' markets of Philly, D.C., and New York. With all the American cheese available, there is still a total shortage of fresh dairy. There are almost no options for consumers unable to drive to rural farms one or two times a week. Around this time, John begins to get a glint in his eye.

We move on to the cheese, though my enthusiasm has waned considerably. I've always hated "Swiss" cheese. When I was a kid, the sliced kind reminded me unsettlingly of unwashed feet, but somehow sweet, which seemed like a very wrong flavor combination. That characteristic "Swissy" flavor comes from propionic bacteria, which emit a pungent, fruity smell.

"Baby Swiss" is simply younger and creamier, aged for less time, so the paste is semisoft and squashy in texture, more like Havarti. I am prepared, especially after my cottage cheese epiphany, to hate it.

Though Baby Swiss is standard issue for Amish producers in this area, guided by the Cheese Guru Isreal, Mark's is different, and good. Very good, in fact. The bone-colored wedge is smooth and elastic, but has not fallen prey to the gummy, plasticky texture that plagues most block cheese of the sort. And the flavor is more cheese than propionic: mild, buttery, with a bit of tang, and beautifully balanced. This is not sophisticated cheese, but Mark clearly has the knack. I am impressed and tell them so. I think Mark is flattered, but he is also eyeing me like a bug the whole time, and he may have just been relieved to see me move on with my day. John, on the other hand, now has the glint in both eyes. Is it really good? Do people buy this kind of cheese? How much do they pay for it? Can it possibly be true that people in cities like New York can't find good local butter? Really?

It's worth noting that nine months later, the newest addition to the Goot Essa line of cheeses was announced. Mark Stoltzfus's Baby Swiss had come on board, and though the butter and cottage cheese would have to wait until an affordable pasteurizer could be found, John had made his first move.

Later that evening, sitting on a stump in the woods behind John's house, full of fire-grilled hamburger patties and melted cheddar, I watch John's eight blond children toast marshmallows and ask him about the Amish tradition of cheesemaking. I am tired, primed for a good story about his

German ancestors who settled their strict communities around the generations-old foundation of woodworking and cheese-making. Before he answers, I confide that I am trying to conceptualize this book I am writing and I realize that I need to go back to the beginning. Before I can coalesce my thoughts about the future of cheese in America, I want to go back to its roots. That's what brought me to Pennsylvania in the first place. The Amish are the closest I could get to origin of American cheesemaking. So what were those origins?

John is superpolite, and he kind of coughs and scratches his beard and says, "We only started making cheese twenty-five or thirty years ago." The Amish are dairy farmers, but apparently milking cows does not equate with cheesemaking. When I point out the well-established history of cheesemaking in Germany, John is fascinated. I'm quite sure he had never thought of it. Yes, he agrees, it is odd that the American Amish didn't bring this tradition with them. But, alas, they didn't. Quite earnestly he looks up at me. "I'm so sorry we haven't been making cheese for longer. I hope that doesn't ruin your book."

On that rousing note, my trip to the Amish concludes, and I am left with the great gulf between my romantic assumptions and reality. Cheesemaking in America has been so referential for so long, looking to the styles and practices of Europe, that I'd hoped to discover true "American cheese." Something better and more honorable in its flavor and practices than Kraft Singles, though simpler and less sophisticated than the single-name offerings most cheesemakers, big and small, are turning out today. I thought I'd find the first real American table cheese, made for everyday eating, within a community that was itself arrested in time. I'd come to the Amish because, I thought, they'd created a world where things are done the way they'd always been done.

Instead, I found out that the Amish are like nearly every other cheesemaker in America: trying to figure out how to make cheese, muddling their way through a tricky, mercurial chemistry experiment that they took up only a generation ago. But unlike nearly every other cheesemaker in America, they're doing it in a vacuum. When I sent John a thank-you box of cheese, I included clothbound English farmhouse Cheddar, so his family could taste something other than the block form they produce. They had never heard of such a thing, and he marveled at the differences in flavor, texture, smell, appearance. For the Amish in John Esh's neck of Pennsylvania, Isreal Kinsinger is where you learn cheese, not in France or England, Normandy or Devon, not bloomy rind or goat milk. It's not the American Cheese Society or *The New York Times* or a segment on the Food Network. It's the cheese that Isreal's dad figured out how to make and the improvements that neighbors may contribute along the way.

The truth is, I haven't found indigenous "American cheese." The closest I've come are blocks of aged cow milk cheese, known as cheddar, dating back to small dairy cooperatives and village factories in the mid-nineteenth century. American cheese began with cheddar types, and if you look at the oldest producers in the country, they're making the same cheese they were producing one hundred years ago. It's only recently that American cheesemakers have cast an eye back across the ocean to the true English cheddars of Devon and Somerset, the big cylinders wrapped up in cheesecloth like R2D2 mummies. So while John Esh joins people he'll never meet in the charge toward better cheese, dozens of other producers continue the tradition of "American cheese" worth eating. It's all cheddar, baby.

NOTES ON AMERICAN CHEDDAR
AND CHEDDAR-STYLE CHEESE

There are blocks of cheddar and wheels of cheddar. Little cylinders that look like concrete plugs called "truckles" or, less romantically, "midgets." There is the regionally driven and fiercely debated color comparison (yellow or white?). The difference, by the way, is that one is tinted with a flavorless, plant-derived coloring called annatto and the other is not. I've already established myself as a white-cheddar girl, though the yellow (orange, really) was, and still is, typical in New York State and Wisconsin. In the past ten years, American cheddar makers have duly noted the magnificence of the clothbound English cheddars made in Somerset, like the famed Montgomery's and Keen's, and have explored traditional English processes, resulting in mammoth thirty- to fifty-pound, bandaged wheels, wrapped and aged in cheesecloth and altogether different from the traditional American forty-pound blocks, which spend a few months or even a few years in a vacuum-sealed bag.

The clothbound wheels have a drier texture and an earthier, mustier smell. There is a distinct whiff of the aging room, and if you nosh the bit just under the bandage, you'll swear you're eating rich, minerally dirt, made firm. Cheddar, as most of us know it, including myself, back to the early Cracker Barrel days, is a bit damp and crumbly, the result of a hermetically sealed cheese whose internal moisture has had no opportunity to evaporate beneath its plastic sheath. The flavor, meanwhile, can be mild and minimal in the case of a young'un (a month or two old) or, as most Americans like it, brawny and sharp!, with stinging, biting intensity and a mouth-watery finish thanks to high, unapologetic acidity.

The thing I'm always cautious about when tasting cheddars is bitterness. So many start placidly, rolling up with a little more body, some lemony, slightly sour notes, or perhaps a mellow, sweeter, butterscotch hum, and then, whap! It's as if someone had you lick a battery. You're left with a dull mouthful of metal, a whiff of nail polish remover, and a slightly dirty, bitter afterglow. You have to be careful.

What joins all cheddar, regardless of size, shape, age, or color, is that they are cheddared. It is, in fact, a verb, and it refers to the cheesemaking technique unique to this cheese. Like Vermont Shepherd, the cheese is coagulated, stirred, and cut, but then so many extra steps go into honest, earnest cheddar that it makes the style extremely slow and labor-intensive. The curds are cut into little cubes, a quarter to five-eighths of an inch. As with any cheese, the bigger curds hold more moisture, and are generally aged for a briefer period of time, the goal being a moister, younger, milder cheese. The smaller curds, when pressed and aged, can get pretty fierce given the proper conditions. The brothy stew of curds and whey is heated and stirred to about 102 degrees, the whey is drained, and then the curds mat up at the bottom of the vat.

Remember my anxiety under David Major's watch to dip and scoop with great expediency? My concern (his concern, really) was that sluggish scooping would give the curds time to solidify into a gluey mass. With cheddar, you want that solidification. Thanks to higher acidity and some heat, the mass that forms is a wonderful, rubbery, squeaky mat. You could rest comfortably on this stuff if it were dry. From that floppy white curd mat, loaf-shaped blocks are sliced (often, excitingly and dramatically with a machete-looking apparatus), and then the blocks are turned and stacked. Then they're turned and stacked again. Sometimes they're turned and stacked a third time. Then the stacks are left alone, lest they get too high, but the loaf blocks themselves are turned. This does two things in addition to developing beautifully chiseled back muscles: (1) The weight of the loaf blocks atop one another presses residual whey from the curd and (2) the warm loaf block of curd in contact with its warm loaf block neighbor encourages and enables the development of acidity. In fact, the cheddaring process ends (is dismantled by the cheesemaker) when the acidity reaches a predetermined level. The whey is constantly checked, and at a pH of .5 to .7 (remember, a neutral pH, neither acidic nor basic, registers at 7.0, so .5 to .7 is superacidic by comparison), the loaf blocks are unstacked and the curd is chopped into smaller bits and milled, like sausage meat. Then it's salted and the squeaky, tart little bits are packed into a form of some size and shape, and aging commences.

All cheddars, great and small, must be cheddared, but the resulting cheese can be many things. Even traditional American cheddar, in block, vacuum-sealed form, appears in many guises. I found myself struggling to write about American cheddars, because so many seem like . . . cheddar. There is a lot of American cheddar, and most of it is bad. That may be surprising, because much of what you can buy in the supermarket is perfectly acceptable. But there are so many potential flaws to cheddar. Atop my list, and previously mentioned, is bitterness. Nail polish remover is the first awful thing I'm reminded of, and bile is the second. Bad cheddar tastes as if you just threw up. It gnaws at the back of your throat, it stings your tongue, it feels dry and jagged to swallow. Some people call that "sharp." I call it gross, unpleasant, and poorly made. Sharpness, acidity, should always be in balance.

The second thing to be wary of is texture. Well-made cheddar, regardless of age, should be creamy. The plastic-sealed kind will be wetter and the clothbound kind drier, but there should be smoothness once you bite down. Cheddar that breaks apart into a thousand identifiably grainy bits is not good. Exceedingly rubbery is also not good. Younger cheddar will have more boing, spring, and bend, but it should yield under tooth. Remember, of course, that Gumby is so called because he was originally invented for toothless infants to gum as their teeth arrived for an inaugural appearance. Young cheddar might be bendy, but it should not be Gumby.

Flavorings are my third area of caution. Second only to Jack cheese (or maybe even first to Jack), cheddar is flavored with everything from pepper to herbs to horrible concoctions like salsa-lime. Flavored cheese is not, in and of itself, problematic.

Sometimes it can be quite delicious and satisfying, especially when it tastes like the flavoring and not an approximation of the flavoring, and second, when you can still taste the milk (the cheese). The flavoring should be in addition to, not instead of, so you get a balance of approachability, savoriness, and a whiff of whatever the flavoring is. Those cautions duly heeded, here are America's best cheddars and cheddar types:

➤ GOOT ESSA
MILL HILL, PENNSYLVANIA

John Esh has the finest barn I've ever been in. The cows dock in an airy greenhouse of sorts, the sides open to cooling cross-breezes, the ground padded with fresh sawdust, everything clean and dry. When I visited, I was so transfixed watching his wife and small children milk their herd that I didn't notice the wasp that crawled up the back of my shirt. I thought it was a barn fly, and so I scraped and swiped, watching his eight-year-old son run from cow to cow, deftly wielding a portable milk can. Not until my back was smarting and stinging did I ask a friend to investigate the damage and pluck the still-humming wasp from his anchorage under my bra strap. Despite the sting, I wanted to sleep in that barn, in the downy piles of bedding protected from slanting sun, with mewling kittens and warm, steady bovine exhalations.

John doesn't make **Goot Essa Cheddar**. He trucks his milk to the Amish cheesemaker Isreal Kinsinger, but I firmly believe that his raw material makes some of the best block cheddar—or cheese, period—I've ever had. It frustrates me that Isreal insists on pasteurizing John's fine milk prior to cheesemaking, but it seems he has been convinced of the danger of raw milk, which is a shame. It's the traditional "American cheddar" presentation: a big forty-pound block, white, not orange, aged in Cryovac packaging for a damp, dense, chewy crumble. In Amish vernacular, the name "Goot Essa" means "good cheese." And it is. It's straightforward but so tasty. Well-done cheddar of this sort has a delicate, brothy flavor that fortifies. Sure, it's a little bit sharp, but you don't taste acid. It's not a pow-pow-pow kind of flavor. It's creamy and savory, releasing the perfect amount of milk fat as the pieces break apart in your mouth. What's astounding to me is that the cheese is aged for three years. Most multiyear cheddars are held to develop that intense, pokey bite. Goot Essa just deepens in its brown-butteriness. Be warned: I played with grilled cheese recipes in search of the Classic (buttered Pullman bread, cheddar, bacon, and tomato), and the rich, mellow twang of Goot Essa dissipated completely when heated. I love this cheese, and I love the stake John Esh has taken in American cheesemaking, but don't heat the stuff. It's too subtle, and you'll kill the essence, leaving only temporarily gratifying ropy melted strings.

➤ 5 SPOKE CREAMERY
WESTCHESTER, NEW YORK/
LANCASTER, PENNSYLVANIA

Had the Great Pyramid been built of cheese, the blocks would resemble **Tumbleweed**. They're enormous squares, six inches high, twelve inches across, and covered with a lovely, delicate marshmallow fluff. It doesn't look like cheddar, neither blocks nor cloth-wrapped wheels, though the interior paste has that familiar yellow chunky crumble. When you bite down on a piece, average age eight to ten months, the texture breaks moistly. I said as much to the cheesemaker, Alan Glustoff, who quickly responded, "I can't tell you what's in there." Alan's background is in food chemistry, with a focus on cultured products. This is no doubt helpful when he loads himself into the car and drives to lower Lancaster County, Pennsylvania, to make cheese for four to five days at a clip, using the grass-fed milk of a single Amish farmer's Holstein herd. Nothing, in fact, is in there. The cheese is raw, and several times a month kosher batches are run, with the rabbi dribbling the starter culture in himself. I can only imagine Alan, the middle-aged former R&D guy for Unilever, a microbial rennet–wielding rabbi, and the Amish guy who owns the cows, the farm, and the whole cheesemaking operation. It must be quite a run.

Alan's plan is to secure some government land in Westchester County and move his operation closer to New York, where city folks can visit the operation and learn a bit more about food and where it actually originates. 5 Spoke makes **Redmond Cheddar**, aged for six months, and **Browning Gold**, a two-year wheel in the English tradition. But when I first tasted Tumbleweed, I was impressed because it was cheddarish without being cheddar. What I mean is Tumbleweed boasted the chunky, feathery crumble I appreciate in cheddar, without any sharpness to speak of. It reminded me more immediately of the French cheese Cantal or Salers du Buron. It has discernible sour, leathery notes and a pleasant yogurty twang. Cantal is celebrated for its muted fruitiness, something akin to dried apricots, and Tumbleweed has that in spades. The whole thing is somehow cooling, like fromage blanc made solid.

> **BEECHER'S HANDMADE CHEESE**
SEATTLE, WASHINGTON

The first time I tasted Beecher's **Flagship Reserve**, I didn't know I was doing it. I was sitting on a plastic folding chair, already sweltering under a stifling tent in a parking lot in Burlington, Vermont. That's not the best place for a tent in the middle of August. It was the American Cheese Society's 2007 conference, and the catered lunch was so ungodly inedible (I was served something that appeared to be steamed white fish in a thick, sticky white discharge) that I was happy to eat everything on the platter of complimentary, unmarked cheeses donated by various American producers.

Popping one nubbly tan edge into my mouth, I was pleased to declare to the entire table that the worst cheddar I'd ever had was sitting before us. I figured if I was going to be hot and miserable and eating unidentified white fish I might as well get folks to try the cheese so they could suffer as well. But first I'd really get them primed:

> *Imagine eating a piece of plastic. Diligent chewing will eventually grind down the microscopic, textured grid formed by the mesh the cheese drained in, until the whole wad develops the gluey chomp of pasta that's three minutes shy of al dente. Starchy. It tastes just. like. dirt. Not evocative of dirt, not earthy, not cavey in its aromas, but loamy and muddy as a carp that has permanently melded to its mucky bottom home. This cheddar fails on all counts.*

I grabbed a second piece, ready to experience the awfulness again, this time with companions who would agree that the cheese was, indeed, profoundly terrible, when I bit into an epiphany of savory cheesiness. I realized, too late to hide, that I had publicly condemned this glorious thing on the basis of its rind. A fatal tasting error, amid a dozen colleagues, and a good reminder that eating the rind may not hurt you, but it can skew your impression of an otherwise great cheese with potentially embarrassing results.

Beecher's itself is a shop in Seattle's famous Pike Place Market, where fishmongers throw whole tuna around to impress the tourists, and Kurt Beecher Dammeier thought it would be neat to make cheese in a public space where people could watch and learn. Kurt also thinks it's neat to own four upscale retail shops, run a restaurant, write a cookbook, own a brewery, and generally pursue any food-related project that catches his fancy. He lived in Chamonix, France, for a month with his wife and adolescent sons so the boys could learn French and they could all focus on downhill skiing, which they love. The guy's a true entrepreneur, with his hands in many pots and vats.

Beecher's has been around only since 2002 and owns about two hundred cows, which are rented by the farmer on whose land they live in Duval, Washington, who then sells the milk back to Beecher's for cheesemaking. Of course, Kurt's already looking to buy a farm so Beecher's can have total control over its milk and move to organic farming without exploding the cost of the milk (and thus the cost of the cheese). Kurt does not, himself, make cheese (the credit there goes to a second-generation cheesemaker, Brad Sinko, and his team of apprentices), but as the idea and flavor guy, Kurt gets credit for the company's **Flagship** cheese, from which Flagship Reserve sprang.

When I tasted cheese with Kurt, I asked him why the cheese is called Flagship. His answer speaks to both marketing (a necessary evil to consider) and flavor (why the cheese is so good). Kurt figures, you call something cheddar and cut it into eight-ounce squares, people dismiss it. Beecher's Flagship is white, comes in big blocks, has no rind, and is sold in small squares, vacuum-sealed in plastic. Those things, in the mind of most consumers, equal sub-par, industrial cheese.

Technically, Flagship isn't *just* a cheddar. The cultures used to acidify the milk are a mixture of typical cheddar cultures but also cultures found in Swiss cheese. Beecher's didn't want to make crumbly, sharp, white American cheddar. It wanted something a little smoother and more meltable, but also sweeter and nuttier.

The leap from Flagship to Flagship Reserve came about when the cheese was made in a wheel, not a block, and cloth-bound, like a traditional English farmhouse Cheddar. It's the lard-brushed cloth that was primarily responsible for my initially awful experience with the cheese. Its fine weave allows for breathability, meaning the cheese underneath hardens into a plasticky crust. You can't tell from looking, though, because the color doesn't change. That microscopic grid pattern I could feel rubbing against my tongue was the impression from the wrapping, and the unadulterated damp soil flavor comes from humid cloth, lard, and contact with shelving over the course of a year and a half.

My second try, when I got the "glory taste," I was actually

getting Flagship Reserve and not just its shell. It's a lovely deep toffee hue, chewy, and toothsome. There's the tiniest bit of elasticity to the texture, so it doesn't just crumble up into wet bits the way block cheddars do. There's a whole range of mellow, savory flavors, hard-boiled eggs and buttered toast, those Swiss cultures keeping it a little bit sweet with the barest background of butterscotch. It manages all the comfort of mac and cheese, without the mac.

Variations on a theme seem to suit this cheesemaker quite nicely. The original Flagship is also jazzed up with flavorings if you're into that sort of thing. I tend not to be but was oddly delighted with the **No Woman** (as in Bob Marley's "No Woman, No Cry"), which is laced not with kind bud but with Jamaican jerk seasoning. I imagine it melted over tortilla chips with braised chicken thigh as the greatest nacho treat ever. There's also **Marco Polo**, which tarts up the sweet, creamy flesh of Flagship with whole black Madagascar peppercorns. It's the crunchy/creamy, spicy/milky, racy/mellow line that's delivered with aplomb.

Also, a quick note on a freaking amazing, "plain Jane" cheese. Jack cheese. Semisoft, elastic, milky, mild, brilliantly meltable, but generally just the goop that holds the bread together. Except not in this case. Beecher's **Just Jack** is awesome, creamy, and whole milk–rich. It's also considerably more expensive than you're likely used to. It is truly worth it. At a recent sampling of a dozen Jack cheeses, Beecher's rocked the tasting. No question, it was the best.

I'm conditioned to assume that Beecher's cheeses' depth and complexity, most notably those of Flagship Reserve, are an instant indication of superior, raw milk. In this case, that's not so. All of Beecher's milk comes from grass-fed cows, with no bovine growth hormones (rBGH) added, so it's certainly of stellar credentials. But the milk *is* pasteurized. They bang out an occasional wheel of **Raw Milk Flagship Reserve**, but otherwise it's all pasteurized, all the time. In Kurt's experience, customers want consistency. Beecher's pasteurized milk helps deliver that predictable (delicious) flavor, week in, week out.

➤ BRAVO FARMS
TRAVER, CALIFORNIA

Sometimes I'm overwhelmed by the enormity of choice in cheddar. Bravo makes five cheddars and makes them all well. It is a superlative example of a cheesemaker producing "everyday" kinds of cheeses with great skill. There are four block styles and one clothbound wheel aspiring to a traditional English flavor profile. Bravo's recipes date back to Bill Boersma's tinkerings as a Fresno-area dairyman turned aspiring cheesemaker. Like many small family dairies, the Boersmas struggled to survive on milking alone. Beginning in the late 1970s, this was possible, but by the 1990s, in the California Central Valley particularly, profitability in cows meant massive confinement operations milking tens of thousands of animals. The opportunities for small dairies shrank as industrial operations expanded. By 1995, the couple turned to value-added products—making cheese greatly increased the value of their milk. Ten years later, having a chance to sell the dairy, the two discovered a neighboring young'un, Jonathan Van Rÿn, who'd studied cheesemaking in college. Their partnership meant several things: the continuation of Bill's cheese, an outlet for his experience and

Is Raw-Milk Cheese
Always Better?

I've been schooled that raw-milk cheese always tastes better. So I was a bit shocked when Kurt Dammeier freely acknowledged that Beecher's Flagship Reserve is usually made of pasteurized milk because it delivers greater predictability, more consistent flavor, and an easier sell. Was this an acceptable admission? Isn't it Beecher's responsibility to showcase the unique if mercurial flavors of its milk? I guess the answer is, if you want to run a successful business with national distribution, providing a more predictable product, then no, not necessarily. And I have to acknowledge that, in Kurt's particular case, he's first and foremost a businessman. He has a point.

But when his antithesis, a former scientist-turned-cheesemaker who makes cheese completely by hand for a dozen or so restaurants and farmers' markets, said a similar thing, I began to reconsider the challenges of raw milk. When I talked to Soyoung Scanlan of Andante Dairy, she reminded me that though pasteurization denatures proteins and kills enzymes, a lot of naturally occurring off-flavors can occur from raw milk, such as rancidity due to the enzyme lipase. And in her mind, flavor comes primarily from starter culture, used in both raw and pasteurized milk cheeses. Ninety-nine percent of Soyoung's offerings are pasteurized because she makes a lot of soft, young cheese, none of which age the requisite sixty days. She has no choice but to pasteurize, nor does any American producer who wants to play in the realm of the moist and buttery.

I have no doubt that raw-milk cheese is nutritionally superior. It is chock full of heat-sensitive folic acids and vitamins B6 and C, which are destroyed during pasteurization, along with enzymes such as lactase, lipase, and phosphotase. It is also teeming with good bacteria that thrive in the gut and boost immunity, fighting off harmful bacteria that may develop. On a purely instinctual level, raw milk appeals to me because it is minimally tampered with. This does not mean, however, that raw milk inherently makes better cheese, and in fact it often makes cheese that varies with the composition of the milk. If your goal is to go national, this degree of authenticity may make life harder rather than easier.

Some say that pasteurizing is lazy. They argue that you don't have to understand your milk as well, you don't have to work as hard to make a good cheese. I don't necessarily agree. There are different markets in America, and if your target is distribution on a national scale, where you can't feed customers face to face and can't rely on middlemen to educate your consumers, you need a cheese that will be tasty all the time. That's Kurt. In this sense, pasteurizing the milk for Flagship Reserve makes all the sense in the world. The two most important things remain: the quality and treatment of his cows and the final flavor of the cheese.

connections in marketing and selling that cheese, and an added value for the next generation to support a family dairy of Jersey cows.

The difference between Bravo Farms **Cheddar** and **Ched-**

dar Reserve is age: the first is an ideal young cheddar. At three months it's still quite moist and extremely mild. There is no acidity, not a hint of sharp bitey punch. It's completely approachable, milky, and sweet. At first I was at a loss for what to say about the cheese. It's just cheddar, right? Right—except that "just cheddar," made consistently well, is a rarity in the sea of options. Most young cheddars are gummy and bland, with a rubbery chew more like eraser than food. Bravo's is almost melting. In fact, I did melt it, over burgers, and it softened into a perfect gooey pool of ropey, lactic delight. There was no separation, no greasy scum, and its hay-ey sweetness remained intact. Jumping up a few years, the Cheddar Reserve is the sharp one. Cautiously I dug out a crumble. The youthful pliability was gone, and I wondered if it would have the trademark burnt toast–pineapple prickle that assaults many of America's aged cheddars. I am pleased to report it does not. The first dry nubbin popped under tooth, still creamy with fatty Jersey milk but fruity and mouth-watery. Any more age and its precarious balance might tip to bitter, but as it is sold, there's a marigold astringency to the nose and zesty pep. It won't be your melter, but it marries beautifully with the Saison Dupont I've been drinking while retasting the lineup. Yeasty, fruity, and bold.

Bravo's flavored offerings look like cheddar marbled with alien blood. The **Western Sage** could be laced with algae or, more likely, pesto, but the first sniff is the tip-off. It smells like really good, sizzling breakfast sausage. The body of the cheese is young like the signature Cheddar, and that simple, creamy backdrop is ideal for the musky herbaceousness of sage. It tastes green but muted and savory. Its second flavored

choice, I figured, surely wouldn't stack up. Here, the cheddared bits of curd are clearly outlined by meandering veins of
circus orange. The cheese looks like bad leopard print. **Original Chipotle**, I thought for sure, would fail to reach my standards of what chipotle should be. See, if you claim chipotle,
you have to deliver two things, in balance. The first is spice.
Sure, it's a pepper. But the second, often elusive, element is
smoke. Smoke like rusty Spanish pimento, as opposed to
American campfire Gouda. And delight! Bravo's Chipotle has
both, in equal measure. The husky smoky comes on first,
chased by tip-of-tongue prickle. The undertone is all savory
roasted red pepper. I imagine that melted on a grilled cheese
with slab bacon, a bit of cilantro purée, and a sliver of tomato,
one might be able to create the perfect nosh. Or on nachos.
That would also rock.

Bravo's "fanciest" cheddar is the **Silver Mountain**, a
clothbound wheel that's gentler in flavor than the Reserve but
far more complex than the Original. The texture is dense and
flakes off in luscious golden hunks under moderate knife tip,
smelling of earth and cellar, with a particular English Cheddar flavor that I've described as cellary. A student misinter-
preted once and shouted out, "Yeah, it does taste like celery. Or
like fresh horseradish, without the spice." And he was exactly
right. It's cellary celery, light and vegetal, with the aroma of
damp, turned soil. I was surprised by ten guests on a recent
evening and threw the contents of my fridge onto the table. It
was the Silver Mountain that was quickly, greedily devoured.
Like all of Bravo's cheese, it's unpasteurized.

➤ CABOT CREAMERY
CABOT, VERMONT

When I first started working in cheese, my mother wanted to be supportive. That meant she began buying the fancy, waxed-block, "Private Stock" cheddar from Cabot Creamery, aged for sixteen months. The one housed in the deli department rather than the dairy case of the local Stop & Shop. Nowadays, she shops at a nearby Italian specialty store, a bold step up and out, but I still remember her pride over the $10 hunk of Cabot. And I remember thinking, "Eeeeeeeee. Cabot." I knew Cabot as the cheese you bought at the supermarket. The cheddar. The Colby. The Jack. The butter. I thought it was passé when I was just getting into cheese. As with many producers, I've changed my tune. Now when I go to the grocery store, I opt *for* Cabot in the dairy department because I know the milk is coming from Vermont, New York, and a smattering of New England family farms while the supermarket private label comes from . . . where? Cabot's history in Vermont dates back to 1919, when ninety-four farmers formed a cooperative, at the cost of $5 per cow and a cord of wood to fuel the boiler. Now more than a third of the state's dairy farms are co-op members, and Cabot owns and operates one of New York State's best-known cheese factories, under the McCadam brand. All told, 1,300 farms own a bit of Cabot made from their milk.

When Cabot was just beginning, there were 17 percent more cows than people in Vermont. Pooling milk to make butter and selling it all over New England was brilliant, lucrative, easy! Or at least a reliable way to support a family farm. By the 1980s, Vermont's family farms had dwindled to 2,000, less than 20 percent of what existed in the 1950s. Cabot has become a relatively large cooperative not because it's objectively huge but because most family farms have ceased to be.

Visiting its Web site, I see the Cabot I know of old. The dairy case Cabot. And as I look for any mention of "the cheese" you need to know about, there's no sign. It's a bit of a secret. It's **Cabot Clothbound Cheddar**. And it represents a singular kind of collaborative partnership between Big Cheese and Little Cheese that will ultimately bring Better Cheese from Family Dairies to All of America. It's really important, and the cheese is really phenomenal. Cabot Clothbound—meaning wrapped in cheesecloth in the English style—has been in the works for ten years. Cabot first approached the small sheep cheesemaker Vermont Shepherd (see "Vermont Shepherd" on page 70) to age wheels for it, an impossibility in its own creamery, where it makes fresh cultured products and couldn't introduce or encourage molded rind development (furries in your sour cream are *bad*). Although aging at Vermont Shepherd didn't work, another cheesemaker with possibilities popped up in the form of Jasper Hill Farm. Jasper Hill helped identify Cabot's finest single farm in the nearby area to provide the raw material. Large by Cabot standards, with 250 to 300 Holstein milkers, the farm proved that it could still produce superior, clean milk. With this single milk source, Cabot makes the cheese and the naked two-day-old wheels are sent to Greensboro for cloth wrapping and a brushing with melted lard. The Cellars at Jasper Hill continues to brush, turn, and age the cheese for twelve to twenty-four months. In 2006, it won Best in Show at the American Cheese Society conference (see "The Rogue Cheesemakers and the Future of American Cheese" on page 346 for more about the important symbiosis between Big Cheese and Little Cheese in Vermont).

In 2008, Cabot Clothbound is still elusive. That's the kicker about aged cheeses. You don't know what you're going to get until they're ready, and if the cheese suddenly becomes the Next Best Thing, you can't respond to market demand for months or even years. By 2009, Cabot Clothbound's availability will skyrocket, as the primary tenant in the aging facility the Cellars at Jasper Hill. When you can nab a chunk, do it.

It's only where the wedge of cheese has been cut that you even realize there is cloth on the outside. It hangs, slightly shredded along the edge, and you can see the microscopic weave of cheesecloth and the flaking layers of russet and ochre molds that look painted on. They have, in a sense, been painted on, because the cloth binding is sealed with regular brushings of melted lard that crust over time to create an earthen shell around each wheel. This allows the paste to breathe and moisture to evaporate, while protecting the insides from invasive molds. The lard-brushed cloth, then, doesn't even smell like cheese and certainly lacks the tangy sharpness I expect of American cheddar. Instead it has the pleasantly musty smell of a damp root cellar full of old potato bags, plus a meaty, jerky whiff. Inside, the pale straw-colored paste has been masterfully pressed smooth. There are no visible clumps or chunks when you look at the cheese, no evidence that small bits were once pressed together to make something solid. Still, a firm knife stroke produces downy snow-flakes of cheese. When Cabot Clothbound was first created, it had a signature candied flavor that has subdued over the past few years of production. I used to feel not that I was eating cheddar but that I was eating those yellow cellophane-wrapped butterscotch candies, with salt, and though it was delicious it seemed nearly artificial in its intensity. Now the sweetness just hangs there, and the first bite is like baked potatoes, tight in their papery jackets, with melted lumps of sweet butter tucked and melting inside. There is just enough acidity, enough pluck and tang, to maintain balance, but the roundness calls to mind an elusive spoonful of perfectly, patiently browned butter, tasting of nuts though there are none to be found. Cabot Clothbound is compulsive, and though I have overgorged, I always return for another small crumble, a sheer shaving, a fourth or sixth chance to detect all the subtleties that make this cheese so delicious.

➤ GRAFTON VILLAGE CHEESEMAKING COMPANY
GRAFTON VILLAGE, VERMONT

Talk about classic, traditional, historical American white cheddar, and you have to talk about Grafton. It's best for me to openly admit my biases right now: the story of Grafton is one of countless stories that illustrate why Vermont is such an enviable, progressive state. People ask me all the time why Vermont is turning out so many excellent and varied cheeses, and I just can't say anything more specific than "Because it's Vermont. They're just . . . cooler there." And please note, when people are inquiring about Vermont cheeses, they're talking about teeny little farms, couples making exotic molded wheels in the backyard, generally not factories making block cheese. They're not talking about cheddar factories, but in this case, I am, because the story of this factory is still proof of why Vermonters are so neat, or, more accurately put, why Vermont seems to lure people in, and back, across decades from childhood to adulthood. Vermont gets under people's skin, and they return to nurture and support this place that changed their life at some point. It happens surprisingly frequently in cheese.

So the story of Grafton cheese begins in 1892 and—this is great—the original cheesemaking was done on the first floor of an old frame house. On the second floor was a dance hall. They'd hold box socials, where the local women would each make a boxed lunch that would be auctioned off to an audience of men. The highest bidder got the lunch and the babe, and then, presumably, everybody danced, while the cheese lay down below. At that time the Grafton Village Cheese Cooperative (cooperative meaning farmer-owned) was a place where local dairy farmers could bring their surplus milk and have it made into cheese and returned for personal consumption. All this socializing, eating, dancing, and general merriment ended when the frame house burned down in 1912, and cheesemaking ceased until the 1960s.

It took a rich, retired banker from New Jersey to bring Grafton (both the cheese and the town) back from the dead. Having summered in the area, he wanted to preserve the town of Grafton Village, and he formed the Wyndham Foundation, which is still Vermont's largest private foundation. The idea was to offer small investments to businesses that would preserve the local architecture, stimulate business, and keep the area alive. The foundation started strong in 1963 and in 1965 had two for-profit subsidiaries: one was the Grafton Village Cheesemaking Company. The thought was that cheese needs to be made by hand, and that need would keep hands in the area. Milk purchased from local dairies kept farms in the area. Employed folks pulling a salary kept money circulating in the local economy, and so, on the blocks of a small local cheese factory, a whole region could be sustained. And it worked.

Grafton made a few cheese choices in 1965 that remain to this day: (1) To use raw milk. (2) To use Jersey cow milk. (3) To age the cheddar for at least one year. In fact, it now makes cheese every single day of the week but is limited to only two batches of cheese a day. The cheesemaking cycle takes nine hours (nearly twice that of other producers I've met), and slower, more gradual acidification tends to yield balanced, even flavor. Add to this the fact that milk arrives fresh each day at 3 P.M. and half of each 50,000-pound load was in the cows that morning. It's an incredibly immediate process for a producer of this size.

That brings me to my tasting notes. I'm sitting here with a slab of Goot Essa alongside a slab of the two-year-aged **Grafton Classic Reserve**. The Grafton is a slightly deeper yellow, more straw-colored than chicken stock, and looks smoother and moister, and so, I would guess, is younger (and it is, by a year). But the obvious difference is that the Grafton is covered in a thin, watery, glistening sheen. The cheese is sweating fat. *That's* Jersey milk. It's 1 to 2 percent higher in fat content than John Esh's Holsteins (the black-and-white cows most people recognize). Then there's the smell. Goot Essa's is minimal: a bit like a bowl of warm mac and cheese topped with buttered, toasted bread crumbs. But the Grafton . . . I know the flavor is going to be spiky, sharp, and intense, because the sweaty slab in front of me smells like pineapple. Pineapple and burnt toast. You know how pineapple manages to be incredibly sweet but makes your tongue feel hairy and prickly? Cheese that smells pineapply is the same. The Grafton, despite its southern Vermont terroir, has the tropical whiff. Sure enough: a bite does none of the crumble of Goot Essa but smears into a fatty, creamy whirl. Hello, Jerseys. There's no tropical flavor; the lushness is all in the texture. Instead, it's like well-made Key lime pie: tart, tart, tart but milky and full. The two-year is my pick from Grafton's one-to-five-year range. I find those burnt-toast smells evolve, the lemon/custard balance dissolves, and the really aged pieces need a generous gulp of brown ale to go down comfortably. But that's me. I'm finding I like softer, velvety flavors more and more with time. I like a little sweetness. If you want a throat searer, you'll relish the **Four Star**.

A word about the Wyndham Foundation's plan for cheese: Grafton still buys all its milk from Vermont farms (twenty-eight now), though the necessary drive is almost three hours to get enough raw material to produce its current 1.5 million pounds of cheese each year. Although eighty-eight dairy farms closed in Vermont in 2006, most cows are absorbed into neighboring herds so milk production remains relatively consistent even as small dairy farms with 50 to 150 cows go under. As Grafton prepares to open a second plant in Brattleboro, it seems that Wyndham's initial vision has succeeded in creating jobs in the southern half of the state, though history indicates that working in the plant may be far more reliable and appealing than supplying its raw material.

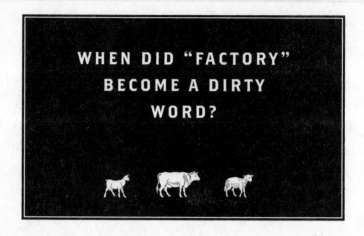

WHEN DID "FACTORY" BECOME A DIRTY WORD?

WHEN I VISITED THE AMISH, I WAS LOOKING FOR SOME DOOR to the past, some way of understanding cheese in America. I've never understood why "American cheese" doesn't mean cheese made in the United States but equates to a Kraft Single. What is a Kraft Single anyway? Or Velveeta? They share a peculiar slippery mouthfeel that disturbs me. They have a texture I can best describe as flaccid. Smooth, slippery, and mildly floppy. It's gross. Even when I was small there was something distasteful about digging my grimy fingers under the thin plastic flap and prying open the hermetically sealed slice that was yellow American cheese. That benignly sweet processed flavor. A perfect half moon of little teeth marks in the limp, cantaloupe-colored sheet. Even now, there are some otherwise excellent cheeses that I'll taste and the texture takes me right back to the open fridge, with a perfectly portioned slice of American cheese flapping about my chin.

When did "American cheese" get so bad? And when did it start to get good again? When John Esh and Raymond Fisher couldn't help me out, I called the oldest curmudgeon I could think of to ask him. Ig Vella. The Godfather of Cheese. That's pejorative, by the way. The Godfather. Ig made sure I got that straightaway. In the early 1980s, he said, they called him "The Godfather," and it wasn't a compliment. I'm still not entirely sure who "they" were.

Now I wonder if they called him "The Godfather" because Ig says what he thinks, and what he thought in the 1990s, when small cheesemakers were becoming all the foodie rage, was that factories could make quality cheese too. Ig remembers when the local cheese factory was the partner of the family dairy farm, rather than some anonymous industrial behemoth that existed to flatten agricultural America. Back in Ig's youth (granted, that was a pretty long time ago), the cheese factory was often a cooperative, turning the milk of twenty or thirty farms, each with forty or fifty cows, into a well-made cheese that generated income into the fall and winter, even as the natural milk supply was dwindling and the cows were drying off—resting for a few months before giving birth to begin the milking cycle anew.

Ig Vella is the current owner of the Vella Cheese Company. When I called California to see if I might schedule some time with the illustrious Mr. Vella, he answered the phone himself. From what I could tell when I was sitting in his cluttered office in Sonoma, he does that a lot. He took a telemarketer's call when we were talking and kept the guy on the phone for a solid ten minutes to make sure he knew who he was talking to. The poor telemarketer was trying to sell a cut-and-wrap machine. Ig invited him to come by anytime and take a step back in time. The sales guy had no idea what he was getting into. Nor, I fear, did I.

Ig reminds me of Rodney Dangerfield, mainly because he has a bulbous nose and big, poppy blue eyes that don't blink a lot when he stares at you. He wears, apparently at all times, a neatly folded paper cap, like an ice cream man from the 1950s. When you talk, Ig just listens. For me, this has the effect of drawing words out, well beyond the point where I know what I'm saying. We sat down, my laptop and I, and Ig asked me what this book was about anyhow. I started to explain that, well, it was about my life in cheese and my observations and stories about American cheese in general. Ig just sat there. I assumed I needed to clarify. "I don't want to write another reference book," I intoned. "I want to contextualize this stuff we call American cheese and talk about the issues that matter." Silence. Ig leaned farther back in his busted brown leather chair. The little cap looked like a newspaper boat some kid might try to sail down a river. "I sent you my list of questions—"

"I lost those. You sent them weeks ago," Ig observed.

"Right. Well. I can print out another copy. We can just run through them. I figure that you've been around since the 1920s. Your father was in cheese. And you might be the place for me to start to understand how cheese in this country developed."

Blank. Utterly impassive blankness. As I was sitting there, the whole idea of a book about American cheese started to unravel, positively fall to bits in my lap. This old-timer thought I was full of crap. And the longer he sat and stared at me, the fuller of crap I became. I could be wine tasting right now, I thought, or hanging out with other yuppie types who want to wax poetic about cheese. I could be teaching starry-eyed servers at the French Laundry. I could be scooting around San Francisco. I could be absolutely anywhere except sitting on this stiff, sticky chair in this warm, still office, with an eighty-year-old guy who's staring at me as if I were a many-legged caterpillar.

And then Ig barked, "Artisan cheese movement. I coined that phrase. And commodity cheese. Up until 2006 we won more medals than anyone else." I started to think this interview might go somewhere.

I didn't go to Ig because I think the sun rises and sets on his cheese. I went to Ig because he is a living piece of history. His story is tied to northern California, but he watched the twentieth century in cheese unfold at his father's side. He bore witness to what I think he might call "the downfall of Wisconsin" alongside the birth of what lots of other people call "specialty cheese in America." Ig comes from a time when everyone had ten or twenty cows. That was how milk was produced and pooled and cheese was made. His father was tight with J. L. Kraft, back in the 1930s, when Kraft was the good guy in a sea of sleazy, mafiosoesque distributors who would stiff dairy farmers on payments for milk. In the 1920s, Petaluma, California, was the "egg basket of the world." All the farms followed the same brilliant model, a three-tier system with three influxes of cash. Grapes or prunes yielded an annual harvest, for which farmers were paid every year. Chickens delivered eggs daily, but distributors paid only monthly. Milk, on the other hand, meant biweekly payments. I perked up at this. The milk, it seemed, was key. It was the cash cow of the operation.

Ig paused long enough to agree. Yes, milk was the cash cow.

There was a particular, peculiar mix going on in northern California in the 1920s and 1930s. Though Wisconsin was America's dairyland, with small family farms sending their milk to local cooperatives, cranking out familiar cheeses such as cheddar and recipes that catered to the Swiss German population such as Limburger, Tilsit, and brick, the population in California was something quite different. There were Italian immigrants working the marble quarries, and there were Italian distributors moving dry Jack, Romanello, Toscanello, and anything else that resembled cheese from the old country. Monterey Jack (Jack cheese from Monterey, California) bore little resemblance to the lush, milky cheese we know as Jack today. There was no refrigeration, and the cheese was firm and rinded. Wholesalers who bought this younger Jack on contract and couldn't sell it let it sit around, aging on wood boards. The firmer, denser outcome was aged, or dry, Jack. After six months it sold well, and so a new style of cheese developed. But as soon as the market latched onto the new product, shortcuts were ferreted out. In California, in the 1920s, the shortcut to dry Jack was a cheese made from skimmed milk. Less fat meant that a similar texture was achieved in three to four months of aging, rather than six. The unintended side effect of this shortcut, however, was that the cheese had no flavor. Kraft saw the opportunity to make a popular cheese faster and began skimming like crazy, short-aging, and producing "American Parmesan." Kraft had discovered a cheaper, faster way to make a cheese similar enough to what people originally wanted that they didn't realize they were buying an inferior product. Flavor was sacrificed for quick turnaround. That, for me, is one of the first moments in the industrialization of American cheese. Kraft wasn't inherently bad, any more than cheese made in a factory is inherently subpar. The failure was in the intention: changing the milk to make the same buck with less work and cheaper ingredients.

While it was making skim, quick-aging "Parmesan" to market to predominantly Italian consumers, Kraft was financing Ig's dad, Tom, in the takeover of a bum plant in Central Point, Oregon. The Rogue Creamery was built by the Rogue River Valley Creamery Cooperative in 1928. In July 1935, Tom purchased the plant and dairy cows with $130,000 loaned by J. L. Kraft. The idea was that farmers could upgrade their milking operations to Grade A and eventually own their cows while Tom repaid his debt and owned the plant. This exchange was achieved while milk production was maximized for cheesemaking at the onset of World War II. Vella accomplished the transition of ownership by deducting a few cents per hundredweight (the measure in which fluid milk is purchased, equal to one hundred pounds) from the price paid to the farmers and a few cents per pound on cheddar, Monterey Jack, Colby, butter, and cottage cheese sold to Kraft. The farmers got a bit less for their milk, but bought their cows in the process. Kraft got premium cheese at a reduced rate. The investment paid off: five million pounds of milk, yielding 500,000 pounds of cheese, were produced under the brand names Elkhorn, Rogue Gold, and Oregon Brand, and every farmer returned the investment. It's a perfect illustration of successful collaboration. The dairy farmers had financial support and an outlet for their milk. Kraft had a direct feeding tube to the stomachs of U.S. troops. Better, more consistent cheese came out of the Pacific Northwest. Everybody won.

Where's the line between the Bad Kraft, manipulating milk to make an inferior product more cheaply and selling it to northern California's dry Jack–loving immigrants, and the Good Kraft, that provided financial assistance and a steady market for small family dairies in Oregon? When did the small family dairy farm selling to the small local cheese factory dry up and disappear? When did "factory cheese" become a dirty word? When did "factory" become "commodity"? And why is that inferior? For most of the twentieth century, American cheese was made in factories, not by individual producers, and it was produced on what I'll call a human scale. Family dairies sent their milk to local factories, many of which were cooperatives and owned by the farmers themselves. Nowadays, factory means massive scale, mediocre milk quality, and uninspiring taste.

Which brings me back to Ig's initial distinction: What is the difference between artisan and commodity American cheese? This distinction has bugged me for some time. There are definitions put forward by the closest thing we have in America to a governing cheese body: the American Cheese Society. According to the ACS, the various categories of cheese may be defined thus:

> *Farmstead cheese:* In order for a cheese to be classified as "farmstead," as defined by the American Cheese Society, the cheese must be made with milk from the farmer's own herd or flock on the farm where the animals are raised. Milk used in the production of

farmstead cheeses may not be obtained from any outside source. Farmstead cheeses may be made from all types of milk and may include various flavorings.

Artisan, or artisanal, cheese: The word "artisan" or "artisanal" implies that a cheese is produced primarily by hand, in small batches, with particular attention paid to the tradition of the cheesemaker's art and thus using as little mechanization as possible in the production of the cheese. Artisan, or artisanal, cheeses may be made from all types of milk and may include various flavorings.

The ACS doesn't provide other definitions, so a cheese whose production doesn't fit "farmstead" or "artisan(al)" must be . . . "commodity"? Built into these definitions and the common opinion of folks in the cheese world are these problematic assumptions and implications:

- Small is better, or at least more virtuous.
- Owning the entire process (animals, milking, and cheesemaking) is the most virtuous.
- Handmade is better, because it is more traditional.
- Cheesemaking in America is defined in a vacuum, without consideration for the impact on a larger community or region.
- What about feed? The environment? The local economy? Cheese is a business, and like all businesses it impacts everything around it.

- Affirmation is given to those who subscribe to respected and lauded practices such as "organic," "handmade," "farmhouse," "artisanal," and "local."

No definition can be all-encompassing, but the few that exist for cheese in America quickly fall apart within a comparative context. For example:

- Is a cheesemaker who owns and milks 1,500 cows the same as a producer that owns and milks 35 cows? They're both "farmstead."
- Is a cheesemaker who owns and milks 1,500 cows that live in an enclosed facility, eating hay trucked in from remote areas, greater than, less than, or equal to a producer that owns and milks 35 cows that graze on grass half-time and live inside eating hay and grain half-time?
- Is a cheesemaker with 1,500 cows living in an enclosed facility, eating hay trucked in from remote areas, greater than, less than, or equal to a cheesemaker that buys milk from 40 small, local dairy farms?
- Which one is a more valuable (or more detrimental) participant in the local landscape? What about the regional environment?
- What if a producer has a big, modern, efficient factory using machines to replace various aspects of cheesemaking by hand but makes tastier and more delicious cheese than a quaint, old-school producer with a few dozen animals in the backyard? What if

the producer using mechanized methods, which is not "artisanal," gets tastier food out to more people across the country? Which one is "better"?

See? It gets tricky fast.

When I asked Ig for his thoughts on the difference between artisan and commodity, he said commodity is computers, big plants, no fingertips in the cheese vat, putting cheese out by the ton, and a focus only on technical specs such as what the prescribed moisture content of cheddar is supposed to be. Commodity is also about "burning milk," not about flavor or good taste. I've asked dozens of cheesemakers a similar question: how would they define "artisanal" cheese? Their responses were surprisingly varied.

The point of words to describe food is an attempt to articulate the spirit of a thing. Unfortunately, when a word catches on with the public, everyone wants to co-opt its power. That's how we have "artisan" breads from Subway. Even as these words get snatched up, repurposed, and watered down, people in American cheese want to hold fast to the virtue of being "artisanal." I'm handmade and therefore superior. I'm smaller and therefore more authentic. But where does one draw the line about how much hand contact makes a cheese "handmade" or how big is "too big"? What is "the tradition of the cheesemaker's art," anyway? The tradition of the art of cheesemaking depends entirely on what kind of cheese you're making and where you're doing it.

I'm frustrated and confused trying to pick the right cheese to buy, based on the words producers and the media offer me. So I'm redefining "artisanal" thus:

Definitions of "Artisanal" from American Cheesemakers

"It's wrong to say you're an artisan if you don't start with the raw material."—Paula Lambert, The Mozzarella Company

"An artisanal producer doesn't change their milk, they change their recipe."—Allison Hooper, Vermont Butter and Cheese Company

"Artisanal is relatively small production, largely made by hand." (How do you define small?) "Small enough to be made by hand!"—Peter Mohn, Grafton Village Cheesemaking Company

"I am not a farmstead operation. I am a cheesemaker. It doesn't matter if it's farmstead or artisanal. It's not industrial because there are no machines. I wanted to work with my hands and brain. I wanted to understand the mystery of life. But I am very small."—Soyoung Scanlan, Andante Dairy

"Artisanal is small scale and a lot of hand work. If it's small scale, you can't afford much automation. Whatever scale you cut off at is kind of arbitrary, but it's hard to claim you're artisanal if you make more than five hundred thousand pounds of cheese a year.... Yeah, I don't know how you define artisanal. There is another factor, and that's the intent of the cheesemaker. An artisanal cheesemaker is trying to produce something special and different."—Mike Gingrich, Uplands Cheese Company

"It's now a buzzword; fast-food restaurants have artisan breads. We make cheese from the milk of our own flock. Some call it 'farmstead.' These are our own cheeses, and we hope you like them."—Barbara Levin, Hope Farm

"Artisan cheese is more creative and more made by hand but I think it could be—more creative is my definition. You can get bigger on a comparative scale. If we get bigger we'll still be tiny."—Kathy Obringer, Ancient Heritage Dairy

"A commitment to the process of making cheese by hand, and that process is by hand from start to finish. It's a process of being connected to a single source of dairy when it's defined in cheese and being connected to that source daily. Understanding what the milk is, how it's different from yesterday and the week prior. It's a process of having—and this is probably where we're different—the process of having an apprenticeship program. Always being committed to being better."—David Gremmels, Rogue Creamery

Artisanal cheesemakers change their recipe, and their cheesemaking technique, to accommodate the shifting fluid medium that is milk. Commodity cheesemakers take all possible steps to forcibly create a consistent fluid medium that can be made into a consistent final product, without modifying their approach.

This, for me, encapsulates the spirit shared by every person I have asked to define the differences between artisan and commodity. There must be a willingness and ability to adapt to the inherently changing medium that is milk. Milk changes over the course of an animal's lactation. Milk changes with the seasons. Milk changes with feed. A commodity cheesemaker will manipulate all of these natural variables and will go so far as to break milk down into its molecular bits and put those bits back together in a new way to maintain an unchanging raw material. From this utterly static raw material, the same cheese can be made the same way, day after day, year after year. In cheese, this drive to make a changing thing unchanging is the enemy and antithetical to what I call artisanal.

My grand redefining isn't going to drastically alter the rankings of which cheesemakers might be called artisanal and which are considered commodity, but it takes the emphasis away from size and away from mechanization, and places it instead on a willingness and desire to work with a changing ingredient. The most industrial thing of all, about cheese or any other food in America, is the complete separation from its source. Milk was not meant to sit in a box on a supermarket shelf unrefrigerated, any more than chicken should cost 99 cents a pound. These things can be achieved, and are achieved every day across the country, but only through a total manipulation and distortion of our food source. To make milk shelf-stable, it must become something that bears no resemblance, in nutritional value, flavor, or perishability, to milk. To make chicken cost 99 cents a pound, it must be raised as quickly as possible (using growth hormones, of course) in environments that are literally lethal, packing the maximum number of chickens into the minimum amount of space. It's cruel to the chicken, bad for the consumer, and devastating to the landscape. This is commodification: rolling over the natural hurdles of food production at any and all costs. What I have found is that cheesemakers who are willing to work with a changing fluid medium generally subscribe to the same tenets of what makes milk (and cheese) better:

- Good milk is fresh.
- Good milk comes from close by (the farther it must travel, the less fresh it is).
- Good milk is clean, not sterile. Clean means having a balance of natural bacteria; sterile means the absence of all bacteria. Healthy organisms include bacteria. Sick and ill-tended animals breed the wrong kinds of bacteria.
- Good milk is free of growth hormones, which exist only to pump more milk out of an animal than it is naturally inclined to give. More milk than is naturally generated can be attained, just like 99-cent chicken. But cyclical, declining milk supply is a major hurdle of making something from a cow (or a goat or a sheep). A producer can deal with it (artisan) or try to get around it (commodity).
- Good milk comes from animals that eat what they are biologically designed to eat. The only reason to feed a cow a solid diet of corn is to push its milk production beyond natural limits or to raise it in an environment that may be more convenient for the cheesemaker; this is life-shortening to the animal.

- Good milk comes from animals that are clean, healthy, and treated respectfully.
- Good milk matters.

One of the reasons I wanted to talk to Ig Vella in the first place is that I have very conflicted feelings about the dairy industry in California. California, and central California in particular, has become America's dairyland. The state produces more milk and cheese than any other in the entire country. Yet, if you've ever visited the Valley, you know that it is a hot, dry, arid bowl. It is completely ill suited to cows, ruminants that are

Good Milk Matters

Lest you think I'm crazy for stating the obvious, let me tell you a little story. I visited a cheesemaker many would call industrial, with a number of factories and cheese that can be found in supermarkets across the nation. But maybe not commodity? This guy stands for so much of what I believe matters:

- All the milk comes from family farms, within a fifty-mile radius of the plants.
- All milk suppliers must sign an annual contract committing to using no bovine growth hormones.
- The milk must be used for cheesemaking the day it arrives. This is nearly unheard of. Most producers, even little ones, can't make cheese every day and often use milk that is one, two, or even three days old.

Then I made the mistake of asking why, as we drove across flat plains of blinding leprechaun green, there were no cows outside. All this grass. Verdant, open, green, green grass. "No," he declared, cutting me off with a sharp flick of his right arm. "Outside is not clean. Outside, they sit in dirt. Inside, it is clean."

Have you ever been in a cow barn? They're big animals, and they make a lot of cow poop. Everywhere. When you walk down the middle of a barn with cows lined up to milk, you walk in danger. All they do is stand around, chew, and make manure. Aren't cows supposed to eat outside? To this guy, inside represents a consistent, controllable environment. What they eat, he says, is not so important, because...

(Here's the point of the story)

"The milk," he intoned, "does not matter. The milk is only ten percent of the cheese. Ninety percent is the aging." I almost died right there. I've never heard such calm and blatant disregard from someone in the cheese business. When we reached one of his plants, we were greeted by his cheesemaker, Josh, a beefy guy in his early twenties, a fifth-generation cheesemaker himself, just back from a tour of Emilia-Romagna, where he had been making Parmigiano-Reggiano.

We cornered Josh and asked why Parm here doesn't taste like Parm from Italy. And smoothly, easily, he breathed, "Oh. It's totally different. The cows don't eat silage in Parma. The milk is just better." Josh makes cheese at one of this man's five factories, running lines of equipment and dozens of men who produce thousands of pounds of cheese a week. But he gets it.

That is an artisan cheesemaker.

built to eat grass and suffer mightily in extremes of heat. In my mind, I have (wrongly) begun to associate cheese factories with the massive operations that Ig calls "milk factories": tens of thousands of cows packed onto enormous cement lots, covered from the sun but also barred from fresh air, where they spend their short lives being milked three times a day. At the age of three, they are sent off to slaughter because their bodies are decimated from two years of accelerated milking. That's America's drinking milk and also the milk that is dried, powdered, or augmented with various stabilizers to become the shreds that top every Domino's pizza in the land, or the blocks of private-label cheddar and Jack in the supermarkets of our country.

Ig reminded me that it wasn't until the late 1980s and early '90s, after years of consolidation of the smaller, local dairies and cheese factories, that these megadairies emerged. For years in America, the cheese factory took milk from nearby and made something for the regional population. In California alone, he said, they never could make a decent dry Jack in the Valley, because their cows, bred for fluid milk, didn't yield the necessary fat and protein. And for his own part, up in Sonoma, Ig couldn't make the cheese Teleme, though it was gaining in popularity, because it required low fat and low solids. You can't just go by the numbers, he warned, and take the fat out, because "the balance isn't the same. Their cows are bred for milking, plus we've got some colored cows around here," and their milk is naturally richer than that of the black-and-white Holsteins most of us know.

By Ig's own definition, wouldn't a commodity producer just skim the fat off and go by the numbers anyway? I guess his point was yes, a commodity producer would do that. But it wouldn't wind up with Teleme. It would wind up with some half-assed approximation of Teleme, and only after it had tweaked and distorted the milk that was inclined to be available in that neck of the woods. One of the last things Ig tossed out about artisan cheese in America was that you can't chalk it up to one of its parts. It isn't the terroir (though Ig pronounced it "terr-e-air" rhyming with derrière) or the breed or the feed that determines artisan cheese. It's all of those things, plus *the history of how these things have been used.*

The history of cheesemaking in America (like that of many things in this country) is remarkably short. If you look at where there's any history at all, it's a history of factory cheesemaking. It shouldn't really surprise me, then, that when new kinds of cheese and new models of production began to sprout up in the early 1980s, they defined themselves in opposition to the old factory style. Add to this the push toward a bigger, faster, cheaper cheese commodity, and the regional cheese factory of twentieth-century America developed a pretty bad rap pretty quickly.

But a lot of these factories remain, making everyday cheeses with milk from hardworking, everyday family farms. And when I think about the value of these cheeses, I come back to the two things I yearn for when I spend my money on food:

- I want it to taste good.
- I want to feel good about what my money is supporting.

Not every piece of cheese will be the rarest, sexiest chunk on the market. But it can adhere to my new definition of artisanal and fundamentally impact the way America eats—for the better. Good cheesemakers may take milk from a broader region and turn it into curd that's run through a machine that mimics the pulling and stretching done by hand in southern Italy. And you know what that cheese is? It's mozzarella. It's mozzarella that lies down in defeat beside the weeping, pearly, shreddy rounds made each morning in Campania. But that mozzarella is a pasta filata (pulled-curd) cheese made with milk from third-generation family farms, and it is 10,000 percent better, and truer to its inspiration, than the pasty flesh-colored vacuum-sealed square block in your local dairy case known by the name Polly-O.

From mild cheddar to Havarti with dill, factory cheese-making in America once represented the finest model of collaboration and craftsmanship we had. These days there are more obscure, local, and exotic cheeses, which is awesome. But I, for one, am ready to get real about all aspects of what matters in American food. Artisanal cheese can't be relegated to the domain of the little guy. We have to remember that there are some factories, driven by principles that really matter, that also happen to turn out really tasty cheese. They produce cheese on a scale that *can* meet the demand of hundreds of supermarkets, which is where most of us still shop, anyway. They're the best of what "American cheese" used to be and a seminal aspect of what American cheese still is. These are the factory cheese-makers that can feed America better cheese.

NOTES ON AMERICA'S BEST
FACTORY CHEESES

➤ VELLA CHEESE COMPANY
SONOMA, CALIFORNIA

I met Ig Vella in the gray stone building where the original Vella Cheese Company began in 1931 and where the company and cheesemaking operation resides today. The impetus for the company's formation was a bunch of disgruntled dairy farmers who'd been used and abused by the Sonoma Mission Cheese Company in the 1920s. The farmers approached Ig's father, Tom (whose brother happened to own considerable stock in the late-paying offender), and offered him exclusive use of all of their milk if he'd open a new factory. Ig made me comfortable with that word, from a time when the factory cheesemaker was a partner with the dairy farmer. Today Vella still is. His small factory uses one quarter of the milk of nine hundred cows from Mertens Farm, just down the road. One third of the herd is Guernsey cows, important for their richer milk (with more solids, it has more fat and protein than that of Holsteins).

When I asked Ig about his milk, his characteristic answer was, "We don't screw around. We get it in and get it out." Mertens is four miles away, and the milk is no more than twelve hours old when cheesemaking commences. Ig told me about the time that they couldn't use Mertens milk (there had been some problem with equipment or refrigeration, I think), so they bought from a milk silo owned by a nearby cooperative. The cheese turned out like crap. It didn't matter that it had been stored at a properly cool temperature; it was simply too old. That was the day his head cheesemaker finally got the importance of fresh milk.

Vella's line of **Jack** cheeses evolved alongside twentieth-century refrigeration. In the 1930s and '40s, customers needed more durable cheeses that would stay good in an icebox during summer months. The largely Italian immigrant community wanted grating cheese as well. Tom Vella created a recipe that was "halfway" as firm as the popular dry Jack, and the cheese **Mezzo Secco** served for everyday eating until the 1950s, when refrigeration became widespread and it was discontinued. Ig revived Mezzo Secco in 1999: a semifirm, rinded wheel that has the milky flavor of young Jack, with a nuttier depth.

Dry Monterey Jack is the classic aged wheel, and Vella has a tier of increasingly aged choices, beginning at seven to ten months and progressing to one year plus (**Special Select**) and two to four years (**Golden Bear**). The rinds are coated in a mixture of oil, cocoa, and pepper and look like scar tissue— waxy skeins laid out over the chocolate brown coat. The pale yellow inside is crumbly and breakable, the texture crumby, with little bits in the mouth and a fruity flavor. It's not almondy like Parmigiano and is noticeably richer. My most recent tasting of Vella Dry Jack, sitting in the Brooklyn Botanic Garden during the cherry blossom festival, felt tropical. The wedge was eminently munchable, not unlike a wedge of coconut oil. Not the coconut meat, exactly, but a rich, liquidy smear of tanning oil made solid. It was scrumptious.

Although the Jack cheese of the 1920s and '30s wasn't the fresh, moist style we know today, Tom Vella turned out a higher-moisture version when refrigeration became widespread. It was golden and moist, milky, delicate, and incredibly mild. Tom focused the company's production on Jack cheese, and the **Original High Moisture Monterey Jack** is one of the best. It's also available in flavored versions, with pesto, jalapeno, habanero, garlic, or rosemary. The wheels are still formed entirely by hand.

In addition to the American Italian-style cheeses Vella pioneered, the company also makes **Asiago, Romanello** (like Pecorino Romano, but using cow rather than sheep milk), **Italian Style Table Cheese** (a Fontina type), **Toma, Sharp Raw Milk Cheddar**, and milder **Daisy Cheddar**.

➤ CALABRO CHEESE COMPANY
EAST HAVEN, CONNECTICUT

I've tasted nearly every cheese from the Calabro Cheese Company. The samples arrived in an enormous box, full cases of chewy mozzarella packed in plastic cups of water, arranged in ascending size from the cherry-sized ciliegine to the cotton-ball bocconcini, just small enough that you can fit the whole thing in your mouth but large enough that you look a little piggy doing it.

At Murray's we've carried Calabro's **hand-dipped ricotta** for as long as I can remember, in big three-pound cans with the fluffy curds spilling over the top like a dairy Sno-Cone. The cans were the bane of my existence when I ran wholesale. When we sent them to restaurants, no matter how many times they were wiped down, each can seemed to pee a milky liquid all over the box of cheese before our delivery guy could get in a client's back door. I recently learned that the cans are actually perforated, precisely so they will pee out a milky liquid, which is whey that sours the ricotta more quickly than one would otherwise wish. Unfortunately, it took me two years to figure out that we needed to transport each can in its own plastic bag.

I feel guilty because I have always assumed that Calabro cheese is kind of questionable. Not because the ricotta isn't fantastic, because it is. The "hand-dipped" is whey and milk boiled down into a light, frothy glop that Calabro hand-ladles into cans, allows to drip drain overnight, and then finishes packing by hand, scooping the snowy mound on top, before lightly vacuum sealing the whole thing (to their disdain, but a requirement by Connecticut law if product is shipped over state lines). A spoonful of the final ricotta is gossamer fluff, with a sweet, milky, ever-so-slightly-cooked flavor, and it's quite perishable, spoiling within two weeks (a good sign when you're dealing in fresh cheese). There isn't a hint of grain or grit, the unfortunate mealy crumble that is the downfall of so many fresh, lactic cheeses.

Despite its apparent successes, I had long written off Calabro for two shameful, shallow reasons:

- It is located in East Haven, Connecticut. I grew up in North Haven, Connecticut (there are also a West Haven, Fair Haven, and New Haven, but no South Haven). East Haven, or, as my father used to parody the local girls, 'Staven, has few redeeming characteristics, except for big hair and Camaros, if you'd call them redemption.

- Calabro has really heinous packaging. Everything it makes looks like something from East Haven, Connecticut, packed on Styrofoam trays with yellow, red, and black fonts, ready to be sold at Costco or Wal-Mart.

Now, both points remain true, but Calabro's cheese is surprisingly, even remarkably, delicious, very much handmade, and born of pretty fantastic local milk. The pasteurized cow milk comes from the St. Alban's Cooperative in Vermont. It's the milk of small farms, and I was shocked but secretly delighted when the small, bossy Italian sales rep from Calabro came to see me and immediately began talking about the somatic cell counts of the milk it uses and its unparalleled quality and freshness. Not what I expected. It has also begun a line of organic cheeses, using all the milk from a single family farm in northern Connecticut. I didn't find particular flavor differences between the organic and the non-, and though the organic version is 50 percent more expensive, Calabro's exclusive partnership with a family dairy less than sixty miles away impressed me.

So, about the cheese. Please, if you find it, *ignore the packaging.* Do not abort mission. Press on, and you will eat something superlative. Calabro makes a bunch of **mozzarella**, including a "pizza" version, which is the anemic, block type that you should avoid, though I will grudgingly give it higher marks than Polly-O. Why? Why does anyone make this?

Because it is far less perishable, which is an issue for supermarkets and big chains that can't move the fresh stuff quickly, and also because pizzerias want a cheese that gets melty and stretchy and ropey. That's what we expect on our pizza. Fresh mozz, in all its milky, liquidy deliciousness, softens into a small puddle but goes no further.

The one to look for is called **Old Fashioned Fior di Latte Mozzarella**. My sample arrived wrapped in plastic, a fist-sized ball. It also comes in a smoked version. When I cut into the ball, it did what Italian mozzarella does: it began to peel apart in shreddy, papery layers. That's good, fresh, pasta filata (pulled-curd) cheese. The curd is shredded, then dipped in heated water, then pulled. The handmade kind bears the mark of that initial shredding, even as it maintains a springy chew. The salting is minimal but detectable, which for me is a necessity. My biggest complaint about Calabro's water-packed mozzarella is its absence of salt, leaving behind the taste of milk but nothing else, which resonates as bland. I know it's authentic Italian not to mar the flavor of good milk with salt, but I am American and my mother is a salt freak, and I like a bit of the ocean with my mozz. It amplifies, rather than overshadows, the flavor.

Calabro's Old Fashioned Fior di Latte Mozzarella has my preferred salty lick, and it's moist, the wet shreds flapping at the edges where I began picking the ball apart with my fingers. At Murray's, we carried Joe's Mozzarella, from Joe's Dairy on Sullivan Street, forever. I love that you can walk over there and watch them pull the curd. But Calabro tasted better, like sweet, fresh milk made solid and dipped, lightly and swiftly, into the sea. It was awesome. In fact, I tasted about twenty cheeses that morning and began cleansing my palate in between samples with bites of the mozzarella. It was better than bread. It brought me back to supreme dairy neutrality, though I did feel kind of sick afterward. There was more from Calabro, though the Old Fashioned Fior di Latte Mozzarella is the pinnacle for me. Their ciliegine and bocconcini share the fine milky flavor but lack the brief salt bath I crave.

What promised to be particularly horrific charmed me faster than any baked Brie or Jell-O mold: Styrofoam trays of **smoked bocconcini**, which looked suspiciously, but delightfully, like pork buns from Chinatown. Peach pit–sized balls squashed flat on top by the pressure of a plastic vacuum seal, they're like a plate of toasted marshmallows. The smoked exterior is a little dry, a little tough, and the inside has the shredded pull of fresh bocconcini but none of the moisture. They smell like the dregs of campfire, and I bit into one and actually tossed it across the table to my colleague so she could take a bite too. They were fun and tasty, in a chewy-smoky-incredibly-kitschy way. I imagined filling big jars on the Murray's counter and selling them for 99 cents each so customers could grab a piece with deli paper and walk out of the store eating a smoked bocconcino like a hamburger slider or a bagel.

The last surprise was the one-pound block sporting a label with a Mexican bullfighter snoozing under a cactus, his sombrero pulled low in the dying sun. Decidedly not Italian. This is a **queso fresco**, something like a feta, though it's not cured or aged in brine. It's a fresh cow milk cheese, crumbly, quite tart, and briny like oil-cured olives. The mozzarella had the tiniest background of salt, but the queso fresco was sharp and zingy. I loved it.

Calabro makes some other Italian cheeses, such as **scamorza** in two ages, which are underwhelming. It was fine, like eating a provolone somewhere between the slicing kind and the robust southern Italian aged versions, but clearly Calabro excels at the fresh styles. The hand-dipped ricotta is hard to find and superperishable, but its **packed-out ricotta** in cups is a solid backup, though drier and a tad grainy. It even makes a fat-free one, which doesn't have a lot of flavor (because it should have fat!) but far exceeds any comparable product I've tasted.

➤ CHALET CHEESE COOPERATIVE
MONROE, WISCONSIN

I visited nearly a dozen cheesemakers over five days on my first cheese-tasting trip to Wisconsin. The drive from Green Bay south to Madison, with dairies scattered along the way, may sound pastoral and picturesque. In truth, these trips always wind up being kind of disgusting because I eat anywhere from three to twenty cheeses at each cheesemaker's and by the end am desperate for a long fast, some wheatgrass juice, and an enema. By day three my body feels so out of whack that I start making extremely poor choices, such as passing time in the car eating golf balls of nuts bound together with tooth-numbingly sweet caramel, coated in milky chocolate. At that point, why not cap off an afternoon's tasting with dinner in a brewpub? In this case, it was the incredible Old Fashioned on the green in downtown Madison, where it seemed a good idea to begin my meal with a Wisconsin signature dish: fried cheese curds. Those are bullet-shaped nubbins of fresh, stretchy cheese, white, squeaky stuff that doesn't taste like much until it's bat-

tered and given a firm dunking in boiling oil. The outside
crisps to a toasty, lightly greasy shell and the interior curd
turns molten and ropey. It's what every mozzarella stick wishes
it could be. Washed down with a few pints of local microbrew,
it seemed natural—no, unavoidable—to order the pub's signature burger, loaded with fat, porky slabs of chewy bacon,
pinky-rare ground chuck, and a healthy slab of Wisconsin
cheddar. It's the manifestation of too much of a good thing.

The following morning, my final day, began at 5 A.M.,
with a forty-five-minute predawn drive to Monroe to visit Myron Olson, the master cheesemaker at the Chalet Cheese Cooperative. It wasn't until I left Myron's and the sun had risen
that Chalet's official location in the middle of nowhere became
apparent. My earnest inspection of each horizon revealed
soggy, sodden green hills, rolling in and out of the thick morning fog and a lone barn that belonged to Chalet.

The cooperative is notable for being the United States' sole
remaining producer of **Limburger**, though similar factories in
Green County turned out eight to ten million pounds of Limburger a year in the 1920s. Germanic in origin, Limburger is a
squat little block (a consistent eight ounces) of cow milk cheese
that is smear-ripened, meaning it looks, smells, and tastes like
a washed-rind cheese, but grows its bacteria rind of *B. linens*
differently. The cheese is dry-salted and then rubbed down
with an ancient bath of water, salt, whey, and little bits of
cheese curd from previous days' scrubbings. Myron is rightly
proud of his vat, which is topped off with fresh brew every day
but builds upon the cooperative's original tanker of schmear
dating back to the 1910s. It reminds me of the *solera* systems
used in the well-established sherry estates of southern Spain.

Each year (or, in Myron's case, each day) a new dose of liquid is added to the original, so the cheese being made today is kissed with the molecules of an ancient sauce: the yeasts and molds indigenous to southern Wisconsin, the hard water typically found there, the granules of salt from ancient scraps of cheese that have calcified like barnacles over three generations. There are no recipes here. Myron knows when the schmear is good by its smell. Too mild and innocuous (not much danger of this, judging by the cheese!), and the brew is goosed: a sprinkling of curdy bits, a handful of salt. Sour or rancid-smelling, and the cheese will be bitter. The result of this nearly hundred-year-old tanker of schmear is a sixty-degree Limburger aging room with clouds of humidity that smelled like Hershey's bars crossed with a whiff of wet dog.

Myron likens the schmear to a mother culture for sourdough bread, and he described the history of Chalet's brine over a 7 A.M. vertical tasting of Limburger, where I sampled slabs of different ages, beginning at two and a half months and going up to five and a half. If dog years can be regarded as seven times people years, cheese years operate on a scale of twenty to one. The first bite was a naked, acidic little thing more akin to feta, and the last had softened into overbearing assertion. All in three months. My choice was middle-aged: old enough for complexity, almost animally, with livery intensity. The oldest piece was unfortunately reminiscent of the shadowy corners of the West Fourth Street subway platform, where more than a few folks have relieved themselves over the years. Myron was quick to point out that by nearly six months, only a mouthful of equally intense flavors (his recs: beer, onions, mustard, and sausage) can tame the mighty Limburger. In Wisconsin, though I've no statistics to prove it, I'm quite certain they keep national Limburger consumption alive with their second signature dish: the Limburger sandwich.

Warily regarding the oldest Limburger, I decided that no one in her right mind would eat such a sandwich voluntarily, but I've firmly established that I was not in my right mind, and so, four hours later, after a brief hiatus to a cheesemaker (see Roth Käse, page 167) who served me a brunch of bread dipped in pools of warm, melted cheese (aka fondue), I took lunch at a bar and ordered, what else? A Limburger sandwich. There are four ingredients: dark, pumpernickely brown bread; mustard; slivers of raw onion; Limburger. The lingering flavor of salt, offal, and sharp raw onion (not to be undone by a final chocolate-caramel-nut bomb) was second only to the persistent flavor of my fingertips. I touched my sandwich, it's true. And though I washed my hands several times over the afternoon, I kept marveling at their smell as I sat on my commuter flight back to New York. It was not a nice smell, but I couldn't stop sniffing. Just to appreciate how bad it was. So bad it was good.

That's kind of how Limburger is, though you must watch for a cracked or crusted rind, as well as the development of russet brown along the outsides. You want some resistance when you squeeze. In this case, firmer is better and certainly will be less alienating to your neighbors. Also, under no circumstances should you melt this cheese. The Limburger sandwich I had was a cold sandwich. I learned this the hard way when I tried a grilled cheese recipe a few weeks ago with melted Limburger. Like the cheese itself, the flavor is absolutely benign compared to the smell, but the hot, melted goo prompted my friends to volunteer that the sandwich smelled "like garbage" or "like something dead." More than a few people apologetically declined to try it simply because of the stink. The sandwich wasn't great, but its mediocrity paled in comparison to the alienating funk that permeated my apartment for the ensuing two days.

➤ **CRAVE BROTHERS FARMSTEAD CHEESE**
WATERLOO, WISCONSIN

A few years ago, George Crave, one of the four brothers referred to in the farm's name, spoke on a panel at the American Cheese Society with Rick Feete (see Meadow Creek Dairy, page 285). There were no punches thrown, but the debate about inside, hay-fed cows versus outside, grass-fed cows got seriously intense. Let's just say, I don't see these two men hanging out over beers anytime soon.

It was a moment that forced me to consider the complexity of cheesemaking in America. Which guy was "right"? Which was "wrong"? They both had salient points, and I walked away trying to sort out the value of their wildly different approaches. I sat down with George and his wife, Debbie, and heard their take on what they do and the comparisons they drew between themselves and many dairies in California. Since I've never farmed, my gut is drawn to the production methodology of a farm like Meadow Creek. But my brain appreciates the methodology of a farm like Crave Brothers. The two farms, at the end of the day, are different cheesemakers serving radically different markets. The "right" way to make cheese, like most anything, is not a black-and-white issue.

George Crave and his brothers have a story that begins,

like many, in Wisconsin or New York State, where there is a long and well-established history of dairy farming. The Craves grew up on a 1950s farm, milking forty cows. In the early 1970s there were 60,000 family dairy farms in the state. More than fifty cows was an anomaly. Today, there are 13,000 farms, averaging one hundred cows apiece. George and his brother Charlie knew enough to know that they didn't want to work for someone else, and so they became self-employed in March 1978 on a rented farm with fifty-five milkers.

Remember: this is a dairy farm we're talking about. Not a cheesemaking operation. Their background was milk, and their farm was, for decades, dedicated solely to the production of fluid milk. In 1980, brother Tom joined the operation and the herd was increased to two hundred cows. More brothers meant more families to support and more cows to milk. In 1988, after finishing college, the fourth brother, Mark, came on board, and again the herd was increased in size.

Crave Brothers now has a herd of seven hundred cows that produce 70,000 pounds of milk a day. They also farm 1,700 acres, growing corn and alfalfa to feed the herd, and would require an additional 500 to 600 acres to grow enough feed to be self-sufficient. On my visit, I mentioned another Wisconsin cheesemaker, Mike Gingrich, who is a staunch advocate of pasturing cows. George remarked that if I visited Mike's farm (which I have), I would see that the land was sharp and hilly (it is). He *should* pasture his cows, George said, but the Craves' land is different. It grows good crops, not good grass.

I think about Jessica Little at Sweet Grass Dairy describing her father as a dirt farmer who has taken fifteen years to learn how to successfully manage his land, constantly enriching his soil to support a herd of cows eating grass. Clearly, pasturing is not as simple as "turning the cows out." In 2001, faced with the reality that they could not grow their herd or increase their land, the Craves decided to grow their business and make cheese, a more valuable commodity than the fluid milk they had grown up with. The distinction George and Debbie kept making, often comparing themselves to industrial milk and cheese producers in California, was this: "They dairy. We farm." The farm is, they reminded me, the only asset they have for their children (from all four brothers). The implication was clear: we'd be nuts not to take care of this one asset if we want to take care of our kids.

Crave Brothers, working within the history and tradition of dairy farming, as milk prices have plummeted and expenses have skyrocketed, is quite progressive. No, it is not a pasture-based dairy. But its pasture season is a mere five to six months, and if it intends to feed the cows through Wisconsin winters, then it had better grow all it can while the sun is shining. Its "dry" cows (the pregnant ladies who are taking a break from milking in preparation for birth) are on pasture one mile away. The milkers live in big, open barns on bedding that is produced by a manure digester.

The digester was installed in 2007, and Crave was one of the first farms in Wisconsin to explore more sustainable uses for the poop of hundreds of cows. Getting rid of manure is hard. Getting rid of it responsibly is harder. The digester makes a lot more than bedding. It actually produces methane gas, which can be burned for energy, and currently generates enough electricity to run the farm and cheese plant, and power an additional 120 homes in rural Wisconsin. Liquid by-products go back onto the fields as fertilizer; solid by-products form the basis of the herd's bedding and can be sold for organic potting mixes.

Unusually, the milk from the Craves' herd is pumped by pipe, under the road, directly from the udder to the cheese plant, where it is made into a number of cheeses that are sold across the country under Crave's brand but also under various private labels. Smaller cheesemakers that have adopted grass-based dairying strike me as progressive and tremendously important. But Crave does as well. It manages a complete cycle of farming, milking, recycling, and cheesemaking, and, at the end of the day, is providing the United States an enormous amount of superior cheese from healthy, well-tended animals.

It has recently introduced the washed-rind cheese **Les Frères** and its smaller version, **Petit Frère**, but where it really shines is in its fresh and pasta filata (pulled-curd) cheeses. All are pasteurized. It makes a **mascarpone** that I would happily eat every day of my life, forever. Many larger producers make mascarpone from whey, the liquid by-product (waste!) of cheesemaking, so it's cheaper. Crave's is made the real way: from cream that is skimmed off milk, as opposed to cream-enriched milk or milk that is beaten and emulsified to hold the signature mascarpone peaks. Post-skimming, Crave's milk is made into lower-fat cheeses such as **Farmer's Rope** and **Oaxaca**. The Rope is like a long string cheese that peels apart into mild, milky strands, still creamy and not at all gummy like the string cheese I grew up eating. But back to the mascarpone. It's like dairy candy, velvety and incredibly sweet. You could cook with it in place of cream, but I tend to just eat it straight with a spoon, like some kind of cool, fluffy ice cream. It's better than any other I've had in the United States and most every imported brand I've had, as well.

Crave also makes admirable **mozzarella**. It's not shredded and pulled by hand, but its mechanized production makes an excellent cheese. I've had others made domestically that are simply awful. Rubbery and bland or mushy and wet are the two likeliest offenses. Crave's has a pearly, glistening exterior without sliminess and manages to be shiny and soft without being squashy. The flavor is clean and mild, a bit walnutty, which I wager is from the dried feed. Most important, you can see the layers. The cheese pulls apart in delicate shreds like a poached chicken breast. When mozzarella falls apart in hunks and chunks, either it's too old or the milk was allowed to acidify for too long. There is a small and quickly closing window to get the cheese right. In addition to regular eight-ounce balls, Crave makes smaller sizes of mozzarella, such as **ciliegine** (cherry size), **bocconcini** (bite size), and **ovoline** (egg size). It also makes low-moisture "logs" that no one should have to eat but grocery stores like for their longer shelf life. Please, seek out the more authentic kind, damply sealed in plastic. This is fresh cheese; it's supposed to be perishable.

➤ EDELWEISS CREAMERY
MONTICELLO, WISCONSIN

The smaller sister company to Maple Leaf (see page 161), Edelweiss, produces 1.5 million pounds of cheese a year. That sounds like a lot, but it's comparable to the Grafton Village Cheese Company, a Vermont producer I still think of as "little." Though it operates in a plant that dates from 1873, Edelweiss Creamery began in 2003 and produced its first batch of cheese in April 2004. At that time, all the milk was coming from a single farm with 450 cows. Today, there are five grass-based farms whose milk is made into cheese under the separate label Edelweiss Graziers Cooperative (see "The Rogue Cheesemakers and the Future of American Cheese" on page 346), and Master Cheese-maker Bruce Workman subsidizes that project with the produc-tion of Edelweiss cheese made from conventional, rBGH-free milk purchased from across Wisconsin. The diet of the cows changes depending on the farm and the time of year, and though it may include pasture, it may also rely on hay, silage, or grain.

Edelweiss is best thought of as the **Emmenthaler** producer, making authentic, copper kettle–cooked, full-sized (that means 140 pounds!) wheels of raw-milk Emmenthaler (that's "Swiss cheese" to you). I need to get my biases out there, so you can con-sider my notes with a grain of salt. I generally hate Swiss cheese.

Even with my natural resistance, I find Edelweiss's Em-menthaler to be superlative. First of all, it's not gummy, a common shortcoming of the type. You want a delicate balance of firm yet pliable, but creamy as opposed to plasticky or rub-bery. Mainly, though, Edelweiss tastes great. It has a really mild propionic note that minimizes the sweet feet quality I particularly resent and instead delivers a subtle nuttiness. The wheels are aged from seventeen to twenty-four months and given the proper time to slowly develop flavor, so you don't get a kick in the face of Swiss-y taste. It gives some of the cave-aged wheels I've had from Switzerland a real run for the money and is an American one of a kind.

While it's producing these mammoth hand-hewn wheels

Why I Hate "Swiss" Cheese

I don't really hate Swiss cheese, as in cheeses from Switzerland, and there are many Swiss-style cheeses (cow milk, cooked pressed, nutty, beefy flavor profile) that I quite enjoy. What I do hate is the quality in slicing Swiss that I was very aware of as a kid and can now only think of as "sweet feet." In my opinion, never should the twain meet. The easiest indicator of a possible sweet feet situation is a cheese with big holes in it. Swiss Emmenthaler, or what most Americans think of as "Swiss," is the most likely culprit. Sweet feet is the result of two simultaneous processes that make Swiss taste like . . . Swiss.

The sweetness comes from the naturally low acidity of cooked pressed cheeses. These are cheeses made with a brief acidification of the milk and lots of rennet coagulation, so there is naturally low acidity or more pronounced sweetness. The feety vibe comes from anaerobic bacteria (*propionic shermanii*) that thrive inside the low-acid paste of this cheese in warmer ripening conditions. The warmth of the ripening cellar is key. Classic European cheeses such as Beaufort and Comté are ripened in cooler conditions, so the bacteria are dormant. Swiss Emmenthaler is uniquely matured in a very warm (high 60- or even 70-degree) room that gets the *shermanii* kicking. These bacteria flourish and cause a secondary fermentation inside the cheese; the carbon dioxide they release causes big holes in the paste, which is stretchy and elastic, and so expands as opposed to cracking. Hence the holes in Swiss cheese. And of course, the somewhat fermented, moist feetlike aroma that completely freaked me out as a child. Give me slicing provolone any day, and I was happy.

of Swiss (which, it must be said, can be cut down into more manageable half, quarter, and eighth wheels, as well as into blocks for easy slicing), Edelweiss also makes "creamed" cheeses. Not Frenchie-style bloomy rinds or triple-crème but cream-enriched table cheeses in the Scandinavian and German traditions: **Havarti** and **Butterkäse**. You know the former, if not the latter: pudgy blocks of rindless cheese, sometimes embellished with flavorings such as dill, caraway, or even pepper. Butterkäse is like Havarti, only without any tanginess and even more cream. I tried them both on my last visit to Edelweiss, and they were lovely in a totally approachable, not-very-complex way. My notes on Butterkäse: "Tastes like milk. Super mild. Really good melter," while the Havarti was "a teeny bit more tart than Butterkäse, but floppy and buttery." For both, what matters is not great nuance but well-executed cheesemaking: a silken, creamy bite, like medium-textured tofu, as opposed to plasticky gum. A soft, milky, buttery flavor with a tangy smack in the Havarti. I've tasted so many bad versions of these classic eating cheeses that the good ones really stand out. Edelweiss makes good ones.

➤ MAPLE LEAF CHEESE
MONROE, WISCONSIN

Actually visiting some of the cheese factories of Wisconsin began to change my mind about what "factory cheese" meant. First of all, there's an incredible tradition of cheesemaking, and most of Wisconsin's Master Cheesemakers are guys who grew up on dairy farms and have spent their entire lives around cows, milk, and cheese. In a time when cheese knowledge is becoming laudable and intellectual professor types write books on dairy science, I find that I can pick up the phone, call nearly any Master Cheesemaker with any question, and sit back as a conversation about hoof rot, titratable acidity, or optimal feed comes rolling across the wires. Case in point: my chat with Master Cheesemaker Jeff Wideman.

What I realized first and foremost is that it's harder to sell people on a producer like Maple Leaf. The primary reason? It makes cheeses like **Gouda** (in red wax), **Smoked Gouda**, and my personal Super Bowl favorite, **Pepper Jack**. These are not the sophisticated cheeses foodies like to crow about—the secret little treasures no one else has yet heard of. These are the pedestrian, the everyday, the cheese you find in the supermarket dairy case. Or are they?

In fact, they're not. Last year I went to Wisconsin to taste dozens of those block cheeses the sophisticates like to mock. I include myself here. I've been known to mock the block. But these cheeses are not all created equal. The raw material isn't the same, the cheesemaking isn't the same, and ultimately, the taste of the final morsel varies radically. There is block cheese. And then there is good block cheese. Maple Leaf is one of the goodies. It's a farmer-owned cooperative that's been around since 1912. There are currently sixteen farms contributing all of their milk, the oldest of which has been shipping to the plant since 1944. The production is big by farmhouse standards—5 million pounds a year—but minuscule compared to the industrial operations that crank out 5 to 10 million pounds of cheese *a day*.

More than the size in one direction or another, I am impressed by both the approach and, ultimately, the cheese. Maple

Leaf farms all abstain from the use of synthetic bovine growth hormones, and they have for years, long before it was trendy to market "no rBGH." The cows are not necessarily pastured in summer; some are, some are not, but the generations-old emphasis on farming is the reality in this part of the country. Jeff's brag was a first for me. He said, "We've got the best ground for growing feed for animals. This is an area of Wisconsin where feed is grown to be consumed by dairy cattle." It's not a by-product or an afterthought but the agricultural purpose of Green County. And the feed is consumed straight from the ground, as well as dried and baled for the winter months.

As for cheesemaking, it involves a lot of machines. It is not cheesemaking by hand. The curd cutting, the vat stirring, the wheel pressing—it's all mechanized. But when the vats were all replaced in 2003, the decision was very purposefully made *not* to go fully automated. Because a machine cannot make decisions about milk, smell, texture, and consistency like a person can. Jeff muttered something that nearly slipped by me. He said it quickly, because it was so obvious, and I almost missed it. He said, "You have to use all your senses. You need to know the smell of the milk when it hits the pan. It's all those little things. I've been running around these vats for forty years. You don't last forty years unless you know what you're doing." And that's more than pressing a button that says "Make cheese now." No point of Maple Leaf's cheesemaking process proceeds without a person deciding it's ready to. Is the coagulation correct? The milk changes all the time. What about the acidity levels? Are the curds cut to the right size? Is the cut consistent? These calls are made with a finger in the vat, a sampling of the whey's acidity, the way the milk smells that day. To me, that's craft.

Cheese is made five days a week, with a milk holdover of two days on the weekends. Jeff had a compelling argument about storage, coming from a place that's been making the same cheeses for one hundred years. The cheeses Maple Leaf turned out in the 1950s and '60s were made with milk taken warm from the cow and transported in open milk cans. The inevitable result was bacterial growth, which ran the risk of erratic acid development and unpredictable flavor. The greatest change in his lifetime has been the improvement in milk hygiene. Transportation now occurs in closed containers, refrigerated, so that unchecked bacterial development is less likely to happen. But greater sterility doesn't necessarily make tastier cheese. Jeff actually prefers to work with milk that's had a bit of time to acidify or, as he calls it, "ripen." The ripening time begins the development of natural acidity before the milk is pasteurized and cheesemaking begins. The milk quality is far superior to what Maple Leaf got with open milk cans and unchecked exposure, but the taste is more like the old days.

The final cheese to really fly on my radar is its **English Hollow Cheddar**. On my last visit, during the World Cheese Championship hosted in Madison, Wisconsin, English Hollow's domination of the one-year cheddar category was announced while I was at the factory. Everyone scurried around the desktop computer to scroll through all the cheddars that were, ultimately, judged inferior to the Hollow. The cheese isn't made like British cheddars in a clothbound drum, nor is it the typical American plastic-sealed block. Instead, each thirty-pound, pasteurized wheel is shelf-cured, left to age on racks, but polycoated with a paper-thin layer of paint-on wax. The cheese ages for a minimum of twelve months, enough time to remain mild but deeply flavored: savory and brothy with a toasted-marshmallow whiff. Maple Leaf has a blend of starter cultures that have been in use since 1982, and it's the blend always used for English Hollow. There is a magic lock-and-key connection between this culture blend and the co-op's milk: it just makes better cheese. Many of the cheddars I've tasted from Wisconsin have a bitter, almost chemical taste that reminds me of nail polish remover. There was nothing of the sort in this fine, mellow wheel. It was, and is, excellent.

In *The Murray's Cheese Handbook,* describing aged Dutch Gouda, Rob and I celebrated "real" Gouda (the aged, imported kind) and griped about the red-wax kind, which looks like candy-wax lips. Oh, how times change. 'Cause I'm about to get down with red-wax Gouda. Gouda is what's called a washed-curd cheese, pressed, dry-salted on the outside, and aged for a brief thirty to sixty days.

I liken this brief settling period to Gouda finishing school. The cheese is made, but it needs to smooth out a little bit. Those smashed-together curds need time to meld into a pliable, even chew. Young Gouda is not the most complex cheese in the world. Don't expect fantastic nuance, a windfall of aromatics, or fascinating mold development. Sadly, it's often bland and gummy, with a texture like heat-softened plastic. The disappointing standard for young Gouda makes Maple Leaf's so impressive by comparison. The paste retains creaminess, is bendy rather than Gummy Bear–ish, and has just the proper undercurrent of tang from residual acidity that results from replacing only *some* of the whey with water. It melts into a pool of ivory milkiness and is consistently rich and well executed.

There is also a smoked variety that, bucking the industrial

What's a Washed Curd?

What's a washed curd? Squeaky clean? Well, sort of. Washing the curd is a process, after stirring and cutting the curd into a soupy stew of whey and solids, wherein the acidic whey is drained off, usually by about a third, and warm water is added to the vat. The process is repeated so the curds bathe in a highly diluted whey solution, which contributes to a lower final acidity (and therefore a milder, sweeter flavor). It also prevents the curd constriction that comes from acid development (harder curd bits) and encourages a softer, more melting texture when the final cheese is made. Not to be confused with washed-rind, which happens after the cheese is made and is a brine washing intended to grow the stinky bacteria, *Brevibacterium linens,* that ultimately impact aroma, flavor, and textural breakdown.

standard, is actually smoked over real hickory chips in a real smokehouse. That's another example of craftsmanship that doesn't happen with mass-produced cheese: real smoke, not liquid. Be prepared for a more persistent ashy essence—hickory leaves a much stronger note than does maple. When I first tasted it, I wrote, "Campfire, creamy, a bit spicy, tastes like rainy day fireplace. Awesome." And it is. That finishing period is even more critical for the smoked style, since it takes some weeks for the smoldering essence to permeate the interior of the wheel. More time equals more flavor development equals more goodness.

Then there's my guilty pleasure: Pepper Jack. And its

even hotter, more ass-kicking cousin **Habanero Jack**. Now, what, pray tell, could be special about a Pepper Jack? It's made like a Gouda, though different starter cultures are used, and the curd/whey bath is heated to different temperatures, but the most obvious difference is the pepper. This is what distinguishes very good pepper Jack from the mediocre stuff. Most producers buy a pepper mix prechopped in brine, drain it, and add it to the vat. Maple Leaf buys the red and green peppers separately and makes its own mix to get the desired balance of color, spice, and heat. The thing I noticed was that the peppers were still crunchy, so as you bite into this firm yet creamy, mild, sweet cheese, you get textured explosions of heat. It pops! The habanero is just . . . hotter.

➤ ROTH KÄSE
MONROE, WISCONSIN
Roth Käse's Web site brilliantly articulates the trouble with larger, regional cheese producers. It says, "You might not know our name, but you know us by our cheese." Well, if a customer can't expect to know a company by its name, what do you ask for when you get to the store? Welcome to the troublesome world of the private label. Many larger producers make cheese under several different names. Sometimes it's for a grocery store, making cheeses under the "Whole Foods" brand, for example. But more likely, it's one of several invented brands intended to capture a certain market, imply geographical origin, or otherwise distinguish itself from the two dozen other cheeses coming out of the same plant. Even knowing all these imprints, I find it pretty confusing.

The spectrum of Roth Käse's brands is like rings on a tree trunk: the more there are, the more time has passed and the more history there is. No piece of cheese will ever say "Roth Käse" on it. Another point for me about Roth Käse's various brands is that they are not all created equal. The company started in 1990 with the intention of making Gruyère. The CEO is Fermo Jaeckle, whose family roots in cheese date back to 1863 in Switzerland. First his grandfather was a cheese ager; then the family established an export company from Switzerland, followed by an import company in the United States, the last of which Fermo oversaw in the 1980s. When he left in 1987 with a three-year noncompete agreement and couldn't work in cheese, he took the time to consider trends in the industry. He observations were: (1) Specialty cheese was going to become a big thing in the United States. (2) European subsidies for cheese exports were going to end (and he was right; in 2006 the European Union did end all export subsidies). (3) Producers in the United States were going to be in a position to compete with their European counterparts for the mouths and dollars of Americans. Fermo knew Gruyère and knew it was in short supply, so he decided to start a small company that would produce Gruyère using traditional cheese-making and aging practices and sell his cheese to distributors who weren't able to get enough product from Switzerland.

That was the original idea. A former Muenster plant was purchased, one that had been making cheese to top Little Caesar's pizzas, and the infrastructure for Gruyère manufacturing was installed. Fermo continued producing Muenster to offset his costs but found that every pound he made lost money. The overhead for labor-intensive Gruyère couldn't be sustained by block Muenster that fetched no money in the market. So Roth Käse began to make Havarti, a small but important step up. The thing about Roth Käse's Gruyère is that while some of it is made into the block, slicing type, much of it is pulled for additional aging. At four months, the better wheels, those deemed suitable for aging, are put into a cure room, where, in typical Swiss fashion, a robot moves up and down the rows pulling, turning, and washing each wheel. The robot, by the way, is named Uncle Sam, with a second robot, Betsey Ross, on the way. But that's only one aging cellar. There are several others, where all the work of turning, brushing, and washing is done by hand. All of the famous mountain cheeses of Europe, from Swiss Gruyère to French Comté, are produced by cooperatives with milk from many farms that is pooled and made into enormous wheels that can age for up to three years. Roth Käse has a similar model but distinguishes ages within the **Grand Cru Gruyère** line to support the costs of additional aging and generate income to support that labor. Within the Grand Cru line, there are wheels aged to a minimum of four (**Grand Cru**), six (**Grand Cru Gruyère Reserve**) or nine (**Grand Cru Gruyère Surchoix**) months. The best are the most aged, generally around twelve months, when the Grand Cru Gruyère Surchoix develops a moldering, meaty smell. That sounds gross, but it's not. It's hearty but dank. Small popcorn kernel eyes pepper the smooth paste, and there are little crunchy bits in the fantastically smooth, uniform, and gently creamy-spitty interior. I wonder what would happen if Roth Käse aged the wheels further or played around with exclusively grass-fed milk. Surchoix has the beginning of fruity, toasty nut undertones but remains in the land of meat jerky.

Roth Käse has half a dozen other lines, including **Havarti** (under the Ostenbørg brand), **Buttermilk Blue, Krönenost Fontina, smoked Rofumo**, a Fontina/Asiago blend called **Fontiago** (under the Mezzaluna brand), and **Homestead**, made and aged in the style of early American table cheese. They're all pasteurized cow milk.

Beyond the Gruyère, the two forays I find particularly noteworthy are the **Solé GranQueso**, made in the style of Spanish Manchego but of cow rather than sheep milk. Whiffs of almond and sucker candies—not exactly butterscotch but caramel—border on artificial in the sweetness that wafts off a chunk. There's nothing added, but the cheese smells like butter and sugar cooked down to a toasty glaze. It's no wonder, since the waxy orange rind is rubbed with cinnamon and paprika. The interior isn't hard or flaky but dense with flecks of crystallized crunch. The flavor isn't as sweet as the aroma; it's leaner, and the ivory paste is an approachable nosher. It's good with salty things—toasted salted nuts and cured ham—though I imagine a drizzle of honey would emphasize Solé GranQueso's essential cheesiness. The overall impression is that you're munching the bastard offspring of cheddar and Parmesan.

The other success story is **Vintage Van Gogh**. Forgive my criticism, but you can tell Roth Käse is going for a broader market because the name is so awful. Here, they're playing to the people who've had Dutch cheese, specifically, aged Dutch Gouda, with its incredibly popular, caramelized, butterscotch sweetness. Vintage Van Gogh is covered in cocoa brown spray wax and smells like a cross between macaroni and cheese and Werther's Original candies. It's young enough that the paste, though firm, is moist and chewy. Smack, smack, smack it goes as I chew. It's a great beginner cheese, well balanced and admirably executed.

Roth Käse's annual production is sizable, and while it used to buy from a single milk cooperative, it now buys from five. The majority of the milk comes from Wisconsin farms, and all of it is free of added bovine growth hormones. There is a pecking order to the milk, just as there is a pecking order to the cheese, and the best milk goes into Gruyère. None of it, however, is ever more than two days old. Even the simpler styles reflect that clean, essential, milky flavor, and the aged offerings grow in complexity from there.

It's worth noting that Fermo's impulses were so right on, in fact, that the Swiss dairy giant Emmi acquired a minority stake in Roth Käse in 2006. On January 1, 2009, it was announced that Emmi had exercised its right to purchase remaining shares, and Roth Käse was sold in its entirety. Emmi will begin to oversee production of American cheeses while expanding its distribution channels of cave-aged Swiss cheeses.

➤ SARTORI FOODS
PLYMOUTH, WISCONSIN

I'll be straight. Sartori Foods used to make me suspicious. It's not even called Sartori *Cheese*. It is, without a doubt, a Very. Big. Company. It has a line called "Intensifed Cheese" that includes products like "IntensaCheddar." According to its Web site, this is "a natural, intensified Cheddar cheese flavor profile featuring consistent performance and high quality in application. This value added cheese has been developed through extensive research to meet the needs and exceed the expectations of food processors." I'm not entirely sure what that means, but from the context of the sentence I can gather that it's a product designed to look, feel, and act like cheddar without having to be (gasp) actual cheddar cheese. No thanks.

So why am I writing about them? Within the big behemoth of Sartori Foods there are departments making cheddar cheese–like stuff (What *is* it? I still don't know) and there are departments—small factories, actually—making some really wonderful cheese. This kind of umbrella organization is incredibly confusing to a consumer because you see only one name—one brand—and it may turn you way off some nuggets of solid lactic goodness. The particular nubbin to which I am referring is now called **SarVecchio® Parmesan**. At Murray's we do not sell anything except Parmigiano-Reggiano under the name Parmesan. And, starting in 2009, by EU edict, co-opting the name will actually be illegal. We sell it under the name Sartori Stravecchio (note there are no rights reserved signs). "Stravecchio" means "very aged," and, at twenty months, it's the oldest cheese Sartori offers. When I first tasted it, the cheese was made by the Antigo Cheese Company, and that's a big hunk of why it's actually so good.

The Antigo Cheese Company was owned by Kraft and then bought out by its northeastern Wisconsin employees in the mid-1980s. Even in the Kraft days, Antigo was known for superior milk and a proprietary blend of starter cultures that made its cheese especially sweet. Kraft used to blend Antigo's milk with other plants' to raise the quality of the overall batch. Naughty Kraft. It should have done what Sartori is now doing: acknowledge that the milk near Antigo and its cheesemaking conditions are so unique that this single plant is capable of producing superior cheese. Rather than water down that greatness, Sartori is harnessing the history of Antigo. Before it was a cheese plant, the Antigo building was a brewery. I believe that there are still molecules and yeasts from generations of fermentation living in that place. And from Antigo's air, local milk, and a history producing Parmesan-style cheese, you wind up with the very best of what a regional factory like this can produce. The company may be Sartori, but the soul is all Antigo.

SarVecchio is laid to rest in a cure room for thirty to forty-five days before its nearly two-year aging run. Unfortunately, most of those months are spent in plastic vacuum seal, which explains the cheese's major shortcoming: its texture. If you look closely, you can see the curd bits that were pressed together to form the cheese. They break apart in an oddly waxy, slightly wet mass as you chew. True Parmigiano-Reggiano is much more aggressively brined and then aged in the air so it develops a rock-hard crust and dry, sandy interior. But I'll come clean: in terms of taste I would rather eat SarVecchio. And lest you think that's just my personal preference, every time I have a class blind-taste the two and they don't know they're eating the Great Italian Classic Parmigiano-Reggiano, they like the flavor of SarVecchio better, too. I'll tell you why: because it's sweet like milk and sugar reduced way, way down at a bare murmur, concentrating the luscious, toffeed roundness. It's succulent and delicious, thoughtlessly munchable except for the moments when you pause and think how much you're into it.

I wish Sartori Foods would take the tradition, milk, and cultures of the former Antigo Cheese Company to the next level. Bust out of the Cryovac. Make the cheese from raw milk. Maybe make a few wheels from grass-fed milk just to see what happens. All the components of a truly exceptional, next-level cheese are there, and I have to give Jim Sartori, who purchased the plant in 2006, some serious credit. He knew Antigo was making one thing very well, and he let it keep doing it. Imagine the possibilities if it started to do it better.

➤ WIDMER'S CHEESE CELLARS
THERESA, WISCONSIN

It was over beers that Joe Widmer mentioned to me that one of the six farmers from whom he buys milk is the grandson of one of the six farmers who sold milk to Joe's grandfather. Joe is the third-generation cheesemaker at Widmer's Cheese Cellars, making typical cheeses like cheddar and spreads but, more interestingly to me, producing two Wisconsin originals. American Originals, in fact.

Joe reminds me of a kindly woodchuck. He has a round face and a close-cropped brown-and-gray beard. His round spectacles top off the whole nice-guy, mild-mannered bear vibe. Then he gets a few drinks in him and gets downright rowdy. He's great. He's also remarkably talented at firing off answers to my questions, which tend to come fast and furious after some brewskies. As in:

Q: What is Colby anyway? It seems like mild . . . cheddar?

A: That's 'cause industrial producers starting bastardizing an American original. Bastardizing it! And the

What's an American Original?

How original can cheese be? With (tens of?) thousands of cheeses made around the world, there is a handful of two dozen recipes that are tweaked ad infinitum to tease out desired flavors, play up texture, minimize bite, maximize nuttiness, and on and on. But there are some known as American Originals, meaning a basic cheese invented in the United States and produced by many cheesemakers. To qualify as an American Original, in this book, you can't be a single producer making a single cheese. Hundreds of cheesemakers are doing that, each putting their own spin on the familiar steps of acidifying, coagulating, cutting, pressing, salting, and aging. I say that an American Original is a type, more famous for the cheese than for the maker. Of the three that come to mind, two originated in Wisconsin and one in Monterey, California.

Colby and Jack (that's the one from Cali. Monterey Jack. Get it?) pull favored characteristics from young cheddar and young Gouda. They are made separately, though sometimes combined into a martial arts–sounding cheese called Co-Jack. Both are made of cow milk, semisoft in texture, and approachably edible with a mild, gentle flavor. That's the result of the washed-curd cheese-making technique. The primary difference between the two is that Colby is always colored orange and is slightly firmer that its West Coast cousin Jack, which is white and nearly floppy in its pliability.

The third American Original is Brick, so-called not because the cheese is produced in a loaf shape but because it was traditionally pressed under the weight of . . . bricks.

USDA greenlit it, even though their job is to prevent this stuff. Those guys starting selling young cheddar as Colby. Colby is totally different. It's a washed curd, to lower acidity and add moisture. Adding salt stops the development of acidity entirely. Colby should have irregular openings, but Cheddar is always closed texture.

While the cheesemaking process differs, Colby looks and tastes a lot like young cheddar, though it's moister and smattered with little open holes. It's never going to be a whiz-banger of a cheese. Joe makes his with flavors, and before dinner that night we tasted his **Colby with Garden Vegetables**. The plain is extremely mild, something like Havarti but not as buttery. The veggie version contained seven herbs and dried veggies that were resuscitated in whey before being added to the cheese. Sprinkling in dried bits would be, Joe warned, like reverse osmosis, sucking the precious water out of the Colby. That defeats the whole purpose of a moist, succulent bite.

The cheese he makes that I really love, and that he makes absolutely better than any other I've found, is **Brick**. The name comes from the shape but also from the fact that true Brick cheese is pressed under weights of the same name. There's actually quite a bit of Brick on the market, and most of it is mass-produced, bland, rubbery stuff, smeared with orange food coloring to suggest a washed-rind. Widmer's Brick is the real deal, comparable to the original recipe that was created by a Swiss-born cheesemaker in 1877. At that time, the common cheese for Swiss-German immigrants was stanky Limburger, and Brick was to be its firmer, milder interpretation. Joe is still using his grandfather's bricks to press the pasteurized cow milk curds. It is flipped by hand three times on its first day and then floated in brine to absorb salt and cultivate the *B. linens* that make a true washed-rind. Additional rubdowns with whey-based paste (called smear-ripening) produce a sunny orange exterior.

That night, we tasted a Brick that was aged for two and a half months. Joe was quick to tell me he likes it better at four and a half or five. I was plenty happy with what I got. The larger block shape means slower ripening, so don't bother before two months. But with time, it gets a marvelous spongy, smushy texture. I kept returning for a bite and delighting in the moist, airy smear as I bit down. The pungency is moderate, and though I can settle down with some rank cheese, I loved how brown the brick tasted. Brown bready, perfectly salted. It was hearty without being acrid, rich without being runny or creamy. My notes say just, "I like this." It was soothing and earthen. There is something called **Yellow Brick**, sort of a young reinterpretation. Don't bother. Also skip the **flavored Bricks**. Get the authentic Brick. Get it from Widmer. It's as satisfying and bacony as any French Pont l'Évêque, as yeasty as any Taleggio.

IT'S 1982, DO YOU KNOW WHERE YOUR GOATS ARE?

SOMETHING HAPPENED IN THE EARLY 1980s IN AMERICAN cheese. Slowly, incrementally, we became a cheese country beyond cows. I want to be able to say exactly what it was that led a handful of people around the country to start making cheese by hand, primarily from goat milk, in the early 1980s. There must have been some collective moment when they all heard the call, from California to Vermont, and began milking goats. But apparently there wasn't. Like all significant change, a few people began doing something differently, something that didn't make much practical sense, with no real awareness of what it might mean ten, twenty, or thirty years down the line. In a few backyards, American cheese began to change at the hands of half a dozen slightly crazy women.

Traditionally, in Europe, women made cheese. The

exception to this is the Alpine cheeses of eastern France and Switzerland, which were produced by small cooperatives of men who tended and milked cows and then made cheese. But most cheesemaking was women's work. That was the case in the United States, too, until the Civil War ripped the country apart, men went to fight, and women were left with homes, families, animals, and, perhaps, the additional burden of cheese to take care of. When local factories were developed, they allowed communities of women to sell fluid milk, pool it, and have someone else make cheese on a larger scale in a larger plant. It was progressive. Industrial. Scientific. Women cheesemakers went the way of the dinosaur. Factories making consistent, predictable, transportable cheese, run by men, became the way, and so things remained for most of the twentieth century.

Until the early 1980s. In my hours of conversation with Mary Keehn of Cypress Grove, one of the first to take up the goat, she mentioned that cheese is becoming cool now because it's real and that people become tired of things that aren't real. Those first female cheesemakers were of a certain cultural moment. Mary mentioned it as if it were the most obvious thing in the world: "We were out protesting the war. We had certain values that were huge. We were activists." So perhaps they were looking for something real a little earlier than everyone else. That may have been the case, but there were few other commonalities. Among these women, some were married, some were single. Some raised animals, some were interested only in cheesemaking. Some lived off the grid, some were pretty mainstream. But there was a clear breaking point from the American cheesemaking that preceded them.

That women were the leaders is unique. Even more extreme was their total inexperience with farming, as was their disregard for the necessity of farming and cheesemaking accompanying each other. Many of these nouveau cheesemakers had no family history with food production or animals, yet they gave cheese a whirl. And then there was their inspiration: for the first time in America, cheesemakers were not looking to traditional, transportable styles such as cheddar or Colby, nor were they inspired to feed immigrating populations with pseudo-Italian, -German, or -Scandinavian offerings. For the first time Americans began looking to France. I have two favorite quotations about cheese, and for both the French claim credit. The first is from the French food writer Jean-Anthelme Brillat-Savarin, who remarked, "Dinner without cheese is like a beautiful woman with only one eye." That's so extreme and absurd I can't help but love it.

The other is from French president Charles de Gaulle, who sniped, "How can you govern a country that has two hundred and forty-six varieties of cheese?" There is nowhere like France when it comes to cheese. Yes, cheese was traditionally (and is today) an everyday food staple, but not in the vein of Italian or Swiss table cheeses: big hunks left out to replace or augment protein at regular mealtime. France is the only country to produce every major style of cheese. Its sheer gloriousness of cheese overindulgence is unparalleled. The French make the fluffy, the sexy, the drippy, the runny, the delicate, the stoic, the crumbling, hulking, racy, lacy, oozing spectrum of goodness that cannot be found elsewhere. France is the Cheese Mother Ship. Its cheesemakers make a lot of cheese, they make the most kinds of cheese, their traditional cheesemaking landscape contained cows, goats, and sheep, every terrain, and nearly every style worth imitating (except maybe cheddar, although they make cheeses such as Cantal and Salers that are similar).

For the first time, in the early 1980s, a sprinkling of Americans turned their eye to this tradition of cheesemaking rather than one of practicality, sustenance, and transportability. It's no surprise, then, that this is the moment when American cheese became interesting. Not all of these pioneers began their experimentation in France, although the best known, the first to garner press and attention, Laura Chenel, did study abroad before she began one of the first fresh chèvre (goat cheese) operations stateside. There were others, however, such as Mary Keehn of Cypress Grove, who lived in the backwoods and started "playing around" with the milk from her backyard goats. Paula Lambert of the Mozzarella Company wasn't inspired by France but was looking for something to do on the eve of her fortieth birthday and remembered with great fondness the damp, milky, lactic marvel that was fresh mozzarella during her postcollege years living in Italy. Miles and Lillian Cahn at Coach Farm had amassed a small fortune turning a dinky little leather company into Coach, now known for superlative and not inexpensive handbags. When they bought 300 acres in New York's Hudson Valley, they recalled the European model of fresh cheese sold to local urban markets and decided to give the cheese business a go. Paula Lambert wasn't making French cheese, or even goat cheese, in the very beginning, but she, too, fits the important characteristics of this cheese change I can summarize in three ways:

FIRST: Freshness
SECOND: Pleasure
THIRD: Total naiveté

Freshness is really important because it flies in the face of generations of American cheesemaking that relied on durability and long shelf life. Fresh cheese, with the possible exception of cream cheese, wasn't part of the American lexicon. Fresh cheese relies on the European practice of small, daily shopping trips to the local market, as opposed to weekly fillups at a superstore with everything from butter to batteries. Making fresh cheese means finding (or creating) a population that eats cheese nearly every day.

Pleasure, I think, was the most powerful fuel for this new kind of cheesemaking. These small, independent cheesemakers began to tinker not because they had to but because they wanted to. Cheese was not what they did as a third- or fourth-generation dairyman. It was what they did because they were seduced by it. All of the first explorers mention how deep their passion ran. Even Miles Cahn, who rolled into the artisan cheese movement an accomplished businessman and whose greatest pleasure, I wager, was creating a second successful business, recalls the European experience of eating impeccably fresh goat cheese at the Parisian table. Mary Keehn started milking goats because her kids couldn't digest cow milk. Practical, yes. But she also showed goats and lost money at cheesemaking for years, persisting only because it was what she wanted to do and she was determined to find a way to do what she loved, be happy, and support her family.

To make a product few know and even fewer buy, which,

from 1980 to roughly 1990, all these producers were doing, requires pluck. And persistence. And arguably a small dose of insanity. But they all loved it, so they kept trying to make it work. Not to be wildly successful, mind you. Just to balance on the edge of solvency. Around 1987, still in her twenties, as she headed up to Vermont to try to make a go of cheese because she didn't want to work for anyone else, Allison Hooper of Vermont Butter and Cheese Company was driven by a single conviction: "I realized, from living in France, that the American perception of goat cheese as bucky and rancid was wrong. People didn't know what they were missing. I realized that Americans needed fromage blanc, butter, cheese. The only reason I felt like we [Americans] needed it was because I needed it." Allison's desire drove her north, but she also had absolutely no idea what she was doing.

Which brings me to *total naiveté*. There was no model, no market, no distribution, no mentors, and no forgiveness on the part of time for American cheesemakers in the 1980s (and 1990s). You milked it, you made it, and you'd better move it, or you'd be left with a big, stinking pile of rotten cheese. Which meant two things simultaneously. It meant that either you developed a local market or you figured out how to sell your product elsewhere. Cheesemakers in the urban periphery stood the greatest chance at success, and Laura Chenel's relationship with Chef Alice Waters at Chez Panisse best encapsulates this. Laura made cheese. Alice wanted to serve local food in the tradition of French country cooking. Alice bought Laura's cheese. Every day. All of it. In the beginning, there weren't choices for fresh goat cheese. Laura was the first maker, and Alice was the first seeker. Miles Cahn banked on a similar symbiosis with the French chefs of Manhattan and was helped along by the iconic cheese guy Steve Jenkins. Jenkins had spent a fair share of his own time finding cheese in France and loved the idea of a fresh local goat cheese, just because it was so cool and European. Not so much because most New Yorkers were going to buy much of it; rather, he wanted to be the first to sell cheese as he'd seen done overseas. So there were signature patrons of these signature cheesemakers, primarily in cities, who were ready to open the door to new and unknown foodstuffs that were still a decade ahead of their time.

The word "specialty" had been used in American cheese since midcentury. "Specialty" was how you described something modeled after European cheese, usually cheeses that were marketed to immigrating populations. Specialty was special, not a plain old block of orange cheddar but something with a more exotic recipe and aspirations. But suddenly there was cheese being made by a single person, in a single place, producing, increasingly, a single cheese. Laura Chenel's chèvre was made only by Laura Chenel. It was finite. It was handcrafted. It was a singular product. Like the artists of the Renaissance, these fledgling American cheesemakers became known as craftspeople. Artisans. Skilled in the creation of a few precious, inimitable cheeses. And many of these were inspired by new, foreign kinds of cheese that came primarily from France. These were not cheeses for shredding, grating, melting, or eating in a sandwich. They did not fit the established framework for what cheese looked or tasted like. Their uses were, at best, unfamiliar (beet and goat cheese salad, hardly de rigueur) and, at worst, completely unclear. What did one do with these cheeses?

The answer can be found in Allison Hooper's reason for

making goat cheese and cultured dairy products in the first place. One didn't do anything with these cheeses except eat them because they tasted delicious and made everyday life better. They existed for pleasure. They existed because they were good. It's just that no one in America knew that yet. The first wave of new American cheesemakers was joined by a second group that cropped up around 1990, folks working with a little more guidance, a few additional resources, and scant echoes of success from the first movers. But, it wasn't until 2000 that any significant market penetration began.

Now, in 2009, firmly astride what I consider the third wave of "backyard" artisan producers who began cheesemaking around 2000, many of the pioneers have evolved into something nearly unrecognizable. Those who began with animals long ago sold them off. Mary Keehn's remaining twenty-five goats were sold in 1993, at no small emotional expense, but because she found cheesemaking to be incompatible with farming. There was no one to take care of the animals when she had to travel, selling her cheese across the land. Many in this first group have become the largest and most accessible "fancy" cheesemakers in the land. Goat cheese is still weird to many Americans, but if you go to the supermarket the choices you'll find come from this pioneering group. Their availability is due in no small part to the fact that they were the first, and nearly all of them found that to survive they had to increase in size and scope. The distribution opportunities for cheesemakers who began even ten years later were ten times as great as for those who started in the early 1980s. Laura Chenel's Chèvre, the local goat cheese supplier for forward-looking Berkeley, was sold in 2006 to the French conglomerate Rians

Group, a company known for buying small farming operations and producing 40,000 tons of cow and goat cheese each year.

The chance to remain a small, local cheesemaker is possible only because the first wave grew large enough to create and then fulfill a national demand for these products. I had expected the pioneers to be the purists: the cheesemakers who insisted on no-compromise, rigid definitions of what the ideal American cheesemaking operation should look like and unforgiving opinions of what made "good" and "bad" cheese. Instead, I found just the opposite. It is the smaller, newer producers who are quick to judge one another with ultimatums about how "artisan" or "farmstead" cheese should be made. The older girls . . . well . . . their attitude is much more "Live and let live." They fought to create and define successful businesses with nothing: no help, no demand, and no real knowledge of what they were getting into. The defining question has always been "How can I make this work?" But running a bigger cheesemaking operation doesn't always make you popular, and some regard the pioneers as sellouts. Mary Keehn summed it up beautifully. She said she felt as though, having been the toddler, Cypress Grove has grown up to be the dorky preteen no one wants to sit with in the cafeteria. Its growth has been due to one thing: it made good cheese, learned how to promote it, and found ways to sell it. The pioneers grew because they were successful. But the challenge for a previously tiny producer is how to stay true to one's roots through the evolution into something different.

As several generations of cheesemakers follow in the footsteps of the pioneers, what I'll call the "French style" remains primary. Milk not just from cows but also from goats and sheep; fresh, soft, and mold-ripened styles; and an interest in reinterpreting specific European cheese recipes. Few cheese-makers are running hobby farms, and their business models are critical to their success, but most pick up the cheese vat because they want to. The love of animals, craft, or good-tasting food brings dozens more fledgling cheesemakers into the fold every year. The total naiveté of the beginning pioneers has become the more manageable challenge of learning something new, albeit with the ability to consult those who have already done it. One fact remains unequivocal: In the early 1980s, America didn't know goats or sheep. They didn't know mozzarella, except the low-moisture, blocky kind. Even French Brie, as opposed to soft cow cheese from Canada or Wisconsin, swept into the limelight only in the 1970s, with its companion box wine and grapes. Small cheesemakers emulating the French were unbelievably premature but essential in paving a winding, crooked road for single-producer cheeses. One maker, one cheese. One flavor profile. No longer "cheddar" or "Colby" or "Jack," these pioneers sought the flavors and styles of Europe's most diverse cheese country, and they did it under their own, singular name. Laura Chenel's Chèvre. Cypress Grove Humboldt Fog. Capriole Wabash Cannonball. Vermont Butter and Cheese Company Crème Fraîche. Old Chatham Sheepherding Company Hudson Valley Camembert. These one-farm, one-named cheeses are precisely what make the landscape of American cheese so indecipherable and so rich. These are the pioneers.

NOTES ON THE PIONEERS OF
NEW AMERICAN CHEESE

➤ COACH FARM
PINE PLAINS, NEW YORK

The story of Coach Farm is about as good as it gets in the cheese world: money, drama, famous chefs, and lots of goats. The farm was among the first of the "new wave" and in 1983 wound up being *the* supplier of local fresh chèvre to New York City. I wouldn't say (and I don't think Miles and Lillian Cahn would say either) that this was the original intention. In the beginning, Miles and Lillian decided to buy a country property, which lots of New Yorkers do. This particular couple was sitting pretty high on the hog, having taken a little family leather goods company and grown it into the famed Coach handbags. They were going to have a farm and shuttle between New York and the Hudson Valley. Like many folks who stumbled into farms and cheese around that time, they self-admittedly had no idea what they were doing.

I get the impression that when Miles Cahn does things, he does them big. Not only did they buy some property, they bought a 300-plus-acre parcel. This happened to be in an area where dairy farms were closing right and left even as the Cahns decided to actively farm their plot. Miles wrote a great little book called *The Perils and Pleasures of Domesticating Goat*

Cheese, and when I called him to talk, he said, "Why don't you just read my book?" The thing about Miles's book is that it describes the phenomenon of Coach cheese as a funny accident that just sort of happened. But you don't wind up with 300 acres of land and more than eight hundred goats by accident, no matter how fertile they are. It turns out the land was really beautiful, and they figured they would farm it and turn the hay they grew into something more valuable. They'd pass it through an animal, turn it into milk, and turn the milk into cheese. Given all the cow dairy closures, they began to consider goats.

Here's where Miles the Businessman isn't entirely present in his book. The "accident" of all those goats was actually the result of this incredibly savvy guy looking around at his new, gigantic piece of land and realizing that if he was going to make more money with animals than with hay, he was going to need a lot of animals. The investment in equipment, facilities, French cheesemakers, packaging, trucks, and so on couldn't be sustained with a dozen goats. No way. This was the couple who took their rinky-dink company and turned it into an international brand. If they were going to make cheese, it would be major. From the outset, they built a barn for eight hundred goats, intending to keep a closed herd, meaning they would breed their does and grow the herd organically, rather than bringing in goats from the outside. (Farms can do this and avoid seriously inbred animals by artificially inseminating. In the process, the male animals are selected for the desirable genetic characteristics they can impart, from fat and protein content to longevity.) Additionally, the Cahns set up the operation for fresh milk, year-round.

That meant segmenting the herd and combating seasonal breeding by keeping the goats under light during the winter to simulate sunshine. (See "Freeze Your Way to Year-Round Cheese," on page 54, for more.)

Coach was the first producer to bring fresh, local cheese to the New York market. My old buddy Steve Jenkins was an early supporter at Fairway, and the city's French chefs were eager to have something beyond stale, imported goat cheese to choose from. This was well before anyone ever used the word "artisanal" to describe cheese, and the notion of a local New York breadbasket—food from the Hudson Valley—was in its infancy. Chefs were just beginning to list their sources on menus, and while Laura Chenel was supplying fresh chèvre to the Bay Area, Coach was feeding the Big Apple. Another chef-related note of interest: the New York chef phenom Mario Batali is married to the Cahns' daughter, and you'll notice Coach cheeses on the menus of all of his restaurants.

In 2007, the Cahns sold what is essentially the Coach brand. They've kept the land, but the cheese operation moved to a facility eight miles away. Of particular interest to me is the future of a producer that has historically been so tightly connected to a particular, local market. Though Coach cheeses are available nationally and additional milk is now purchased from goat farms in New York and Pennsylvania, the competition that has developed in the past ten years is significant. Coach is no longer the only option, and its products claim a premium price. Its cheeses have remained relatively unchanged for twenty-five years, although it introduced a triple cream several years ago that is truly one of a kind.

Coach still hand-ladles and packages all but its vacuum-sealed cheeses and distinguishes itself from other comparably sized goat cheese producers for never using frozen curd. Part of the impact on price of the **fresh cheese** is the hand wrapping (and perishability) that accompanies the approach. While it makes the typical Cryovac'd goat cheese logs you know from the dairy case, their fresh **discs, logs,** and **pyramids** have a moist, airy, fluffed-up feel because the cheese hasn't been packed together and squished into plastic. The downside of this is that the mild, slightly crumbling, milky, mouth-watery cheese is extremely delicate and can't sit around in refrigeration for two months. With prolonged exposure to air, it will sour and mold.

Coach's entire **aged** line is encased in the formidable bloomy rind, and though it has mastered the technique pretty well (not too thick or snappy, no ammonia, bitter, or plasticky flavor), the cheeses remain clean and neutral, without the fungal lull I expect from the rind. My favorite is an oddly dated version flecked with **green peppercorn**. Each nugget imparts a burst of verdant spice, though softer and more vegetal than what you'd get from black pepper. It's a surprisingly delicious combo with the milky zest of goat cheese. We brought it to Murray's recently, and no one agreed with me. I think it's hard to persuade people that flavored cheese is anything other than novelty and therefore would cost anything more than very little. Coach's newest addition is the **triple cream**, which comes in a personal pocket-sized six-ounce version and a larger three-pound wheel. It is, like all of Coach's cheese, pasteurized. I've had inconsistent examples over the past year, due primarily to an overactive rind that leaves a chewy film and bitter finish.

More recently, though, the triple cream has been solid, both texturally and in consistency. Although the milk is cream-enriched, the cheese is not limp. It's beaten-egg-white stiff, and not until you bite down does the whole mouthful sort of dissolve into a lemony, milky whirl. The flavor, too, benefits mightily from all the fat. It does a better job than Coach's traditional aged goat cheeses in delivering the perk of salt and citrus undercurrent of the milk itself. It manages to be rich while remaining tart.

➤ CYPRESS GROVE
McKINLEYVILLE, CALIFORNIA

One of the first cheeses to gain national recognition and national distribution, the poster child for a new kind of American cheese, began in the backyard of a woman whose log cabin had been built from tree trunks dragged from the forest by horses. The goats whose milk would be made into cheese existed in that backyard only to feed her four children, who had trouble digesting cow milk. Once there were a few goats, the milk outpaced the family's drinking, and cheese was the natural way to use it up.

Fresh cheese, to be precise, because it could be made quickly and easily, but then blue cheese because this hippie lady just loved to eat it so much. With a burgeoning clientele of one French couple, one local restaurant, and one bagel shop that sold the fresh cheese in lieu of cream cheese, she laid off the blue altogether. Even the simple stuff was a battle. That was 1983. And this lady continued losing money on the fresh chèvre that nobody wanted.

Then she heard about a show for food—fancy food—a show that still, in fact, goes by the name the Fancy Food Show. She wrapped up some goat cheese in several layers of supermarket plastic wrap and brought it in her purse, though it leaked milky juice everywhere, to this show, and found a distributor who seemed interested in selling the cheese beyond her remote northern California environs. San Francisco was a promising market but still six hours south.

This woman with cheese in her purse was Mary Keehn, and during this time she was, unwittingly, leading a revolution. Even when she found herself suddenly the divorced mother of four girls, with goats that needed milking and cheese that few people would eat, she wasn't willing to give up her gig. Fresh chèvre was the first tentative investigation into French-inspired, non–cow milk cheese. Then Mary went to France with Capriole owner Judy Schad. While Judy was falling in love with the stoic, natural-rinded goat cheeses of the South, Mary fell in love with the experience and discovered soft cheese. From Swiss Alpine goats picking through lavender fields came the milk for the softies, and though Mary spoke no French, she learned to make bloomy-rinded cheese on the farm family she was visiting. On the plane ride home, she fell asleep and dreamt of the cheese she would make when she landed. It, too, was soft-ripened but a much larger wheel, five pounds, taller and sturdier so it could be transported. Enrobed in a delicate ivory skin, the insides packed like snow white cheesecake, the cheese was divided by a wavering line of black ash, an homage to the French cheese Morbier. Mary dreamt of the cheese in every detail, gray and foggy as the Pacific coasts near her home, and when she returned she began to make the cheese she called **Humboldt Fog**.

These days, Cypress Grove's selection extends beyond one cheese, but most are variations on the theme. Mary is a big proponent of the European approach to doing one thing and doing it well. So she'll tweak size and shape, but she always works from the same basic recipe. Although she began shrinking her goat herd as the business grew, it was in 2003 that she sold her remaining twenty-five animals, mainly because she found a single buyer who would take them all and who sent a fancy veterinarian to escort the goats back to the East Coast. I see the Selling of the Goats as Mary Keehn's turning point as an American cheesemaker. It's the moment she became a regional rather than a backyard business. The responsibility of animals plus cheesemaking plus parenting was too much for one person to do well, and as Mary's focus narrowed on making and selling, the cheese got better. She began to develop a network of farms whose milk Cypress Grove bought and has worked with farms that could not support themselves on cows to convert, or at least add goats to their mix.

"If I started because I loved the goats," she told me, "I still have that commitment even if I don't have the goats anymore. I just have to do it. That's my job." I've pressed her, several times, to help me understand how Cypress Grove went from a backyard hobby to the job she refused to let go to a flourishing company. As with so many things, her answer was ridiculously simple: the only way to make income was to grow. And she had four kids to feed. In 1986, the farm did $63,900 in gross sales. It was "grim," but it was also, Mary reminds me, "what I really, really wanted to do. I wanted to make a living doing what

I wanted. I had certain things I wasn't willing to compromise."
In 1987, having cut down the milking significantly to concentrate on sales, that number doubled to $124,000. I keep insist-
ing on knowing how she had gone from teeny-tiny to national,
and Mary just laughed a mellow little chuckle. "It's been twenty-
five years." I guess it doesn't seem so fast when you're doing the
work every day.

So now Cypress Grove is a "big" artisan cheesemaker,
and Mary recognizes the discomfort of growth but revels in
the impact her company can make. She mentions the Green
Award it was given for saving open space in their community
and the company's profit-sharing plan that exists now that
there's a profit. She's direct and matter-of-fact about it: "I may
not be back to the land in the farmstead way, but our employees play soccer on their lunch hour. I love that."

I think cheese in America would have exploded without
Mary Keehn. But she has been a major driver, pushing forward
to do what she believes in and to have as good a time as possible while doing it. Mary looms large in my worldview of cheese.
She has stuck to her guns, she makes consistently excellent
cheese, which is really hard when it's going out across the
country, and she's used her size to stand up, first and foremost,
for goats and secondarily for the local environment and the
people she works with. Plus she doesn't bullshit around, which
I really appreciate.

Inside the world of cheese (and food), where I often find
myself, or even in New York, where everyone likes to prove
how much he knows and where my doctor breezily tells me
that Humboldt Fog is one of his favorite cheeses, I still think
Mary's cheeses are special. They are incredibly tasty. They are

I'm Not Afraid to Admit I Use Frozen Curd. Doesn't Everyone?

My e-mails and chats with Mary Keehn had been going pretty well when I decided to take the plunge and ask her the "risky question." I was nervous. I'd heard that when industry people and other cheesemakers made the six-hour pilgrimage to McKinleyville, Mary wouldn't let them into the making or aging rooms. I'd heard she guarded her cheese recipes like precious jewels. Did I dare to ask her the obvious question? Which is: If goats provide milk seasonally, how can she supply the entire country with her cheeses year-round? Does she use (drumroll and ominous clashing) . . . frozen curd? I thought for sure she'd be offended, or perhaps she would deny it and move on. Instead, she thanked me for asking. And the answer, by the way, is yes. Her calm observation was something about selling four to five times as much cheese at Christmas (when the supply of goat milk is rock-bottom low) than at other times of the year and how this was impossible without frozen curd. I used to think using frozen curd was a cheat or a dirty little secret, but in fact it's pretty standard. Steve Tate at North Carolina's Goat Lady Dairy mentioned freezing curd completely casually, and he's a small-time farmers' market cheesemaker. Mary's assertion is that every year-round goat cheesemaker must, at some point, use frozen curd. And it's no big deal: "We make really good cheese using frozen curd in a specific quantity, mixing it with fresh . . . all the French cheeses everyone adores use this method." Mary's concern is focused on guaranteeing her farmers a consistent price for milk all year round, regardless of supply. So she pays as much in summer, when milk's raining from the heavens, as she does for winter milk, when it's scarce and precious.

How is there any in the winter at all, you may wonder. The answer is that goats can be tricked into thinking it's spring or summer if they're exposed to light for most of the day. In this way, a cheesemaker can encourage breeding at a time when the animals would not normally be so inclined. This is a distinction Miles Cahn from Coach Farm made about this cheese in the early days.

For Mary, excess summertime milk is simply preserved for later use. I appreciate why this is necessary for year-round production. I really appreciate her candor. But most of all, I appreciate that the acceptance of seasonal animal milk means paying a premium even when supply is high. Because that premium keeps farms alive when supply is low.

simple in their range and similarity. They are very well made. Some might call them passé, which only proves how well this woman has done in twenty-five years, coming from a time when no one wanted cheese from a goat.

Humboldt Fog is the granddaddy, the classic, and it comes in its original five-pound wheel and a one-pound mini that restaurants love because it's so easy to portion. It is a bloomy rind, but unlike Brie or Camembert, the fresh cheese is dusted with ash before the rind begins to grow. When the whole thing is fully ripened, the white is undercut with foggy gray, and the whole cheese is divided in half, widthwise, by another line of ash. It's like a two-layer goat cheese cake. Which is fitting, because a mouthful of Humboldt Fog is like tropical frosting: light and smeary but bright. Sunny, with a lemony, citrusy tang. That bloomy encasement softens the zest, though, so it manages to be herbaceous as well. My lips smack like a horse's when I dig up the crumbling bits. **Bermuda Triangle** and **Fog Lights** are comparable though variously shaped, with less ash than the original.

Truffle Tremor is another variation on the theme, albeit a relatively new one. Is it a cheap shot? Yeah, maybe. But cheap shots work. It's Humboldt Fog minus the center line of ash, plus flecks and specks of black truffle. It's a perfect marriage of highs and lows. The truffle is actually pretty subtle, so you get the fungal, earthy hum alongside the singing high of crumbling fresh goat cheese. It makes me want to snuffle under leaves.

Of Cypress Grove's fresh cheeses, I must call out the **Purple Haze** for being such a magnificent illustration of flavored cheese. It's a squirty little puck of fresh chèvre, super-creamy and flavored with lavender and fennel pollen. In my mind this is the expression of Mary's first trip to France, the one that inspired Humboldt Fog in the first place. It's sweet and aromatic but manages to be substantive and of a place, like driving through Provence with the windows down. It's transportive, really, which is impressive for such a little swab of cheese.

And then there's **Midnight Moon**. Those of you out there who know a bit about cheese think you're about to bust my ass for including in this book the crunchy little gem known as Midnight Moon. Because it's not actually made in America, right? So why is it here if it's made in Holland? It's here because I think it's notable that one of America's pioneering goat cheesemakers began a production line overseas and imports and markets this line under the Cypress Grove subbrand Cypress Grove Creamline.

The Dutch goat Gouda (there's a sheep Gouda as well called **Lambchopper**) began in 1992, though the concept for the project dates back to 1988. Mary met a young Dutch couple with the potential to make this incredible aged goat cheese that Mary couldn't manage in her single-style-focused facility. Its acquisition promised a broader range of cheeses, but there was real economic practicality as well. Cypress Grove had outgrown its facility, and a newer, larger one was planned, but Mary couldn't finance the expansion on the original plant's volume. The Cypress Grove Creamline was a brilliant way to make more money without having to physically produce more cheese. When Midnight Moon was introduced, the euro cost 80 cents, and in addition to being extremely tasty, the cheese was remarkably affordable. That's far less the case these days.

Like all good Dutch Goudas, Midnight Moon is cloaked in wax, in this case black, as the cheese name implies. I'll be straight, this isn't my preferred style. As goat cheeses age, they develop a distinctive, nearly candied sweetness that seems shockingly inappropriate, and this wheel is no exception. I prefer grassy, minerally notes. But people love the intensity. The cheese is firm and chewy, punctuated by the occasional eye like a chickenpox scar, with an intensely raisiny flavor. It's a brilliant and approachable choice, especially for professed goat cheese haters. But for the bone-colored paste, they will not know the difference when they're served.

➤ KENDALL CHEESE COMPANY
ATASCADERO, CALIFORNIA

In the late 1970s, Sadie Kendall was en route to a degree in philosophy with the intention of attending law school. Accidentally, passionately, she fell in love with cheese. It was the combined persuasions of the Beverly Hills Cheese Shop and a backyard Nubian goat that felled her. Redirected to Cal Poly to study dairy science, Sadie drove up from L.A. and slept in her VW van between classes, studying French for the sole purpose of reading old journals in the library that yielded secret, ancient cheese recipes. At Cal Poly all they made was cheddar, though Sadie's self-designed senior project was to make Camembert. In 1981, after finding an old cheese plant and refurbishing it, Sadie left school a few credits short of a degree to begin making her own goat cheese. I asked why.

Sadie speaks in short intense jabs, and I heard her suck in air before she fired off the answer. "It. Made. My. Soul. Sing. I'd never felt that way before." In the beginning, she *was* Kendall Cheese Company, making a goat Camembert using blue mold (the milder *Penicillium glaucum*) rather than traditional white fluffy *candidum* mold, and a hybrid Stilton made of goat and cow milk. Even she admits this was beyond the market. While Laura Chenel was building steam making fresh chèvre, Sadie wanted to make more complex recipes. Plain old goat cheese was kind of boring to her. Maybe so, but it was the first tiny, tentative step retailers and restaurants could handle, and by 1988, Sadie was struggling to sell cheese and cultured butter. She found the lactic wonder crème fraîche on a trip to San Francisco and set about making it for the sheer joy of being able to eat it every day.

Here's what makes Sadie an exceptional craftswoman. She wrote her own recipe for crème fraîche, working backward from the final flavor and texture she imagined, through the various starter bacteria that might tease those qualities from the cream. Crème fraîche isn't cheese, it's cultured cream, meaning the cream is acidified to a thick, spoonable fluff. I couldn't believe that the woman who now makes only crème fraîche, and in fact has made only crème fraîche for more than twenty years, could do this without getting bored. This is the woman who didn't want to make fresh goat cheese because it was too simple!

Sadie's crème fraîche is known by all of the country's top chefs as the uncontested best. I wondered what makes such a simple product so superior and thought for sure there would be critical characteristics of the milk, the animals, the hand ladling. But that wasn't the case. Sadie's cream comes from a third-generation family farm in the California Central Valley, and she's been buying from the same farm for the entire time she's been making crème fraîche. The cows are Holsteins. They aren't grass-fed, and Sadie thinks this is part of the reason her crème fraîche is so good. Cows on grass and colored cows, breeds like Guernseys and Jerseys, make milk with more diacetyl, the flavor of butter. Good crème fraîche, Sadie says, shouldn't taste too much. It's there to play a supporting role. "If it isn't white, it doesn't work for the chef," and, as I so well

The Magic of Crème Fraîche

Sadie Kendall blew me out of the water with her unadulterated enthusiasm for crème fraîche. She has made
crème fraîche four to five times a week, every week, since 1988.
That's twenty years of crème fraîche. When she talks about it,
her words fly like bullets, and she kind of chokes toward the
end of her sentence because she's so short of breath. She
radiates the delight and unbridled passion that I so strongly
associate with the early 1980s change in American cheesemaking. Sadie's amazement with crème fraîche goes something
like this:

"Cow cream doesn't have the same flavor variation that
goat milk does. I wasn't that interested [in making crème fraîche]
except that I wanted it [to eat myself]. It's a challenge to work
out the recipe, and along the way I was sharing it with chefs and
no one else was making it.

"On the surface it's as simple to make as fresh chèvre, but
it's not like that at all. Crème fraîche is amazing. Its function—this
cream is the most astounding—you can make the whole palette
of classic French sauces—you don't need roux, you don't need
thickeners—it's the most astounding product—you can whip it—
it is béchamel. You can make velouté. The thing with the classic
velouté is that it's going to take several hours to cook the flour
out of the roux, and by the time you do all that, you can just
temper the crème fraîche into your stock. It's the most astounding product, and I am in awe of it.

"With a few exceptions, including the French, there is no one who understands this product. It's not a garnish, it's an ingredient. If you have an emulsion that breaks, just put in a little crème fraîche, it fixes it. If you're making mayonnaise, add a little crème fraîche at the end. Whipping it. It whips to twice the volume of a heavy whipping cream, and you can leave it in the fridge for days and you have a fine dense foam that will never collapse.

"When I started with it [crème fraîche], I thought it was kind of boring, but it's magic. Even if you study the science of cheesemaking, you never get over the magic of it. Just add a couple of things to your vat or bucket of milk, and it's cheese. I learn new things all the time from it."

relate to, the chef "will hate you" as a result. The cream she gets is pasteurized, and then, by law, she must pasteurize it a second time. As the company has grown, the production process has become automated, with machines replacing hands; Sadie indicated that this actually made the product more consistent.

So in central California, Holsteins, no grass, double pasteurized, automated make process, and still . . . Kendall crème fraîche is the best. It was for me an important illustration that "the best" raw material depends on the product you're trying to make. For crème fraîche, the best (and most important) facets are consistent raw material and consistent starter culture. One of the trickier things for Sadie is that she's "old" and the companies that she bought starter culture from thirty years ago aren't all around anymore. So that's complicated. Managing temperature and fermentation is the challenge to be mastered for consistently excellent crème fraîche. Sadie's is snow white, thick, and airy, with the ideal balance of nutty, light, lovely, lactic flavors. Crème fraîche manages to be tart at first, like sour cream, finishing sweet like mascarpone, all the while with the tug of something delicately browned, like hazelnuts. Driven by Sadie Kendall's unflappable interest in this apparently simple dairy product, Kendall Farms makes one thing, and it makes it better than anyone else.

➤ THE MOZZARELLA COMPANY
DALLAS, TEXAS

Paula Lambert is a smallish, bustling Texan, and though I've seen her work her drawl to great advantage, she's a tough cookie. So I was shocked to hear that in the midst of her conquest to learn more about cheesemaking from various Italians, she found herself alone and near tears in a desolate mountain cheese plant as snow piled up outside. Paula's not a crier, but I guess we all have our breaking points. Hers came in Liguria, in January 1985. She'd been sent there by an importer she'd met in the States and had managed to check into, in her words, "a godforsaken hotel in the middle of nowhere." In her sixties now, Paula bursts and bubbles with energy. She talks a mile a minute and throws all of herself into whatever's caught her fancy. In 1985, that was goat cheese. She wanted to expand her cheese line, and the fresh mozzarella she was making back home in Dallas hadn't exactly caught on. I'm not sure why she was thinking that goat cheese was going to help, but the woman was driven.

Unfortunately, she was also a complete goat novice. So she found her way to this small factory and walked into cold emptiness, with a lone Italian hanging around, who looked at her and said, "Lady, don't you know goats don't give milk in the winter?" Clearly she did not. So she got back into the car, en route to friends, and nearly got killed on the autostrada. If it were me, I would have resigned myself to the fact that the goat dream wasn't happening and started drinking lots of wine alongside plates of homemade ravioli stuffed with sage and butternut squash. But Paula's friends, who had nothing to do with cheese, found her, by the next morning, a cheesemaker/gentleman farmer who gave her free run of his plant and plant manager, and when she got home, Paula started messing around with recipes. You know how there are a million ways to make apple pie? Paula says cheese is like that.

The Ligurian goat trip was actually her second visit to Italy to learn cheese. The first came during Christmas 1981–New Year's 1982. At the age of forty, Paula was about to be kicked out of the Junior League, where she volunteered, and, having lived in Italy in her twenties, thought it would be neat to start a fresh pasta company. Then she found out another Texan was already onto this plan. Crushed, she went to Italy for the holidays and when a ball of fresh mozzarella was plopped in front of her decided that *this* was what Americans didn't have. And what they needed.

Can you imagine? A forty-year-old woman, in 1982, deciding that Dallas, Texas, really wanted milky, lactic, spongy fresh mozzarella. Most Americans today haven't had fresh mozzarella and don't feel their lives lacking as a result. But Paula thought it was important. As she went on a self-guided quest from one cheese plant to cheese professor to another, an important model for cheesemaking was formed.

In Italy, mozzarella isn't made by the guys with the cows (or buffalo). Instead, the cheesemakers drive around to small local farms, collect milk, make it into cheese, and sell it within a day. It was this concept of "cheesemaker" that firmly established itself in Paula's mind as separate and distinct from "farmer." Paula never considered getting animals, because she had no intention of being a farmer. What she aspired to be was a cheesemaker.

Despite modeling her Mozzarella Company after the Perugian model she was trained in, Paula's 1982 idea was, in fact, a bit nuts. Her plan to sell to stores dissolved completely when stores couldn't handle her cheese and its unmanageably short shelf life. By 1984, her customer focus was squarely on the chefs, so she returned to Italy to learn about goat cheese and expand her cheeses.

With handmade mozzarella and goat cheese, Paula tirelessly worked the chef-and-restaurant angle. The concept of "regional cuisine" had begun, slowly, and southwest chefs were beginning to incorporate the seasonings of Mexico and Texas into their cooking. Paula joined them. In talking about the restaurants and how essential they were (and now, by choice, still are) to her business, she said, "You've gotta dance with the one who brung you."

That's an incredible southernism that means, I think, that those guys bought her cheese when no one in the general public would touch it with a twenty-foot pole, so now she does business with them even though the grocery stores have finally come calling. The Mozzarella Company has actually gotten smaller in the past seven years, and Paula regulates demand by raising her prices. Although it's making 200,000 pounds of cheese a year, the work is all done by hand, and apparently, a lot of her employees are getting older and slowing down. She's managed that slowdown by selling directly to customers and screening out companies that aren't willing to pay a premium price.

The cheese that landed the company on the map, and inspired its name, is its **mozzarella**. There are lots of places that "make" mozzarella by hand. You can watch as the curd is chopped by hand, dipped by the fistful into hot water until it's pliable, stretched, by hand, with a paddle, pinched into balls, dipped into cold water with nimble fingers, and immersed in brine for a dose of salt before being packaged.

That is not handmade mozzarella. The reason I say so is that those "handmade" producers begin with curd, not with milk. The Mozzarella Company starts with raw milk that is delivered every three days by a local cooperative, and cheese is made four times a week. By starting with raw milk, a cheesemaker can achieve the correct level of acidity and convert all the milk sugar (lactose) into lactic acid. Those starting with curd have the right acidity, but acid has been poured into the milk and the lactose has not converted. It's easy to spot mozzarella with lactose—it won't melt and turns brown when heated.

It's a far more difficult process to add starter culture and let the milk's acidity fall slowly, lactose converting all the while. There is a brief window the cheesemaker must hit: start too early, and your mozzarella is tough; start too late, and you wind up with a ball of mush. The Mozzarella Company's whole process takes six to eight hours per batch:

1. Pasteurize/acidify the milk (30 minutes).
2. pH falls (acidity is building).
3. Add rennet (25 minutes).
4. Cut the curd and leave it to mature (3 to 4 hours).
5. Pull off most of the whey and make ricotta.
6. When the acidity of the curds is 5.2, put them on table, chop by hand, transfer to vat, add hot water (180 degrees), stretch by hand with a paddle for 5 minutes.
7. Transfer from vat into bowl, pinch into balls.
8. Toss in cold water.
9. Immerse in brine to salt.
10. Package.

The resulting mozzarella has the proper stretch and chew, the outer layers peeling back in papery shreds, the flavor clean, milky, and mild with enough salt to earn my appreciation. Paula now makes a slew of other Italian-inspired lactic marvels, including **burrata**, a mozz-like ball shaped around a lump of sweet-cream butter, a **mixed-milk mozzarella** made from goat and cow milk, **ricotta, scamorza, crescenza**, and flavored **caciotta**.

My favorite cheese from Paula's second wave of regionally inspired cheese is **Hoja Santa**. A small hockey puck of fresh, pasteurized goat cheese, the package is wrapped in a green leaf, saturated with water from the cheese it contains. The leaf is called *hoja santa* (meaning "holy leaf" and pronounced "O-ha

Saan-ta"), and it's typically used in Mexican cuisine for wrapping chicken or fish. It's appreciated for its sprightly, minty, licoricey twang. When I was tasting it with my friend Angie one night, she looked up at me with the triumphant expression of someone who has just nailed the impression of a cheese's flavor. "This is a good cheese for vegetarians because it tastes like fennel sausage. Vegetarians are always looking for meat replacements." Hoja Santa is lighter and more delicate than most meats I know, a little curdy, kind of whippy, with a leaf that is alive and fresh-tasting, almost juicy, and the cheese beneath utterly clean and zesty. I love it in the spring and summer, when we carry it at Murray's.

➤ REDWOOD HILL
SEBASTOPOL, CALIFORNIA

Jennifer Bice's experience with kids, of both the human and the goat persuasions, is extensive. She's the oldest of ten children and the daughter of a pioneering goat dairy that began in northern California in 1968. By 1978, she assumed ownership and, along with her partner, Steven Schak, began making more than goats and milk. The making-of-goats part is no joke. Redwood Hill is a premier breeder of dairy goats, and Jennifer's been showing goats since she was a kid in the 4H Club. She regularly judges at snazzy-sounding events like the American Dairy Goat Association National Show. I look forward to the day this is aired on ESPN after Westminster. Her brother Scott now oversees the breeding while Jennifer does the cheese and yogurt, but their Alpine, LaMancha, Nubian, and Saanen herd is exceptionally well groomed for milk flavor and production.

Like the other goat adventurers of the 1980s, Redwood Hill began making fresh **chèvre**, which has a great, thick, extremely creamy, smearable texture. The line has expanded to focus more on the aged goat cheeses, most of which are small format and mold-ripened. The **Bucheret** is cloaked in a blend of white *Penicillium candidum* and brainy yellow *Geotrichum*. A soft, furry coat covers each drum-shaped barrel. I prefer it to the **Camellia** for its brighter acidity and zesty tang. For soft and creamy, go Camellia. Think little goat Camembert, with a slightly thick but doughy, yielding rind. It's incredibly mild, almost shockingly so for goat cheese, which makes it good for the leery. Good salt, mild, and bready, it's extremely approachable. Although all the young guys must be pasteurized, there are a few raw-milk options. The **feta** (which can be made pasteurized) is salt water–brined for eighteen hours. It's incredibly light and oceanic, with the clean, high hum of mouth-watery goat milk. Then there's the relatively new **Gravenstein Gold**. Of course, I'm inclined to like it because of the washed rind, in this case with cider made from Gravenstein apples. It's firm from several months' aging, and the rind is a crusty terra-cotta smear atop bright white, apparently crumbly insides. In fact, when you bite into the thing, it's smooth and pressed, like Spanish Garrotxa or Ibores. It's the best of the lineup and a highly unusual find in the United States. Washed-rinds are typically cow milk, so the funky/browned apple aromatics combined with the dry, hazelnutty goat paste is delicious.

➤ VERMONT BUTTER AND CHEESE COMPANY
WEBSTERVILLE, VERMONT

Allison Hooper is one of the goat mothers. She founded the Vermont Butter and Cheese Company with her business partner, Bob Reese, in 1984, though at that time they did not make butter. Allison is so nonplussed about her accidental foray into cheese that it's rather hard to believe, even though it's true. Allison began Vermont Butter and Cheese because "I wanted to make this cheese. I was so into the product that the business side was secondary. When you make a product, it's incredibly gratifying. Twenty years ago, people weren't talking about cheese, much less American cheese. Today you're kind of revered. Twenty years ago, if it wasn't French or Italian, it wasn't cheese. It wasn't edible."

Allison's life in cheese started when she was a college junior studying abroad in France. She liked it there a lot, and wanted to spend the summer but needed to make money. Several family farms responded to her inquiry, but it was one in Brittany, with animals, that trumped the veggie operations. That was 1980. Allison graduated the following year, and, after a brief stint in Taipei, during which she realized that learning Mandarin was impractical if she didn't want to live in Asia, she returned to France. First the Ardèche; then back to Brittany.

By now it was 1982. Allison's mother sent her a clipping from *Gourmet* about the California goat cheesemaker Laura Chenel. At the ripe old age of twenty-two, Allison "thought that was so cool but didn't quite dial in to doing it myself." Nonetheless, she came back to the United States and ruled the roost at the fledgling Union Square farmers' market in

Manhattan, selling goat cheese for a "large" (150-goat) producer in New Jersey. Wanting autonomy, she headed up to
Vermont in search of her own gig. She met Bob Reese by accident, he got her to make goat cheese for a dinner, and they
decided to start a company together. She knew cheese, he
knew business plans. They complemented each other and together had a grand total of $1,200 to put into the operation.
Their intention was never to own animals but instead to buy
milk from Vermont farmers. Allison summed up: "We were so
stupid. We didn't think about it. We just started making
cheese."

Make they did, and in 1984 they took their cheese, which
at the time was fresh chèvre, to the farmers' market. "We
didn't sell shit. It was awful. In 1984, no one bought at the
farmers' market. It was a place for summertime produce, not
other products. Plus, cheese alone wasn't something people
were doing or buying." The cheese was piling up with nowhere
to go.

Enter the consumer highs and lows. On the one hand,
they began buying cream to make the French staple **crème
fraîche**, known and desired by no one but French chefs in Boston and New York. These chefs didn't actually want an American product, but the dollar was gaining in strength, the cost of
imports was climbing through the roof, and French cheese,
especially Brie, was being recalled right and left for suspected
listeria contamination. On the other hand, in 1988, Americans
took a liking to a Boursin-inspired spread Allison and Bob
began making: fresh goat cheese, garlic powder, thyme, salt,
and pepper. It was, according to Allison, "awful." But people
recognized it, and they bought it.

Their success with chefs, after much wheedling and cajoling, led to the addition of French-style cultured butter in 1991 and Italian-inspired mascarpone (a thick, sweet, cultured cream) soon after that. And though the cow milk products became an essential part of the business ("The market wasn't ready for goats. Goat cheese alone wouldn't cut it"), the Vermont Butter and Cheese Company almost went bankrupt when the bank pulled the plug on funding for its plant expansion and new equipment. A second bank offered a bridge loan if the partners could raise $150,000 in two months. They did, with the money of high-risk investors, but it forced them to grow the company more quickly than they might otherwise have done. What had begun as a lark, with little thought, driven by the passion for good dairy and goat cheese, became an exercise in managing cash flow. VBC didn't have the liberty to poke around and sell a little bit here and there. It focused on the products that sold and rode the luck of being in the right market at the right time. Fine-dining, particularly French, chefs greedily consumed their fresh, lactic marvels, and though VBC's aged goat cheeses became popular in the 1990s, the partners nearly shut things down a second time.

Bonne Bouche was one of the very first cheeses the Frenchies went for. When I sold it to Ducasse and Daniel, I knew American cheese was on a roll. They liked it because the small, ashed rounds were like local Selles-sur-Cher. Pasteurized, perhaps, but crinkly and walnutty, with an oozing little drip under the gray, hairy rind. The Loire Valley counterparts we carried often suffered tremendously on the transatlantic journey, and lo, this Vermont upstart began to look pretty good. When VBC abruptly announced it was ceasing production, everyone was mildly traumatized, myself first and foremost. What American cheese could I sell these restaurants now? This was 2002. There wasn't a ton of soft-ripened American goat cheese and even fewer worth eating. But VBC was coming down fast because the aged cheeses, with their molded outsides, were contaminating the neighboring fresh cheeses. As Allison said, "It was bringing us to our knees." Either you get serious, or you stop playing around with molded rinds. Until VBC could expand its aging facilities, the Bonne Bouche was out, and I was back to square one with the restaurants.

The heart of the enterprise is VBC's range of fresh, pasteurized goat cheese (**chèvre**) logs, available in plain and herb. There are also cups and tubs of **creamy goat cheese**, meant to emulate the luscious, spreadable smear a chef once created by mixing their chèvre with ricotta and heavy cream. The cow milk muted that glorious, mouth-watery pucker, so VBC came up with its own recipe. It feels like a spread that would shame you, but it's just really, really delicious cheese. There are also some compulsively edible flavors. There's one with **olive and herb**, which I find a tad watery in its brininess, but the **roasted red pepper** is insane, sweet and smoky, with big chunks tucked into the cheese. I've eaten a whole cup by myself on several occasions.

And then there are the cows: milk and cream from St. Albans Coop in Vermont that are turned into **cultured butter** (meaning lots of tang and a bit of nutty). The one in the little basket, liberally sprinkled with coarse, briny sea salt, is like dipping cool churned butter in the ocean. We often eat a baby tub at lunch with a baguette. Life at Murray's can be rough.

Then there are **mascarpone, crème fraîche, quark**, and **fromage blanc**, the last of which, regrettably, is made of skim milk (the French chefs still lament that choice).

Happily, Bonne Bouche made a grand comeback in 2007, along with a line of other mold-ripened goat cheeses. The prior year, VBC had added a new 4,000-square-foot creamery dedicated to aged goats (the cheeses, not the animals) and brought in a young Frenchwoman, Adeline Folley, to manage production and aging. Bonne Bouche is different from what I remember, which was dense-packed clay, the rind more white than bluey gray, the flavor delicate limestone. Now this morsel has a goatier complexity, the flavor rolling out from mineral to high acid and then receding at the perfect moment, leaving a glaze of tangy ice cream and mown grass. Mind the rind. If the cheese gets warm or sits without exposure to air, the rind expands into wet, fat rolls, gnawing away at the milk proteins until each little piece drips milky liquid as you push through the damp, papery skin. Should this happen, blame only yourself, the retailer, or the restaurant. Bonne Bouche begins its life with far greater austerity.

Other aged specimens, made without vegetable ash sprinkled on the exterior or with a combination of ash and a yellowy mold called *Geotrichum*, include **Coupole, Bijou**, and **Crottin**. Coupole is my favorite of the three. It's a little globe and looks like Honeydew's head (of Muppets Beaker and Honeydew fame). The rounded dome is dusted with ash, and then *Geotrichum* takes over, so the cheese is parchment-colored, with a creamy layer and then an incredibly dense center. Think papier-mâché, almost starchy in its chewiness. The typical goat-lemon acidity is muted, the flavor more akin to chickeny risotto, but incredibly vegetal and grassy. I'm always surprised at the complexity pulled from the freshly pasteurized milk. Bijou and Crottin look similar: smallish, squared-off gumdrops with way more acid and a chalky center that doesn't quite dissolve. I'm left with a thick skim of goat tang on the roof of my mouth.

Like Cypress Grove, Vermont Butter and Cheese has become a big player in the little world of good American cheese. And like many big players, it can make a big positive impact— or not. Part of the advantage of size and present-day success is VBC's ability to help goat farmers develop workable business plans to begin, or grow, their operations. It pays a premium price for milk with a higher protein content, and VBC keeps an employee for "farm relations" who works with the dairies on nutrition, breeding, and milk quality to deliver richer milk with more solids for cheese and less water that eventually goes down the drain. Two thirds of VBC's goat milk comes from twenty Vermont farms and several New York Amish farms as well. The feasibility of 100 percent Vermont goat milk is a challenge, and Allison is quick to point out that she'd rather put off new business than grow to the point where she must buy enormous amounts of curd from far away. The inherent seasonal restrictions on goat milk are dealt with in two ways: (1) rotational breeding and (2) mixing frozen curd into milk. The great advantage of rotational breeding is not just a steady annual supply of milk. It also ensures a mix of milk from animals at varying stages in their lactation cycle. Milk becomes increasingly richer (more fat and protein) during lactation until it plateaus and begins to decrease in both supply and composition. Rotational breeding evens out these natural spikes, so the final cheese is more consistent in flavor and texture. The incorporation of high-moisture, frozen curd made from excess summertime milk is viable only for the fresh, rindless stuff. Allison's original vision was to help struggling Vermont dairy farms convert from milking cows to milking goats, but this hasn't worked, given the complexities and differences between the animals. Nowadays, VBC partners with its milk suppliers and helps them become better, more productive, and more sustainable goat dairies.

➤ WESTFIELD FARM
HUBBARDSTON, MASSACHUSETTS

I'd be unlikely to accurately guess the number of American producers making simple, fresh goat cheese, but every restaurant and store that sells it should find a cheesemaker as close as possible that makes cheese as often as possible, to get something of unparalleled quality. For me, at Murray's the fresh goat of choice has always been Westfield Farm's **Capri**. This is handmade goat cheese. Not the Cryovac logs with the infinite shelf life that are squeezed through a tube (the official term is "extruded") for a slick, almost glossy appearance and thick creaminess. No, the handmade stuff has more air in it, like fluffy clouds rather than goat milk hot dogs. Westfield was one of the first, and Letty and Bob Kilmoyer began making chèvre in the late 1970s, when, you guessed it, no one had heard of the stuff. By the mid-1990s, they had grown their business to a large enough scale that the original goats had been sold (all but three) and they purchased milk from four area goat farms. But they were ready to retire.

Enter Bob and Debby Stetson, who were getting, in Bob's words, "antsy" with Boston life. They'd built a successful business themselves and sold it, and were looking for the next thing to do. This is a man who had never had goat cheese, who didn't know what it was. An ad in the paper led them an hour west of the city to a three-hundred-year-old farmhouse and a lifestyle that just seemed . . . better. Their attitude of "best not to ask too many questions when making a big life shift" led them to buy the farm and apprentice with the Kilmoyers for a mere month before they were left alone to make cheese. The couple still buys from four area farms milking Nubian, Alpine, and Toggenburg goats. They pay a premium for the milk because they're smart enough to understand that goat farmers can provide milk only if they're paid a living wage in return. And the cheese is still made by hand, nearly every day. At Murray's, our weekly shipment arrives in New York two to three days old, and we sell it in a week rather than stockpiling it and risking its quality.

Recently, I planned to reacquaint myself with Capri, but that day I forgot my cheese at work. The following Monday I brought it home but was too busy to taste it. Almost a week later I dug the paper-wrapped slab out of my fridge and worried. Was that vinegar I smelled? Sniffed again. Nope. The cheese looked a little glisteny. Was it too wet and weepy? Apparently not. When I dug a schmear out of the plump slab of snowy white chèvre, it was everything I expect from Westfield. Fresh, fresh, and supercreamy, silky, even—not a bit of graininess. Just enough cultured flavor, a little sour cream on the finish, but soft. Balanced. Sweet, even. It's utterly simple and in that way one of the hardest things to do well. There's simply nowhere to hide. This cheese, it seems, never has to.

Westfield also makes the **Classic Blue Log,** rounds called **Hubbardston Blue** (in goat and cow, the latter with milk purchased from a neighboring dairy of Ayrshire cows) and little gobstoppers called **Bluebonnet.** All follow a similar recipe: fresh, pasteurized cheese blanketed in a Technicolor coat of blue mold. The reason they don't have internal veining like most blue cheeses is that they are never pierced with needles, a critical step that allows the oxygen-loving blue mold *Penicillium roquefortii* to grow inside a cheese and not just on its rind. Unlike the salty, piercing bite of most blues, these taste like mild, sweet, fresh cheeses with just a bit of the mushroomy damp. They get soggy and compromised within days if they're allowed to sit around, but fresh from the farm they're plump and delicate.

FIGHTING THE FRENCH: CONQUERING AMERICA'S CHEFS

MOST FOOD PEOPLE AGREE: IT'S THE CHEFS WHO INTRODUCE us to the way we are going to eat. It's a slow trickle-down from the finest four-star enclaves to the national chains, but trickle it does, and suddenly one day McDonald's owns a chain of Mexican restaurants whose primary focus is on freshly prepared food made with hormone-free, humanely raised meat. The chain is called Chipotle, lunch comes quick and tasty with a healthy side of virtue, and many tenets of the past thirty years, from Alice Waters on down, are translated for the American public.

When Laura Chenel began making fresh goat cheese, calling it chèvre, which no one had ever heard of, it was in fact Alice Waters at Chez Panisse who first began buying it. When Paula Lambert, the Dallas owner of The Mozzarella Company, decided to make cheese like those she'd eaten in Italy, it was an importer who'd begun a steady trade in a new exotic known as "sun-dried tomatoes" who sent her to a contact in northern Italy. When she returned with a handful of recipes, this same dealer of foreign sundries introduced her to the chefs who would be her primary buyers for the next fifteen years.

For all food trends worth considering, chefs are the first barrier to entry. They are the most likely to take a risk and the most curious, they often have the greatest access, and they are more likely to pay a premium than a random supermarket shopper is. In 2009, these denizens of fine dining are wholly, comfortably, and inarguably Americanized, but still, in 2009, three of the five New York City restaurants to boast four stars from the *New York Times* are French in soul, leadership, and ultimately cuisine. The other two? One is sushi, by way of Japan, and the other owes much of its discipline and approach to classic French methodology.

To be French and succeed in America, some adaptation must occur. There must be some flexibility for local breeds, some concession to regional adaptations, such as fromage blanc made with skim rather than full-fat milk, and, hopefully, a generous celebration of inimitable perks, such as spring ramps or stinging nettles. There must be, and has been, some massaging of tradition, so Daniel Boulud's or Jean-Georges Vongerichten's food is no longer what his grandmother might have made, though the principles remain very much alive.

French chefs—all chefs, really—may be malleable in their ingredient sourcing, but in the early days, even they are resistant. In the beginning, some menu items remain a bastion of tradition, right down to their very presence on the menu in the first place. Say, for example, the cheese course. The very concept of *fromage* as a midcourse between dinner and dessert is un-American, as we have been groomed to scarf a few heavy wedges before dinner to really get our fat on. In the beginning, cheese was foremost among the foods that simply couldn't be made locally. The cheese course was the place to showcase one of Europe's most refined traditions and no place for experimentation.

I've never met the great French chef Alain Ducasse. I've always wanted to, because everyone in the industry speaks so highly of him and his horn-rimmed glasses give him an intellectualism that's especially appealing to me. Though I was often in the kitchen of his now-shuttered Alain Ducasse at the Essex House, we never crossed paths, but the uncompromising discipline for which he's known permeated the slick, blue, humming space. There was a fantastic private dining room, glassed in, at the back of the kitchen, where the *über*-rich could entertain parties of eight or ten while they watched legions of ramrod-straight, string-bean French lads reduce, sous-vide, mince, sprinkle, and craft their priceless meals to perfection. I remember several things about the guys at Alain Ducasse. One, they were silent. When forced into a situation where they must acknowledge or interact, they were exceedingly polite. Many of them had fingers stained tannish yellow by smoking. I think they took cigarette breaks in lieu of eating. They all had dark circles under their eyes. No one seemed particularly unhappy; they all accepted that to participate in a four-star Ducasse kitchen they'd better show up, work mercilessly, not talk, go home, and then come back and do it again. The place quivered with the relentless pursuit of perfection. At the time it was New York's most expensive restaurant, and it had been dealt a blow when its executive chef announced his return to France. He was an intimidating guy to work for but universally respected by his staff.

The replacement chef was more decorated than an admiral but brought in from the outside, which can really screw a restaurant because everyone has to find the rhythm of the new leader. The thing I've learned from standing around kitchens with my bag of cheese is that all present take their cue from the chef. But if he's brand new, how do you learn what not to do? I'll tell you how. You do the wrong thing, and he makes sure to correct you in front of the entire back of the house. Loudly. I inadvertently crossed that training line a few short weeks into his tenure, when I rolled uptown with some cheese samples. I was there for a tasting, to see if any changes to the cheese cart were in order. I swept through the dining room, which, it must be said, was one of the uglier dining rooms in New York at the time. Every time I was there I thought of the move they teach little girls in dance class: Jazz Hands. Yeah! Jazzy! The carpet was yellow, the chairs were covered in orange and red, the window that looked onto Fifty-eighth Street was decorated with random musical instruments positioned on stands like artwork. It was really weird and very Harlequin, though the massive pedestal vases stuffed with roses were expensive, lush, and beautiful.

Swing a left through the double doors, ten steps down, and the hum of the kitchen opened to my left. The guys prepping at the counter were always masked by cabinets that hung down, so I could see a skinny midsection swathed in thick, starched chef's whites, and hands with nails bitten to the quick pulling lobster meat from tail shells, scraping paper-thin sheaves of dirt from mushroom caps. As I ducked my head under, the chef de cuisine, Sebastian, would smile back. He always rallied for me, and though I wouldn't call him ebullient, he was warm. Also very tall and seemingly better fed than many of the others. So we'd say hi and I'd walk around to his side of the pass and begin unwrapping my crumbling wedges and unctuous rounds. This time I got them all lined up, mildest to strongest, and we started tasting. We were maybe two or three cheeses in when Chef appeared. I rarely call chefs "Chef." Not out of disrespect but out of familiarity. It's like calling your husband's mom "Mrs. Smith." That would be strange. With the French chefs, however, I'm often lacking the warm fuzzies. I call Daniel Boulud by his first name now, but it's taken a few years, plus he's a pretty approachable, down-to-earth guy. This chef? Not so much. Neither familiar nor down-to-earth. So I worked the big, fake smile that suddenly appears on my face when I'm in a formal and uncomfortable situation, and said, "Hi, Chef!"

Mind you, it was late afternoon. We were getting on toward dinner service. Sebastian and I always taste cheese, and then I get out. These guys don't mess around with espresso and bullshitting. But he looked at me, this small man, as though I were a downtown roach in his spotless midtown kitchen, and asked, "You are not going to have me to taste cheese in my own kitchen?"

Eek. I had inadvertently violated the Do Not Cross line and offended this man's ego. Score Direct Hit.

Shit. So I was already sweaty and awkward, and I stammered a bit (unlike me) and tried to recover and said that I assumed he was far too busy to taste, but, yes, would he like to join us? Because I would like him to join us. Because it would be fantastic to show him some of the new seasonal cheeses I'd brought from a local producer, which are just perfect at this time of year and—

And he raised his barrel chest up to a full height that was less than my own and spat, "Who do you think you are? You come into my kitchen, and you taste without asking my opinion, and you bring this American cheese. This is sheet." He didn't really throw anything, but he sort of wiped his arm across the counter and flicked his pudgy hand at the cheese and I stood there, absolutely mortified. Every head in the place went down, eyes on the counter, knives tapping faster, and frankly I don't remember what I did or said because I was so focused on not bawling all over myself in the middle of the Alain Ducasse kitchen.

The moral of this story is: clearly I should have asked the guy to taste the cheese, but I didn't know. The submoral of the story is that American cheese was, for many years, a very hard sell. Ironically, this man's predecessor was one of the first chefs to embrace Vermont Butter and Cheese Company's Bonne Bouche, and this man's successor prioritized American cheeses on the cart, continuing to this day at Alain Ducasse's new New York outpost, Adour, at the St. Regis.

Chefs used to have a nasty reputation for being drunks and druggies, arrogant pricks who slept with the hostesses and threw sizzling cast irons at incompetent line cooks. That was the rep Tony Bourdain so hysterically described in *Kitchen Confidential*. But the truth is, cooking became legit in the last two decades in America, and the French chefs are especially lauded for their discipline. What I found as I got to know many of them is that they embody a charming combination of uncompromising work ethic and incredibly intimate memory. Many of the old guard grew up in rural France, surrounded by women who planted and dug, whipped and baked. I kid you not: every time I taste cheese with Philippe Vongerichten, the younger brother of Jean-Georges and maître de maison of his four-star mecca on Central Park West, he tells one of a handful of stories about his Alsatian grandmother. One story is about coming home from school as a boy and scarfing down her crème fraîche, made by hand that morning. The other story is about placing a wheel of (the incredibly sticky, pungent, stinky) Alsatian Muenster, sent from home, on his radiator in New York to soften the thing up and get it ripening a little, only to receive irate phone calls from the downstairs neighbor, whose apartment was inexplicably scented with the diseased funk of a raw-milk washed-rind. Philippe tells both stories with nostalgic sighs and apparent amazement that it all happened so long ago.

For all the formality that so often intimidated me when I went into French kitchens, these men remember what it means to cook with ingredients from the immediate area. It's what they grew up with, and it's a model that makes sense to them. Especially when you're talking about dairy: why bring it from far away if you can find good milk, cream, or fresh cheese nearby? Mind you, they don't throw anyone bones just for being local, and as the American cheese resurgence was building in the 1980s and '90s, they were just as picky with the struggling fledglings as they were with the seasoned suppliers of Europe. But: they remembered their training in France, and they understood having a face-to-face relationship with a local farmer.

Then there was the up-and-coming American contingent. Guys whom no one had heard of then, but are becoming common names now, such as Charlie Trotter and, here in New York, Dan Barber, Peter Hoffman, and Bill Telepan. These guys began to plant a stake in the ground of the nascent local-food movement. Among other things, they prioritized American producers, not just of cheese but of heritage breeds of chicken and pork, foraged mushrooms, and upstate veggies. They balanced out the French chefs, they were forgiving, they were willing to ebb and flow with cheesemakers who were finding their stride, and they committed to carrying cheeses none of their guests had ever heard of. They embraced the French tradition of the cheese course, and made it their own.

Between the two groups of chefs, cheesemakers had an audience that didn't yet exist at the retail level. In many cases, in the beginning, these producers survived on the patronage of restaurants alone. But as is so often the case, when the chefs take notice the press does, too, and slowly the downward trickle begins.

In 2003, when I took over the nascent wholesale business at Murray's, I bounced around among the chefs, and it was often at their urging that I sought out new American producers of whatever they needed for a recipe or cheese cart or special wine dinner. Their preferred cheeses were as diametrically opposed as the chefs themselves: one group considered and then embraced traditional French styles such as ashed goat cheeses and oozing washed-rinds, while the other clamored for the weirdest, funkiest range of American originals I could dig up.

The cheese course has become de rigueur in fine-dining destinations across the country and has even started to appear at chains such as Ruth's Chris steak houses. For me, the advent and legitimacy of American cheese began with the chefs I've known the best or longest. These are the favorite cheeses of New York City's first adopters.

NOTES INSPIRED BY
NEW YORK'S CHEFS

➤ ANDANTE DAIRY
PETALUMA, CALIFORNIA

Cheesemakers are a generally approachable crowd. But I have always, at least until very recently, been completely intimidated by, or rather mildly terrified of, the cheesemaker from Andante Dairy. Which is kind of amazing, especially if you visit her Web site, which shows a tiny woman with a round, open face, laughing deeply as she sips a cup of . . . tea. Soyoung Scanlan scared me for many reasons. The first is that, if you open the seminal book *On Food and Cooking* by Harold McGee, you will see it is dedicated to Soyoung. This book is the first, best, and unfailing reference for all things technical and scientific about food. Anyone who knows so much about the technicalities of milk and cheesemaking that she's helping Harold Mc-Gee understand it is someone who knows an unprecedented amount. Second, there's the issue of where you can find Soy-oung's cheese. Most often, the answer is nowhere, because the very best chefs in the Bay Area, plus a few transplants to New York City, buy whatever she will make for them. The rest goes to the San Francisco farmers' markets. Plus, Soyoung is an intense woman and I was pretty sure she didn't like me, so I was surprised, relieved, and nervous when she agreed to let me visit her operation in Petaluma, California.

This visit involved opening a locked metal gate to someone else's property and driving my rental car basically across that person's front yard and up a steep, muddy dirt road that snaked through open fields of livestock. When I reached the top of a hill and saw a lot of goats, I simply shut off the car and started walking. The goats belong to neighboring Volpi Ranch and dozens of them pick their way about the open, airy building she's constructed for cheesemaking and aging. Recently, they decimated her vegetable garden.

It turns out that Soyoung does not dislike me, and she is not, in fact, especially scary. Her intensity, however, hums like a quiet vibration. She was studying for a Ph.D. in biophysics and hating it when California's Department of Agriculture gave her a sizable scholarship to focus her work on the membrane of fat globules. With the state's growing dairy industry, it wanted to learn how to make good low-fat cheeses, and Soyoung was the person who could learn how the structure of fat could be modified. With one semester of her prestigious grant remaining, she decided that the purpose of her study was backward. I believe what she actually said was that the whole culture was sick. I think what she meant is that learning how to restructure the natural order of things so people can eat uninhibitedly (and tell themselves they're doing so without repercussions) is crazy. So she abandoned the money and the degree and headed up to Sonoma to help dairy farmers understand their milk and make better cheese. The power of her realization overrode any idea that the farmers might not be on the same wavelength. Sure enough, she found that dairy farmers can be pretty inflexible. Often, they do things the way they've always been done and aren't so quick to change. She thought it better to use their milk and make her own cheese than try to modify their cheesemaking practices.

How this woman learned to make cheese is impressive. She knew the structure of fat but nothing of cheesemaking, so she went to Europe and tasted five to seven cheeses every day, very intently, and from their flavor and texture started writing recipes for how she thought they were made. Don't ask me how she did it, but this was her method of learning. As precise and technical as her background may be, what moves me about Soyoung and her cheese is a kind of mysticism. She began making cheese because she wanted to understand the mystery of life: life in nature, life in society, the relationships of beings. She does this over ladles of milk in sun-filled silence while her daughter plays quietly in a room built as a nursery. Cheesemaking is so technical, so prescriptive, so scientific, yet it must be improvised as tiny factors in and around the cheese shift and change. Her new aging rooms were inconsistent in their humidity and temperature, so Soyoung set up a cot and slept with her cheese, seeing how the air felt on her skin every few hours. This, she said, is science.

Her cheese is handmade on the most unforgiving scale and her methods are, by Soyoung's own admission, diametri-

How Do You Define Good Milk?

Soyoung Scanlan is refreshingly unwilling to define quality cheese with the labels I've come to rely on: grass-fed, raw milk, artisanal, farmstead, and so on. She did, though, go to the slippery heart of the matter and managed to describe the things that feel most important to me when I think about cheesemaking in America. As to what makes good milk:

Care of the dairy farmers. Love for the animal. The notion that whatever you put in comes out. Soyoung's example? Holstein cows. "People say they're no good for cheesemaking, but in England farmers love their animals, feed them right, and the milk is the best." Healthy animals live thirteen to fifteen years and make less milk as they age but better milk. You can carry the flavor into the final product.

"Is one hundred percent grassfeeding possible? Here it is not. In Vermont it is not.

"Artisan is about tradition and history. It limits your growth. You can't make money. That is the sacrifice. It's a very American problem. It's hard for me to look at people and say 'Sorry,' and not run home and make ten times as much [cheese]."

cally opposed to those needed for feeding the masses. When I saw her, she had not had a day off in seven months and was making cheese every day. The milk came from Spring Hill Dairy's herd of four hundred Jersey cows over the hill, milking was done at 3 A.M., and by 8:30 Soyoung had her raw material in the pasteurizer. Everything is hand-ladled, because she believes the integrity of Jersey milk is destroyed by sloshing in a truck or rumbling through a pump. She copes with the milk's seasonal variation and unusual fat structure simply because she loves the Jersey cow and the texture, color, and smell of its milk. This is the romantic ideal of small-production cheese in America. The reality is that any producer subscribing to these tenets can make only a tiny amount of cheese for restaurants and farmers' markets. And at the end of it all, with her peculiar balance of scientific acumen and spiritual wonder, how is Soyoung's cheese? It is, rather like the woman, remarkable. Her cheese is unlike any other I have had, not because she makes a style I've never heard of but because the flavors of her cheese are thoughtful. They are quiet but incredibly complex. Often, when I am tasting, I have the impulse that this time, this cheese, is not quite right, it's going to be bitter or flat, and just as it seems to begin to head in that unwelcome direction, the flavor changes, softens, dips, and I'm left with a mellow intensity. I've noticed that her cheeses often taste of coconut or are deeply savory, like burnished, slow-roasted garlic heads.

She also does neat things such as making triple-crème cheeses not by adding cream to milk but by adding Sadie Kendall's crème fraîche so the final texture is of stiffly beaten buttercream frosting, the richness of the fat undercut by a cultured twang, not unlike that of sour cream. That's true of two of her cheeses I'm most familiar with: the **Minuet**, which is a goat milk triple crème, made so by the addition of Kendall crème fraîche, and a cheese Soyoung began making exclusively for Murray's in the summer of 2008 called **Trio**. "Trio" refers to the blend of cow and goat milk, plus crème fraîche. She often makes one-off cheeses like this, exclusively for restaurants such as the French Laundry. The two cheeses are extremely different. The Minuet captures the brighter, higher acidity of goat cheese, but in dense, fatty fluff. And because that additional fat is cultured, there is a browned-nut essence that brilliantly complements the green-grassy goat flavor. Soyoung's goat cheeses have an old-world complexity that's hard to describe. There are many flavors, and my initial impression that they might go awry disappears as new layers of taste unfold. When I last tried her goat cheeses, they were redolent of coconut. Not the dry, shredded junk you get in a bag but a fat wedge of the nut itself, milky yet firm, oily yet light, the flavor of coconut clean and delicate, nothing like a piña colada.

The Trio, although it's blended milk, sits heavy on the tongue like good New York cheesecake. It's yellowy white and looks innocent, creamy, and milky. You think it will be mild and light, perhaps a bit salty. Easy but ultimately careless. And it's not! It instantly recalled an unusual raw-milk triple crème we can no longer import from France, a little puck called Délice de Saint-Cyr, that always amazed me for its earthen complexity. The square Trio shares that leathery, horsey quality, like smelling an empty barn with freshly polished saddles lined up for show. There are countless others, and my understanding is that Soyoung invents new cheeses when the fancy strikes her, because this is what she loves. In other words, you're about guaranteed that any cheese from Andante you can find will be excellent. That gives you two much-needed excuses to (1) go to fancy restaurants or (2) go to San Francisco and visit the farmers' market.

> **CONSIDER BARDWELL FARM**
WEST PAWLET, VERMONT

Abutting New York's Washington County, Consider Bardwell Farm sits in the Champlain Valley of Vermont, where it was established in 1864 as the state's first cheesemaking cooperative. It now happens to be owned by my literary agent and her husband, but that's not why I'm interested in their doings.

The farm first caught my attention several springs ago, when Angela Miller popped up at Murray's with little discs of fresh goat cheese. Given the life cycle of this style—from teat to table in a couple of days—it's one of the most common offerings from fledgling American producers. No aging is necessary, and the immediacy of cheese helps the cash flow. It's ironic that the cheese no one could sell twenty-five years ago is often the cheese that floats cheese start-ups these days. I taste a lot of fresh goat cheese. So here was Angela and her **Mettowee**, which at the time was made only in a perfect four-ounce patty. Nowadays it's made in larger-format sizes as well. It was spectacular in its simplicity. This was around the same time I discovered buckwheat honey, a thick, brackish spread smelling like molasses and made from bees pollinating buckwheat fields in Washington State. I tried the two together, and the combination was symphonic. Mettowee is clean and milky but somehow more complex than the typical lemony notes of chèvre. It has a slight muskiness to it, like damp tree bark, and conservative salting, so you really feel as though you're eating goat milk made solid. The astringency of the honey is intense and was so perfectly offset by this cool, creamy morsel. Then the farm enlisted Peter Dixon, whose resume as a roving cheesemaking expert is long and storied. From there, they started playing around with aged styles and have nailed the cheese they call **Manchester**.

Some of my favorite impossibly hard-to-find cheeses are the raw, aged goat tommes of southern France, particularly in and around the Ariège Valley. Because they have some months on them, they're available long after the goats go on nonmilking winter hiatus. With age (in this case four to six months), the acidity of goat milk softens into an incredibly sweet, rich paste, replete with hazelnut and chestnutty depth. They're washed-rinds, so a bit pungent, but balanced and savory. It's a very French style and one that I don't find a lot from American cheesemakers. Manchester is as good as my favorite Tomme de l'Ariège: incredibly dense, a bit musty, and buttery with a little acidic zip at the end. It's truly awesome, and because of its age (anywhere from three to six months) can be made of unpasteurized milk.

In the past year Consider Bardwell has begun producing cow milk cheeses in addition to the offerings from its seventy head of pastured Swiss Alpine goats. The goats produce milk only from spring to fall, so cows help with the cash flow, even when there's no milk flow. Consider Bardwell buys all its milk from the Jersey Girls, Lisa Kaimen's herd of twenty pastured Jersey cows in Chester. During the winter, the cows are fed dry hay and some grain. There are four raw cow milk choices, all in the semisoft range, with rinds composed of various collections of natural mold. **Rupert**, though it's aged from six to twelve months, is the mildest, more like an Italian Fontina Val d'Aosta than anything else, and **Pawlet** has a naughty similarity to butter. Tasting it cold from the fridge (which you should never do), I felt as if I were biting directing into a stick of chilled butter. The milky, slightly fruity flavor is appreciably more complex than that of butter, making it a good nosher. But the one that really moves me is **Dorset** and its new variation, **Chester**. On its Web site, the farm describes Dorset as being made in the style of Taleggio. It is much better than that, considerably more earthy and complex, albeit firmer, thanks to three to six months' aging. Dorset has an orange basket-weave rind, smooth and tight, with a bright yellow grass-fed Jersey cow interior. The Chester is made with more water in the cheese curd and brine-washed only once so wild molds and yeasts can bloom on the drier surface. It looks more like French Saint-Nectaire, lumpy and bumpy like a moldy quilt. There is a thick cream line under the rind and a tart, chalky interior. The high water content means it hits market at a bare two months, so buyers get the creaminess before the flavor tips to bitter. The Dorset tastes somewhere between Pont l'Évêque and ribbons of fat-framed, acorn-fed, Spanish *jamón*. Chester has much more yogurt to it and a mushroomy, fungal note to its perimeter of ooze. Sixty percent of Consider Bardwell's cheese goes to farmers' markets in Vermont and New York City, while the other forty percent is doled out to retailers like Murray's and others along the East Coast.

> ➤ **COWGIRL CREAMERY**
> *POINT REYES STATION, CALIFORNIA*

Wave two of French-inspired American cheese began in the early 1990s. Chenel, Keehn, and Hooper were on their way (see "It's 1982, Do You Know Where Your Goats Are?" on page 178), and the next group of pioneers stepped up to the plate. It was right around the time that Rob Kaufelt bought

Murray's Cheese, a period he describes as the height of fat phobia and margarine embracement. I believe his father told him he was "completely nuts" to buy the shop. Same time, different time zone, Peggy Smith and Sue Conley were wrapping up two decades in the Bay Area's Berkeley food scene. Peggy coordinated the kitchen at Chez Panisse, and Sue owned Bette's Oceanview Diner. This was just the place, and just the time, to see and touch the microcosmic changes happening in American restaurants. Local food, the notion of a cheese course, and organics were beginning to take a tentative hold.

Sue moved to Point Reyes Station, where she met Ellen and Bill Straus, who had recently taken their family dairy organic. Peggy joined her to open a new business, Cowgirl Creamery, at first conceived as a café that the two launched as a marketing vehicle for local cheesemakers. But they also wanted to make cheese themselves. In the beginning they kept it simple with fresh, pasteurized cheeses made with organic Straus milk: **cottage cheese, crème fraîche, fromage blanc**, and **quark**. A dairy scientist intern from the Netherlands pushed the pair to create an aged, soft-ripened style, which became **Mt. Tam** (named for Mount Tamalpais, that weird jutting hill just over the Golden Gate Bridge).

I'm lucky enough to revisit Mt. Tam on a rainy evening when my fat little wheel appears perfectly ripe. My guess is three to four weeks old. It looks like a double-stacked, generous hamburger, and the pads of my fingers stick ever so slightly to the papery white rind. It's a tricky line to walk because perfectly ripe means the cream-enriched insides have broken down into a thick uniform schmear and the white, bloomy rind is dappled with sandy brown patches. Is it too ripe? Up close, under my flaring nostrils, there's the unequivocal smell of ammonia. But as I tell classes at Murray's, if you have to jam your nose up under the cheese, don't consider it ammoniated. That whiff is the natural by-product of *Penicillium candidum* mold. I want at the goopy little wheel that guts itself on my knife. The fun part is bathing your tongue in the luxurious ooze of thick, white insides. I don't bite the thing but lick at it. No one else is home. But alas, it's gone a little too far. What should be a perfectly balanced swath of salt, cream, and butter has the edge of bitterness, and the rind carries that ammoniated parchment flavor up the back of my nose on the exhale.

I love that the Cowgirls opt for Straus Family Dairy pasture-based, certified organic milk. It's yellow and sweet and generally superlative. That Mt. Tam is a triple-crème means the milk used for cheesemaking is enriched with cream, something to which I am rarely opposed.

My warning is thus: by the time this cheese has ripened all the way through, the delicate custard puff is tainted with the acrid bite of ammonia. As the cheesemakers themselves caution, Mt. Tam is not meant to be runny like Brie. If yours is, don't buy it. It should be a firm, fluffy wheel, with minimal give under prodding. Straus milk is so fantastic, and the balance so well executed, that you can eat the thing young, with a slightly chalky core, and savor the balance of sour cream and high butterfat, without any sting on the finish.

The ultimate success of Mt. Tam led Cowgirl Creamery to work variations on the theme. All four of its soft-ripened cheeses are whole, organic, pasteurized Straus milk. There are two seasonal cheeses: **St. Pat** in spring, a bloomy rind wrapped in stinging nettles that are washed and frozen to remove the sting (and taste like butter and artichoke), followed annually by **Pierce Point**, made in the fall and winter, washed in muscato wine, and rolled in dried herbs from Marin County. But the one you hear the most about is **Red Hawk**. Of all the triple-crème cheeses in the world, the only one I know of that is not a bloomy rind is Red Hawk. It has all the thick, slippery, insidious slick of room-temperature butter, plus the salt, complexity, and meatiness of a solid washed-rind. Brine washing grows that sticky cantaloupe exterior, and man! when its texture is like stiff custard, you know why it won Best Cheese in America in 2003.

Next to the Mt. Tam, there's a perfect comparison of ripe and too ripe. The Red Hawk has a half-inch core of firm white, and I thought when I tasted it, it would be crumbly and young with no flavor. How wrong I was. The Mt. Tam was in fact past its peak, and the Hawk was flying high. I've eaten four pieces, trying to pull individual flavors out of the ooze, and it's really hard. They've blended into this supreme *umami* of salt, butter, bourbon, and some kind of sweet, cured meat, like really luscious Italian mortadella.

When this cheese is great, it's very, very great. And when it is bad, it is rotten. Avoid any kind of ruddy, brown, or rusty-looking Red Hawk, and certainly reject dry or cracked specimens. Seek out the slightest bit of core, and when you can't see the thing, squeeze it. You want some resistance. There's only one in the world, and I want you to have the best one.

➤ FRANKLIN'S TELEME

SAN LUIS OBISPO, CALIFORNIA

I remember my boss Rob Kaufelt talking about an American cheese that was one of the first to sweep in and blow everyone's mind. The cheese itself wasn't new. It began in the 1930s, when Giovanni Peluso learned of a soft cow milk cheese being made by a Greek family in Pleasanton, California. Ig Vella (see "When Did 'Factory' Become a Dirty Word?" on page 124) told me that the cheese was "Nick the Greek's" failed attempt at feta. The cheese, nonetheless, was popular, and Giovanni Peluso decided to attempt a version and compete. His son Frank joined him after graduating from high school in 1933. The father and son failed at making the Greek family's cheese but produced another soft, milky offering that they dusted with rice flour and called **Teleme**. It was a hit with the Italian immigrant population south of Paso Robles.

Though the family took a cheesemaking hiatus in the 1960s, the desirability of anything called Teleme was undeniable. Other area cheesemakers began making high-moisture Monterey Jack they called Teleme Jack, though it had nothing to do with the Peluso original. In the mid-1970s, Giovanni's grandson Franklin Peluso decided to get back into cheese. A broker offered to help him sell it *if* he would learn Giovanni's original recipe from his father, Frank. Franklin did and began selling Peluso Cheese Company Teleme in the early 1980s.

Although the California market changed and the focus of the Peluso Cheese Company turned to Hispanic-style cheeses, Teleme remained the cheese everyone knew about. Rob waxed nostalgic about the milky white slabs that would show up via overnight carrier at Murray's. Young and firm, they were laid out in a dish to ripen before customers' eyes. Harmless spots of blue and green mold would develop atop the rice flour as the insides slowly liquefied, weeping and running from cracks in the fine white crust. The cheese maintained its sweetness, even as it developed into mushroomy silk. Rob made it sound like the greatest cheese in the world.

The Teleme I've had has been consistently underwhelming: bland, kind of rubbery, with the rice flour no longer a delicate blanket but a gritty powder atop the tough outer skin. Even so, many of our chef clients wanted the stuff, so I searched far and wide. A few years ago, the supply from East Coast distributors dried up, so I called California. The phones rang and rang. No one answered. No one returned my calls. It seemed that Franklin Peluso and his Teleme had vanished.

And then I found out what had really happened, why the cheese had taken a turn for the worse, and how the Teleme has returned, though it's no longer Peluso that you should seek. What you want is called **Franklin's Teleme**. In 2005, father and son Frank and Franklin sold the original Peluso Cheese Company in Los Banos. A shadow of its former self, Teleme bearing their name continued. That's the disappointing bland one described above. Franklin moved to Maine that October and resumed production under the name Franklin's Teleme, but I never knew he was a mere six hours away. After one winter convinced the family that they didn't much care for the cold and isolation of Maine, they moved back to California in 2006. His Teleme production resumed, this time at the dairy plant of Cal Poly. Franklin no longer uses his last name to market the cheese lest consumers get confused (no kidding, they might). Now he goes by his first name, which is good enough for me, because the cheese is back! Franklin's in the process of getting an aging room to make a washed-rind Teleme (like a Taleggio), and has begun exploring his dream of making a goat Teleme with the milk from a tiny farm outside Petaluma. Presently, Franklin's Teleme is made from the milk of Cal Poly's on-premises dairy. There's a herd of approximately one hundred cows, a 60/40 split of Jerseys and Holsteins.

My sample arrived like a lump of dough, wrapped in aluminum foil and tucked into a shoebox. It was like getting a very special, slightly drippy present from an old friend. The cheese was on the younger side, no surface mold yet, but the sweet rice dusting tasted like Dairy Queen ice cream cones. During cheesemaking, the curds are washed to remove whey and lower the acidity, then salted, turned into their square form, and pressed overnight. The flour comes onto the scene after four days of drying. My piece was sticky and moist, pale yellow and lactic, with the clean whiff of sour cream. I knew enough to guess that in a few weeks I would have a limpid pool, more intensely buttermilky, fungal, and even more delicious. I'm so relieved this cheese has been resurrected. It's slathery and wonderful, and I remember in my first days of cheese turning a heaping scoop into a bowl of steaming garganelli. Plus salt, pepper, and a big handful of parsley equals happiness.

➤ HOLLAND'S FAMILY FARM
THORP, WISCONSIN

I have never received a random box of samples from a cheese-maker I've not heard of (that no one else has much heard of, either), opened the box, tasted the cheese, and had every single one be excellent. And made in a style that's becoming increasingly better known and much beloved by American eaters. It's a seriously rare occasion.

Yet this happened to me with the cheese from Holland's Family Farm. You might guess there is a connection to Holland, and that connection might involve Gouda. Both guesses are correct! Holland's Family makes a slew of Goudas, the aged versions of which rival our best imported specimens from the Netherlands. It was a fantastic delight. The wizard behind this cheese is a lovely young woman named Marieke Penterman (pronounced "Mareeka"). She and her husband, Rolf, both grew up on small (sixty-cow) dairy farms in Holland. These days, Holland has six million people, plus another six million cows, while Wisconsin is seven times as large and has five and a half million people. Space in Holland is seriously tight, and land is prohibitively expensive at $30,000 an acre.

Wanting to farm, Marieke and Rolf came to the United States, their brother-in-law having worked on a farm in Baldwin and found affordable land in rural Thorp. They started farming in 2002, had twins in 2003, and found cheese in 2006 as a way for Marieke to work on the farm but be close to the kids (there are three now). She traveled to Holland twice, first to train with a woman milking ten cows and later to study on a farm with two hundred. She made her first batch of cheese in November 2006.

It's astounding that in less than two years the cheese has become so good. Marieke makes cheese once a day, with warm morning milk straight from the cows. She and Rolf have a herd of 710, and the rest of the milk goes to the milk cooperative.

Only 8 percent of that single morning milking goes into cheese. I'll be honest and admit that I wish their cows were pastured, at least some of the time. The nonmilkers go out, but the rest of the girls are in a free stall barn eating hay grown on the Pentermans' 500 acres of land. Additional hay is trucked in from North Dakota and southern Wisconsin, and Marieke mentioned that buying additional land and expanding the farm would be preferable to buying hay, especially as feed and fuel skyrocket in cost. The advantage they see to indoor, hay-fed cows is that the milk is more consistent for cheesemaking.

All of the farm's **Gouda** is sold under the Marieke brand, and comes in thirteen different flavors, including some wacky ones such as foenegreek (a native seed of Holland that tastes like maple) and burning nettle, which I'm guessing means stinging nettle though I've not tasted it. They are also all raw milk. What I have latched onto is its aged varieties. The two-to-four-month range includes the flavored Goudas and the **Smoked Gouda**, which is subtle, creamy, and sweet, the smoke more toasty than anything else. The four-to-six-month version already has the smooth *dulce de leche* caramel of the Dutch brands Prima Donna and Old Amsterdam, though it's younger. And then there's the nine-to-twelve-month, which is simply awesome. It has tons of crunch, huge, crystalline hunks that pop and sizzle under tooth, plus an intense sweetness and the burnt oak/Woodfood Reserve bourbony edge that keeps this style of cheese interesting. Holland's Family Farm is making, without question, the best aged Gouda I have had from the United States.

➤ JASPER HILL FARM
GREENSBORO, VERMONT

Jasper Hill Farm is currently the collective work of more than a dozen people, but when I first ran into it, it was a farmstead operation in northeastern Vermont struggling to stay afloat on the backs of four people: two brothers, Andy and Mateo Kehler, Andy's then-girlfriend and now-wife, Victoria, and Mateo's wife, Angie. The Kehler boys had family roots in the Greensboro area, and while Mateo was working in Southeast Asia on the economic redevelopment of small villages, he realized that the family's summer haunt in Greensboro was disappearing beneath waves of real estate development and evaporating family farms. He came home and developed several business plans with Andy, and only after realizing that they could not survive producing beer or sheep cheese did they settle on cows, buying what is now Jasper Hill Farm in 1998. The consideration of a sheep dairy is especially interesting, as their research found that six hundred sheep would be necessary to support two families, while forty-eight cows could do the same.

Angie supported Mateo while he worked at London's famed cheese store Neal's Yard Dairy, in 1998 and 1999, and again when he visited cheesemakers in 2001 and 2002. The brothers chose Ayrshire cows, a breed that's uncommon in the States, but used in Scotland expressly for cheesemaking. Their cheese-specific use is unusual because many breeds, such as Guernseys and Jerseys, are bred for butter making (high fat content, thick cream, easy skimming), while Ayrshire milk has smaller fat globules that stay suspended better. It is, as Mateo describes it, "naturally homogenized." The upshot for aged

A New Definition of Terroir?

Terroir is a concept discussed with growing fervency in the American food and wine scene, and its implications for American cheese loom large. The French idea of a place, with unique characteristics of climate and soil, animals and feed, and microorganisms that flourish in milk, thrive in aging caves, and ultimately impact the color, texture, and flavor of a cheese, begins to explain the importance of the connection between soil and food. Terroir staunchly argues against a uniform, consistent product across the land and across time. Mateo Kehler of Jasper Hill considers another facet of terroir in his definition: its economy. When Jasper Hill Farm was merely an idea in the minds of two brothers, the economy of the local Vermont landscape was as much a defining attribute as the microbiology of the soil. And the economy of Greensboro, and of Vermont in general, in Mateo's opinion, is ideally suited to cows. Mateo pointed to France as an example: the regions that have the grass to support cows specialize in cheese from their milk. It is the marginal climates that have learned over generations to succeed with goat and sheep dairies.

Greensboro's land and facilities (barns, milking parlors, etc.), as well as the local infrastructure for off-season feed (primarily hay), could support a herd of forty-eighty cows. And this herd could support both Andy and Mateo. The financial and structural investment required for a sheep dairy—animals that give markedly less milk for a significantly shorter period yet require year-round feeding—far exceeded what the Kehlers could raise. Part of Jasper Hill's vision for the future is a network of small family farms, each producing a single cheese whose recipe has been tested and tweaked for maximum market impact. This vision is built around the terroir of northeastern Vermont and the unique economies of scale that cows represent.

cheeses (whose fat molecules undergo a longer process of enzymatic breakdown) is a more stable medium with less likelihood of developing rancidity and bitterness, especially in blue cheese, which the Kehlers intended to make from day one. They bought and bred fifteen heifers in July 2002 and made their first batch of cheese less than a year later, in 2003.

When Jasper Hill hit our radar at Murray's in the summer of 2003, Mateo the cheesemaker/sales guy was offering a very unusual, labor-intensive, bloomy rind called **Constant Bliss**. He seemed to have mastered the art of the rind.

He was also peddling (sigh) *another* blue cheese. We were inundated with American blues. Those and fresh goats seem to be the first styles fledgling cheesemakers try. Murray's just didn't need any more of either. My colleague Amy Sisti was doing the American cheese ordering back then, and I remember the day she came to me and said, "Mateo says if we don't buy their blue, they're out of business. He won't let us just buy the Constant Bliss. So I got some blue. I felt bad." I was entrenched in wholesale and remember being annoyed that now I was going to have to push another blue, when all the chefs wanted was the soft, creamy stuff.

The Trouble with Bloomy Rinds

Most people love a little scoop of something soft and milky with a bit of salt and a lot of butter. Even if they do not love the rind itself, most people love a bloomy rind cheese. I certainly do, though I prefer mine on the side of moist and fungal, like some truffled milk bomb secreted under a clean, protected rock. It's a hard love in American cheese, however. Bloomy rinds are not easy to make, and there aren't many cheesemakers who have mastered the high-wire act of thin, slightly papery, cohesive skin, a little bit of luscious ooze, and a stiff but creamy paste that doesn't leak liquid all over the plate. The challenges are numerous: texturally, the rind can be too thick, so it's tough and chewy, or worse, snappy like a hot dog skin when you bite in. It might be too thick, so there's an eighth inch of white moldy dough before you get to the cheese underneath. That amount of excessive mold might lead to overactive breakdown of protein and fat (proteolysis and lipolysis, respectively), so the cheese underneath unravels at accelerated speed and falls out of the rind like a gooey nut from its shell. And then there's the flavor to beware of. So many bloomies fall prey to bitterness, soapiness, an unfortunate chemical whiff reminiscent of pool chlorine, and the good old-fashioned harbinger of decay: ammonia. To find an American bloomy rind with no flavor at all is quite an accomplishment. To find one with good, complex, balanced flavor is another triumph altogether.

Mateo offered to come to New York, I offered to take him around to meet the restaurants, and together we would sell this funny new kind of American blue called **Bayley Hazen Blue**. It looked more like Stilton with its brown crusty rind than the foil-wrapped, juicy-sharp wheels of American blue we were all used to. Fine. We would try. Mateo showed up in a baseball cap, T-shirt, and Carhartts, with scarily big forearms and a renegade eyebrow hair that stuck out about two inches. It reminded me of a grasshopper feeler. He still has it. The man also smelled like milk. I don't know how to describe it, except to say that his very flesh, not to mention his hair and clothes, emanated the persistent smell of warm, coagulating milk. I liked him immediately, and we went tromping around the city, me in heels and Mateo hauling a freezer bag with samples of his cheese.

It's funny to recall, because our jobs are so different now, but I feel for him the fondness of a best friend from camp. We started out together and in our own separate ways have grown up in cheese. But what about Jasper Hill Farm's cheese?

A few people, most loudly and persistently my sometime ball-busting boss Rob, have suggested that I may harbor a wee crush on Mateo Kehler. I do harbor a crush on him, and Andy, and the whole operation, mainly for how smart they've been in their approach to cheesemaking. They did an enormous amount of research on something they knew nothing about and approached it like a business, which it is. They identified the components that mattered—rotational grazing and grass for their cows when the weather cooperates, a clear and manageable herd size, and the kinds of cheeses that are lacking in the American market. It's the school-nerd part of me that so greatly appreciates their approach. That and the fact that they produce consistently excellent cheese. Really. They don't make bad cheese. They don't even make mediocre cheese. They make superlative cheese all the time, except, in the beginning, at the times when the demand for their cheese was so great that they released it too early and the blue in particular came to market slightly bitter as a result of its youth. They now have that under control.

Bayley Hazen is so different from most American blues, which I think of as the "Maytag contingent." There's no foil wrapping, instead a stony white crust of a rind, thin and actually edible and quite delicious. Unlike the crust of English Stilton, with its brackish color, occasional damp spots, and ammonia whiff, I feel comfortable trying the rind of Bayley Hazen because it's dry and powdery. The flavor is pleasantly wheaty, like unpopped popcorn kernels. This cheese is so good. It's what's called an "open-curd" blue, which means there are meandering pockets and rivulets of mold that lend a stony minerality to the otherwise butter-sweet paste.

Bayley is dense and dry, the slightest bit crumbly, but as Cynthia Zaran wrote in her *New Yorker* article about Murray's, it's "velvet on the tongue." Slightly smoky but more like unsweetened chocolate than anything else. All of Jasper Hill's cheeses are named for local landmarks. In this case, Bayley Hazen is the Revolutionary War–era road that runs from Greensboro straight into Canada.

While Bayley is made year-round, there is a second blue, **Bartlett Blue**, that is produced seasonally. The cheesemaking season begins in May, and the sixteen-pound drums hit the market several months later. They are not only larger than Bayley

Open Curd, Closed Curd

Jasper Hill makes two blue cheeses. Bayley Hazen is the smaller of the two, weighing in at around six pounds, while Bartlett Blue requires some chest hugging to haul its sixteen pounds. They're both cylindrical, but one is an open-curd blue, while the other is closed-curd. So what's the difference? During cheesemaking, Bayley is cut and stirred, the whey is drained, and the curds are packed in a cylindrical form. The cheese is then dry-salted on the outside. The result is pockets of air trapped between the curd bits. When the cheese is pierced to allow oxygen inside to jump-start blue mold growth, pocks of blue form in those air spaces. Although Bayley is fudgy in texture, it's much more crumbly than Bartlett, and the milky white insides are punctuated by powdery blue holes.

Bartlett Blue is also stirred and cut, but the curd is then milled through a sausage-grinder type apparatus, and salt is added to the puréed chunks in the vat. These are then packed into a cylindrical form. The small, ground curd bits are packed closely together, and when the wheels are pierced, the resulting blue develops in thin striations, marbled veins that run like rivers through the inside of the cheese. The "closed" texture makes for a denser, creamier mouthfeel and an even, leathery flavor, while Bayley alternates sweet cream milk and minerally pop.

but denser and thicker in texture. The "closed curd" means an even blue veining and succulent richness more akin to Stilton than the powdery alkaline notes of Bayley. It shares the natural rind, though darker brown and a bit damp, without Bayley's pleasant nuttiness. I avoid eating it and keep to the saltier, almost peanut buttery insides. In the beginning, Bartlett Blue was based on the English cheese Wensleydale, a crumbling, cheddary type, and I didn't care for it as much as I do now. It seemed too tart, a bit bitey, and sharp with mold. The recipe has since been tweaked, the target acidity lowered, and a moister, richer texture has followed in the wake of this change. It's grown on me considerably, and I think I may even prefer it to Bayley Hazen these days. Far from annoying me, the fleeting availability is a welcome treat, and wheels roll into Murray's just as the autumn air gets that nip and bushels of pristinely crunchy apples hit the farmers' market.

Constant Bliss is the cheese that everyone coos over, though its romantic implications are far from the cheese's true namesake. Constant Bliss was a young Revolutionary War scout killed and scalped in the town of Greensboro. An unlikely beginning for a remarkable cheese. Constant Bliss the cheese is pure pragmatism, with a small cylindrical shape that is all about functional cheese aging. In this case, there's a cheesemaker whose goal is to produce exclusively raw-milk cheeses. But this cheesemaker is also enamored of the soft, mushroomy greats of northwestern France, cheeses like Brie and Camembert that are essentially patty-shaped. There is a high rind-to-paste ratio: a skinny little middle enrobed on the top, bottom, and sides with carnivorous white mold. The whole ripening process for this standard patty shape is a mere twenty-five to forty-five days. That's just not long enough for a raw-milk cheese to be legal in the United States.

So Mateo decided to make a bloomy rind with a cylindrical shape, like a squat Donkey Kong barrel. The molded rind has a much larger, denser interior area of paste to digest. The ripening process takes longer than for Camembert, though I'll tell you that Bliss sings at forty-five days. But you have to have an in to eat the illegal stuff at Mateo's dining room table. Yes, Constant Bliss can last the requisite sixty days for sale, but it's a ticking milk bomb. At about seventy days, the rind develops a damp sandy ridge along the edges, and a fierce peppery finish follows, blowing the incredible delicacy that makes it such a singular cheese.

A piece I recently tried had that brown, sticky warning sign at its edges, and I wondered if I'd taste all the goodness this cheese can offer, only to be bitten in the back of my throat after swallowing. Because of the lower rind-to-paste ratio, Constant Bliss never ripens all the way through. It always has a snowy, chalky lump at the center. This is a good thing. A fully runny Bliss would be bitter and astringent. The small core of my little guy was another warning sign of potential over-ripeness.

There was no help from my nose. I couldn't tell what was in store any more than I could by looking. It had a glorious, mossy milk smell, like a cool subterranean milk river. Lovely. No ammonia. So I proceeded. The inside was silken, yielding, all cream and mushroom. It seemed the greatest impact of more advanced age was a noticeable concentration of salt. Not overly salty, but a bold seawater quality that carried the lactic notes forward. The rind was surprisingly approachable, though there was a little soapiness on the finish. It must be said that one of the reasons this cheese is so good is because Mateo has the rind touch. Many American producers of bloomy rinds struggle to get it just thin enough, just cohesive enough, that it's not chewy or bitter or snappy. It's very difficult, and few nail it consistently. Constant Bliss is one of the few. So at the end of this taste, despite the appearance of a potentially overripe cheese and a potentially sharp, aggressive finish, Constant Bliss wound up tasting nearly perfect, as it so often does: a rush of luscious texture and incredible complexity, delicately fungal, hay-ey, and sweet-cream ice cream. I do tend to prefer softer cheeses, but this cheese balances on a high-wire intersection of potential shortcomings. It's a risky cheese to produce and age, yet, more often than not, it is mind-blowingly delicious. If you get an old piece and a bad taste, you've no one to blame but your cheesemonger because the Bliss itself is extraordinary.

I don't have godchildren, but if I did I imagine I would feel the affinity reserved in my heart for **Winnimere**. Winnimere is my godchild cheese. Yes, I love it, and it hits my sweet spot of squashy, runny, washed-rind, pungent, salty, woodsy perfection. But I get to claim a tiny bit of the credit because I gave Mateo a piece of one of my all-time favorites, a Swiss stinker called Forsterkäse, and he set out to make its American doppelgänger. Winnimere is that twin. It's also the lake that Andy and Mateo grew up swimming in each summer.

To make a washed-rind that manages to maintain the sweetness of milk under a robe of salty, bacteria-laden stickiness is no easy feat. Then throw in the flavor variable of wood— wet, Christmas-tree piney bark that binds the whole thing together so it doesn't squirt away—and maintaining the milk flavor is even tougher. Winnimere does that. It knits together sweet, stinky, and sprucey in a thick, nearly lappable consistency.

Winnies are made in large format (about two pounds) or small format (about twelve ounces). I prefer the smaller as a personal pan pizza of sorts. The rind is very subdued, powdery white mold atop tacky sherbet, the whole thing lashed together with a two-inch band of bark—actually the cambium (third, inner) layer of spruce trees from the property at Jasper Hill Farm. Sawing through the bark is absolutely worth the effort, because the brown skin underneath is the tastiest part of the cheese. It's like eating butter and cedar, and the essence of woods runs through every bite of Winnimere. The wheels are initially washed in a whey brine to get the bacteria growing, but after three weeks the washing is done with a spontaneously fermented beer. An open vat is left in the aging room to ferment with yeasts from the wheels of cheese. A good deal of residual sugar is left in the high-alcohol beer, and this cheese-fueled brew is then fed back to the cheese via regular washing.

Like all of Jasper Hill's cheeses, Winnie is always made of raw Ayrshire cow milk. Unlike most of the farm's other offerings, it's seasonal. Production begins in November, and the first batch comes to market in February. We have it through June, and then it's gone for another year. The short season is due to a few things. Number one: when the cows are on grass in summer, the changes in fat and protein don't accommodate Winnimere so well. Reason number two is a bit more devious. It is, as Mateo explains it, an opportunity to train customers on the virtues (and challenges) of seasonality. Cheese changes. And cheese isn't always available. After the requisite aging, Winnies come to market just after Christmas. It's a little carrot to keep retailers buying after the grueling holiday season, but it's also a way to break them in to the experience of having cheese only some of the time. The season is predetermined, the cheese comes, and then, sadly, the cheese goes. Get it before that happens.

➤ LIVELY RUN GOAT DAIRY
INTERLAKEN, NEW YORK

Even in summer, New York's Finger Lakes region is mired in damp fog, with huge, fat gray clouds roaming across big sky. The air is full of spritz, but somehow it never rains as I skirt flat fields of corn and stubby patches of itchy-looking wheat stalks on my drive to Lively Run. Sitting on the porch waiting for Suzanne Messmer, I take in the scrubby green yard, the neon yellow Goat Xing sign, four ducks asleep in the weeds, their beaks tucked under their wings so they look like the broken-necked Pekings in Chinatown windows. When Suzanne steps out of the cheesemaking room in a hairnet to say hello, her hands are sticky and damp from the fresh curd.

Her whole operation is quite small, the herd of fifty-five goats inside the barn picking through hay and the clever ones practicing how to open fence locks. Suzanne and her husband, Steve, an engineer in Syracuse, acquired the farm in 1995. They undertook a six-week crash course in cheesemaking from the Feldmans, who'd started Lively Run in 1982 and then ran off to Africa to pursue mission work. Suzanne's very frank, with a broad face and no-bullshit demeanor. She's German and met her husband when he was a soldier patrolling the Berlin Wall. They moved back to the United States in 1991 and have several hunks of the Wall now sitting about their living room. Suzanne liked the idea of farming as a mission-driven space to train people, though the post-9/11 world has been tricky and the Egyptian refugees who first came in 2000 were not so welcome by the U.S. government a year or two later. Now Suzanne works with local help, including her sons, making three cheeses. The fresh **chèvre** and **feta** are solid offerings for the small farm store she runs and from which impromptu tours are given. But the cheese that has always captured my heart is the raw-milk **Cayuga Blue**, so named for the local lake. It has a fetalike paste, the characteristic bright white of goat cheese, with the dry center gnawed out with jagged pocks of blue.

The pierce points through which air is introduced to develop interior mold are long, straight entry wounds across the surface, now filled with the cerulean blue of *Penicillium roquefortii*. This salt-and-mushroom kazaam is balanced by the non-bluey parts and the baby-powdery alkaline quality I like in aged goat cheeses. Unlike the full wetness of most blues, Cayuga Blue's drier texture translates into a softer, lighter flavor, something akin to unsweetened chocolate. It's available seasonally, from April to September or so, not just because of seasonal goat milk but because it requires summertime humidity for proper aging. Things simply get too dry and crumbly come winter. Plus, Suzanne pointed out that since she is now buying some milk from three local Amish farmers (two of whom are certified organic), it's in her best interest to stop milking for the winter so she can take a vacation.

Why Is Goat Cheese White?

Ⓞne of the most happily reliable ways to guess what kind of milk your cheese might be made from is to look at the color of the interior, or paste, of the cheese. Snow white, bone white, china white paste, and you're almost certainly looking at a goat cheese. Unlike pasture-fed cows, whose beta-carotene-rich milk is deeply yellow, goats—even those munching pasture and leaves—convert beta-carotene into vitamin A, which has no color and is therefore not visible. They may be fueled by the same tender forage as their cow counterparts, but you can't see it in the cheese. I find goat cheese the easiest to identify, because it tends to be younger and is often shockingly white compared to everything else on the plate (or in the cheese case).

➤ OLD CHATHAM SHEEPHERDING COMPANY
OLD CHATHAM, NEW YORK

Old Chatham holds a special place on the cheese menus of Manhattan because it was the second maker to emerge from the Hudson Valley, bringing local cheese to the city in 1994. Tom and Nancy Clark began with 600 acres and 115 sheep in 1993 and have grown their flock of East Friesian crossbreds to more than a thousand since then. Although it is the largest sheep dairy in the country, the demand for its cheese far outstrips its milk supply, so it purchases sheep milk from the Wisconsin Sheep Dairy Cooperative, as well as neighboring dairies. Its supply is further extended by blending it with Holstein cow milk for its signature **Camembert**, making a mixed-milk cheese, which is still hard to come by in the United States. The liquid by-product (whey) from the Camembert production is used to make **ricotta**, so nothing is wasted.

The signature bloomy rinds are both pasteurized. **Hudson Valley Camembert Square** is a small six-ounce square, and its larger counterpart, **Nancy's Hudson Valley Camembert**, a three-pound wheel. The danger of the little square is breakdown by molded rind; the pasteurized insides are slippery and glossy and wonderfully whippy like room-temperature butter. But with only a few days' ripening the lovely, creamy interior is eclipsed by intense bitterness from the rind. I prefer the larger wheel from Nancy because the taller, thicker format takes longer to break down under *Penicillium candidum* so the flavor remains focused on the buttery fat of sheep milk. Old Chatham recently reintroduced its blue, **Ewe's Blue** (and its raw-milk counterpart, **Shaker Blue**), which one of our wholesale managers blind-tasted with the chef at Alain Ducasse's restaurant Adour. He was solidly convinced that the cheese was Roquefort, on which it is modeled. I think it's Old Chatham's most complex offering, with rivulets of cool, spicy mold and the balanced punch of good blue: sweet, fatty milk, sharp salinity, and a stony minerality from the mold.

As a larger producer with national distribution, Old Chatham has taken a different path from the little Vermont Shepherds of the world but remains a critical player in the introduction of sheep milk and sheep cheese, still relatively unknown to the American palate. Plus, it must be said, it makes an incredible line of yogurts, the best of which is touched with maple syrup.

▶ POINT REYES FARMSTEAD CHEESE COMPANY
POINT REYES STATION, CALIFORNIA

I wondered if it would be wrong to admit that I fell in love again with cheese from Point Reyes because it sent me a cup of their **Original Blue Dip**. Was it shameful? Was I trivializing this family, its incredible farm, and its cheese by shouting from the rafters that its dip made my spring? Could everyone just be happy about the fact that I spent an entire weekend jamming fistfuls of New York State's first romaine of the season straight into the plastic tub and ripping apart the watery, crunchy lettuce ribs while flecks of Original Blue Dip dripped on the kitchen floor?

Maybe it is wrong. But it's the truth. The dip brought me back to Point Reyes's cheese. It's the only deviation the family has taken from making a single cheese—**Original Blue**—and its turn in the road was brilliant because it took a good thing and possibly made it better.

I remember Point Reyes from the beginning of my life in cheese. The farm is now owned by the four daughters of Bob and Dean Giacomini, whose dairy farm it was beginning in 1959. Forty-one years after they started, the couple wanted to retire, and it was with no small amount of reservation that the children came home, concerned about losing the family land and tradition but with no real knowledge (and dare I say without much burning interest) in milking cows. But cheese offered a fortuitous compromise. What if they took the milk of their 250 Holsteins (which, by the way, wander and ruminate across the most beautiful, sea-salt-air-drenched, foggy, verdant land I've ever seen in the Bay Area) and made cheese out of it? What if they pursued the production of a single cheese and did it really, really well? Would that be feasible? It's still mildly amazing to me, because I remember the Giacomini girls (women in their thirties and forties) swinging into Murray's during New York's annual Fancy Food Show. They were all so pretty and wholesome and well dressed, with simple pearl earrings and big, wide smiles. They didn't look like cheesemakers. Turns out they weren't. They figured their way into this cheese gig, and part of the mastermind was bringing in a recent California import, Monty McIntyre, to make their one, blue cheese. Monty cut his teeth at a little place called Maytag Dairy Farms, which had been making rindless blue cheese since 1941. Monty was quite a catch.

Despite the company's significant growth, Point Reyes continues to make its Original Blue by hand, with raw milk straight from its cows, which are milked in the middle of the night so cheesemaking can begin promptly in the early morning. The milk is set and the curd cut and sorted by the frantic hands of Monty's cheesemaking team into molds where they are packed to sit and take shape for a day. Then they're turned out of the plastic forms and taken to a curing room for three weeks of hand-salting, turning, and piercing, to introduce oxygen so the blue veining can begin its development. Five to six months later, the cheese is sold.

Despite all that time, it has a remarkably white paste. The molding is mere striations of yellowy green *Penicillium roquefortii* within a damp, crumbling paste. Original Blue has punch. It's fruity, almost alcoholically so, like a bizarre and salty after-dinner drink. So why my histrionics about the dip? Quite simply because it is the best blue cheese dressing–type thing I've had, and usually I make my own. It has all the right ingredients, what you would put in dressing yourself, but it's better. I'm convinced it's the cheese, which is drippily commingled with mayonnaise, sour cream, lemon juice, cider vinegar, green onion, Dijon mustard, Worcestershire, sugar, and pepper. The pop! that you get with the cheese itself (that indescribable differential between naked, creamy white cheese and liquescent moldy vein) is evened out, distributed across the milky drizzle that becomes Original Blue Cheese Dip. For God's sake, don't be snobby. Get some, and eat it on crunchy green things or even mixed with a tangle of steaming egg noodles.

➤ RIVER'S EDGE
LOGSDEN, OREGON

My first memory of cheese from River's Edge is inexorably linked to two people, neither of whom probably remembers the day. It began in the basement of Murray's Cheese, where our aging caves are and where, midmorning on some random autumn weekday, I opened a box of samples from this tiny producer in Oregon. The cheeses were promising: various rounds and pyramids of mold-ripened goat cheese, tied up like lovely little presents in carefully folded cheese paper. But there was one that was just stunning. I remember being overcome with delight at the exquisite leaf-wrapped parcel. Bursting out of the cave room with this thing in my hand—I had to tell someone, anyone—what a treat we had, I ran smack into Tamasin Day-Lewis.

Tamasin is a noted British food writer, and at one point she spent a great deal of time in New York and at Murray's, where she developed recipes for our kitchen. She has a wicked tongue and a razor-sharp mind to match. She also has incredibly fierce standards for all things edible (and some not) and has never, in my experience, wasted a moment sharing her (often withering) commentary. I was regularly given the task of recommending restaurants for her to dine in, and I waited dolefully to hear, the following morning, that her meal had been simply rubbish. For a while I enjoyed the challenge, and then I resigned myself to the fact that I would never find a place that blew her mind. She always found them herself, often the simplest little dives dishing up falafel or fried chicken, and I cursed my failure to recommend them before she discovered them unassisted. That day, it was too late to stop. She saw that I had the gleam in my eye and immediately demanded to know what brilliant cheese was on hand. I pulled up, nonplussed. It was, I faltered, a little pasteurized goat cheese. It was . . . smoked. She probably wouldn't like it, even though I found it to be a flawless balance of delicate, milky crumble and evocative campfire depth. She picked a crumb up and tasted. And then another. And then she smiled. Broadly. I'd done it! I'd passed the Tamasin Test! We scrambled up the stairs to show everyone.

That cheese was **Up in Smoke**. It is, in fact, a hand-squashed little ball of chèvre, smoked and then wrapped in a maple leaf that looks to have been plucked from the ground. The whole package is smoked a second time and then spritzed with bourbon to tease out a woody, barrel-aged nuance. It tastes like New England fall.

When I tried it again recently, my first memories were confirmed. I wrote, "*This!* Is why food is so important. It's so intensely, powerfully evocative. It's that first damp, autumn day, when some of the leaves have fallen but most are on the trees, all red and vermillion, and you catch, on your trek home, the first wisps of a nearby fire. It's all wool socks, spicy red wine, crunchy apples, and heavy sweaters. It has nothing to do with goat milk except that the intensely creamy, tart, cream-cheesey mouthful can better take you on the November walk home."

Later in the day of first discovery, one of the great neighborhood chefs in the West Village, Galen Zamarra of Mas, stopped by. I'd called him, saying he had to come over because I had this amazing cheese. Galen is as gentle and teddy bear–like as Tamasin is sharp and wiry. He ambled up to the classroom, which we use for tastings of all kinds. A boutique producer of Oregon Pinot Noir had been by and several bottles stood there, half full. Galen and I split the remaining half bottle, trading sips of liquid earth with smears of Up in Smoke on crusty baguette. It is an incredibly fond memory.

By rights, the cheese from River's Edge is precisely the kind we should not carry at Murray's. Its production is very limited, largely fresh or briefly aged cheeses that don't travel well and are quite expensive once the exorbitant costs of overnight shipping are figured in. But there are some things I'd rather not go without, and as long as Pat Morford will send cheese to us, I will happily buy it. She makes a warm-weather cousin called **Spring Crottin** that is equally gorgeous. A golf ball of fresh, pasteurized goat, the cheese is heaped with fresh herbs: fennel fronds, thyme, and bay leaf, with the barest bit of truffle oil. It manages to be tangy and clean with just the briefest bit of anise and musk, and once I unwrapped it, it pained me to cut the thing apart. Each leaf was placed just so, like something fairies had made and stowed for safekeeping under a woodland fern. There are so many to choose from, denser, creamier specimens cloaked in bluey gray ashed rind with names like **Cape Foulweather** and **Siletz River Drums**. Another that took me by surprise was a heart-shaped trinket called **Heart's Desire**. The rusty orange edges just visible under the thin white rind were the work of paprika, and the interior of the cheese was nearly hard, dry, packed goat cheese with the smoky warmth of chorizo, though none of the spice.

From the milk of forty goats, Pat makes nearly twenty cheeses. And she's just decided to add some sheep to her mix, a little bit for diversity ("You have to stay on top of stuff in order to keep people interested") and a little bit for pleasure ("I just love sheep's milk cheese"). What's kind of amazing was her acquisition of a young dairy ram, who was summarily introduced to Pat's five geriatric ewes to get things rolling. Apparently the old girls still have it in them! River's Edge cheese can be found at Oregon's summer-season Lake Oswego Farmers' Market and the Beaverton Farmers Market from May until October.

➤ ROGUE CREAMERY
CENTRAL POINT, OREGON

Can I pause here to mention how obsessed I am with the guys from Rogue Creamery? Rogue Creamery, as its Web site attests, has been making handmade cheese since 1935. Remember my talks with the droopy-eyed, paper hat–sporting Ig Vella? The man has a major hand here. I think part of my fascination has to do with the anomaly between Ig Vella and the guys from Rogue Creamery. There are two main ones now: Cary Bryant (CEO/cheesemaker) and David Gremmels (president/cheesemaker).

When I was in high school, I was lucky enough to have a choice of foreign-language focus: Spanish (practical), French (classic), or Italian (based solely on the fact that I was in North Haven, Connecticut, and half the kids spoke Italian at home anyway). I took Italian. Mrs. DiGennaro was my teacher, with floaty green and blue skirts and a salt-and-pepper feathered mullet. At the end of one particularly auspicious year, I bought her a thank-you gift. I thought it was riotously witty: a ten-inch magnet of Michelangelo's David, right hip thrust out, enormous paw draped against the thigh, perfect abdomen front and center. And with the magnet came a fabulous ensemble: boxer shorts, denim jacket, keys, underwear . . . it was totally Village People. Turns out the brainchild behind Dress-Me-Up David was a lanky young man named Cary Bryant. In 1992, Dress-Me-Up David was as loved by everyone else as it was by me, so Cary had a little extra money to play with. He decided to play with food.

So there's the staunchly traditional Ig Vella, second-generation cheesemaker and son of Tom, who turned this little plant in Central Point, Oregon, into a major success story for Kraft (and small family dairy farms) during the World War II era, and then there are Cary and David. Cary, of Dress-Me-Up David acclaim, and David, who at Murray's has earned the nickname "Magical David" because he's so quiet, slow-talking, and groovy. It's all good, man. It's magical. That's what talking to David is like. He cracks me up. Although Ig received offers to buy the Rogue plant, he turned them all down, knowing that buyers wanted just the name and the recipes. Though he never wished to close Rogue, he couldn't run it successfully from his home in California. And he didn't want to give the name away. Then Cary and David wandered in, doing research on cheeses for the wine bar they planned to open. They were duly impressed and said, "Mr. Vella, we'd like to buy your cheese for our wine bar." Apparently Ig said, "Goddammit, if you boys want to buy my cheese, you're going to have to make it yourselves. I'm shutting her down." David and Cary were certifiably insane to consider this offer, as they knew nothing about cheese. But they both had in spades what Rogue Creamery lacked: business, marketing, and manufacturing experience. They eventually made Ig an offer, and the agreement was to try cheesemaking and stick to the offer if they liked it. On July 1, 2002, the three made cheese together, and Cary and David enjoyed it. They walked with Ig to the front porch and bought the plant on a handshake. With solid intentions and a real commitment to the local economy, their employees, and good-tasting, handmade cheese, David and Cary embarked on the Next Generation of Rogue.

Although they still make cheddar, including Magical David groovy flavors such as lavender and chocolate stout, made with Rogue Brewery's Chocolate Stout Ale, Rogue Creamery is best known for blue cheese. That's where the Vella factor comes in. There was an established history of cheddar production in all of Kraft's midcentury plants, but in 1956 Tom Vella headed off to France for three months to study Roquefort production and returned to the United States with a bag full of blue mold spores. Blue cheese production began with the signature **Oregon Blue Vein**, which is still, like all of Rogue's blue cheeses, made of raw cow milk.

The partnership between local cheese factory and small local dairy farmer continues today, despite the encroachment of suburban sprawl and real estate prices that far exceed that of cow milk. Hedged in by developments, Rogueview Dairy milks a herd of two hundred Brown Swiss and Holstein cows on one hundred acres and sends all their milk over to Rogue Creamery. Although the Creamery doesn't currently use all of the milk for cheesemaking (its production isn't big enough), it pays a premium for everything and sends any excess to a fluid milk cooperative. From March to October, weather permitting, the cows graze on pasture, and during the winter their stomachs are filled from troughs of hay and some grain.

The evening I revisited Rogue's blue cheese lineup, I did in fact taste them all in one fell swoop. It was intense, but an effective way to force out the distinctions among six rindless, raw-cow blues. I have my favorites, but I'll begin with the classic: Oregon Blue Vein. Like most of Rogue's blues, the flavor is what I'll call moderate. It doesn't leave you wheezing from moldy pop or parched for water to wash away the salt. This is good. Blue cheese should be balanced. OBV has a substantial perimeter of white, curdy rind that looks almost cheddarish and a mild flavor to match. The blue-pocked insides are melting and creamy, a little like ranch dressing. **Oregonzola** pays homage to Italian Gorgonzola, with a deeper yellow paste and smooth, creamy texture; it's a bit sweet and minerally—neither as luscious and ploppy as Gorgonzola dolce nor as toasty and meaty as Gorgonzola piccante. **Crater Lake**, named for the deepest lake in the United States, is also solid, though not as mind-blowing as its namesake (which, by the way, is one of the cooler things I've seen, intensely deep, infinite, brooding blue water; the bar is set pretty high). Like OBV, it has the straightforward white curdy exterior, but this one tasted Annie's mac and cheesy, with faintly butterscotchy pockmarks of blue. **Echo Mountain** is spiced up a bit because it's blended with goat milk, with a flat, flakey crystal to it, like good *fleur de sel*. The goat milk makes it a little dirty (dirty in a good way), with an animal piquancy and a smoky finish. It's made in very limited quantities with goat milk from a herd of seventy-five Alpine and Toggenburg goats at Applegate, a mere twenty minutes away.

Now my special favorites. When I feed Rogue cheese to people, these seem to be their favorites as well. First up is **Smokey Blue**. You'd think from my drama about River's Edge Up in Smoke that I am obsessed with smoked cheeses. That is not, in fact, the case. But here's one more reason not to believe me, because Rogue's Smokey Blue is its second best cheese and overall one of the best in America. Like all Rogue blues, it's raw cow milk, rindless, wrapped in foil. This makes sense, because the cheese starts life as the signature Oregon Blue Vein. Then it gets sixteen hours of cold smoking over Northwest-grown hazelnut shells. What happens over the course of a day's smoking is the incredible elevation of this traditionally punchy blue into a whirl of toasted corn husk and roasted nut shells. Smokey Blue tastes blue, but more. Deeper and richer, with all the astringency and pucker of mold softened into earthy, autumnal savor. If you hate smoked things you will not like it, because the smoke is clearly there, but it's more like a whiff from the chimney on a biting cold night. You catch it in little ghosty puffs. Don't even get me going about what happens when you lob a chunk of it over charcoal-blackened steak and it melts into a pool with those rosy pink juices. It's heaven.

Playing the other side of the flavor spectrum is the final, greatest Rogue triumph: **Rogue River Blue**. From the name you'd think this was its signature cheese, but it's actually the most elusive and very limited in production. It's also a symphonic meeting of flavors from the Rogue River Valley. Produced during the autumn equinox and winter solstice, the wheels are aged for twelve months before their release the following September. The late-summer milk swims in herby, floral notes, sweeter and rounder than at any other time of year. Each wheel of cheese, which also begins as Oregon Blue Vein, is wrapped in Syrah and Merlot grape leaves that are hand-harvested from a neighboring vineyard. I've been told that the leaves are plucked only when the sun has shifted in its heavenly arc so the remaining grapes, now unprotected, are not burned on the vine before harvest begins. The leaves are then macerated (basically, allowed to loll and stew) in pear brandy made by Clear Creek Distillery in Portland. The cheese is then blanketed in brandy-saturated leaves, tied with raffia, and allowed to mature over the ensuing months. Upon release, the alcoholic burn has evaporated, and you're left with an intensely creamy, mellow blue that is permeated with the essence of golden autumn pears, the kind that juice down your arm when you bite into them. The salt and sweet, fruit and minerally smoke, coexist in perfect, tenuous balance. A classic, if somewhat passé, pairing is blue cheese with pear and walnuts. Rogue River Blue delivers the essence of that pairing without the fruit and nuts. It's absorbed deep within each wheel. Production is so limited that we place our orders for Murray's a year in advance. We usually make it through Christmas, but supplies are gone by early winter. Then we sit back and wait for the cheese to cycle through again. It is one of a very few cheeses worth the pain of a nine-month absence.

➤ TAYLOR FARM
LONDONDERRY, VERMONT

What's the difference between an "artisanal" Gouda and a factory one? I remember when the topic of Taylor Farm's Gouda first came up at Murray's and everyone protested because the style wasn't fancy enough for us. Gouda was the giant, processed, tubular cheese cut into discs, all floppy and limp, the only smoky attribute the spray-on brown skin. But could Taylor deliver something better?

The answer was yes. Vermont's only farmstead Gouda producer, nestled on a 180-year-old farm in Londonderry, Taylor was making familiar cheese in an increasingly unfamiliar way. Sixty cows, grazing on clean pasture, their morning milk pumped straight into the vat to commingle with the previous evening's haul and become a range of Goudas. The first thing that piqued my interest was that the farm owned its cows. The second was that its milk wasn't pasteurized to make styles that I had come to regard as young, bland, and vapid. So we tried it out. Jon Wright, the cheesemaker and owner, has told me that he thinks the traditional red wax–covered **Vermont Farmstead Gouda** is actually its best. The **Maple Smoked** is the one I really know. The name comes from the maple hardwood chips over which it is slow-roasted. When you peel away the chocolate brown wax, there is only a distant linger of smoke. It's an echo of flavor, while the cheese retains the mellow, cushy sweetness of well-made Gouda. Most smoked cheeses meet their maker over hickory, which is markedly stronger, more like eating the fire pit than catching a whiff. The finish of Taylor's is cheese, not smoke, and the buttery chew is firmer and more decisive than most I've tasted. Taylor Farm also makes **Chipotle** and **Garlic Gouda**, which I'm less intimately acquainted with but know to have the same impressive balance *with* the cheese and not just a head bashing of added flavoring.

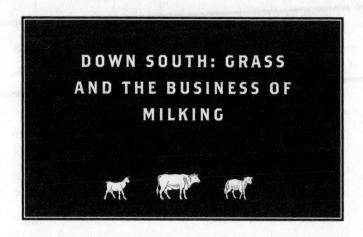

DOWN SOUTH: GRASS AND THE BUSINESS OF MILKING

AS I DRIVE DOWN SHARP RURAL ROADS OVER WINDSWEPT hills dotted with bushy black cattle, it feels desolate and more remote than the Hudson Valley, Vermont's Northeast Kingdom, or the backroads of Wisconsin. It's not as warmly Mediterranean as northern California nor as close to urbanism as northern Connecticut. This sliver of the Blue Ridge Mountains teetering between North Carolina and Virginia is wild, like Wyoming, sans big sky and big mountains. It is a little bit rocky, with stumps that are a little more gnarled. There are a lot of conifers.

In early spring, the landscape is pointy. Straight, upright trees, with spindly skyward branches that are naked but for little dabs of Kermit the Frog green. All the splotches and drips and snips of color are delicate and washed out, the tree trunks ashen. There are a few tight white dogwood buds, fine, small leaves, and occasional riotous patches of skunk cabbage popping up like globs of apple-flavored Laffy Taffy.

The grass of the North Carolina foothills reminds me of Kentucky. There it's called bluegrass, and here it has a similarly aggressive heartiness. When the sun hits it just right, each fine, fat blade is bluey green. The acres roll by on some two-lane highway, vibrant health in each lot, and I wish I could eat the stuff, all shimmery and verdant in the bright, wide light. Down dirt paths, as I curve past the Hickory Grove church, there are obscenely tall towers of wisteria. In my childhood, wisteria crept up the side of the house, silently, insidiously choking every electric wire and gutter in its path. Here they wave like strippers. Seriously, they're taller than anything else around. Wisteria is a vine, mind you, not a tree, though the bases here are thicker than my thigh and there is no house to cling to. Instead, they grow straight up, maybe fifty or sixty feet, and toward the top the heady, old-lady perfume of each dripping purple-flowered cone wafts out across the land. Standing nearby in the late afternoon, with the wind whipping through, I see colonies of stooping violet blooms shaking amid the pine trees. Getting over my delight at their sheer excess, I inquire at their enormity, and a local cheesemaker snarks that they invade like biblical locusts, or at least like dandelions. Thankfully, the pigs nose about their roots and the cows stomp the ground so relentlessly that most teenage wisteria crumple and die. I understand the annoyance of weeds but can't help my admiration for the excessive purple spills so high in the air.

As I head north up into the mountains, things change.

Many of the incoming leaves have an oddly autumnal palette, pale russets and orange, some staid green, legions of twiggy brown trunks. But even here, sprinkled down the side of I-80, appears the work of some second-grade punk straight out of ballet class. It's as though she had been given her choice and told to pick any spray paint she desired; the loudest, tackiest, lilac-fuschia hybrid was selected, and she proceeded to run across state lines, haphazardly spraying trees along the way. As I drive down this austere road, my eyes keep darting to the right, every time I see a redbud tree in garish spring bloom. There she is! Again! It's the exact color of the Lee Press-on Nails I would have bought when I was nine, had I been allowed to decorate my fingers. The little sprays of tree are gaudy, but I love them for every fake nail I was never allowed to have.

Coming to the South was supposed to be a short getaway and a chance for me to meet some cheesemakers who make so little cheese they won't ship to New York. They know Murray's Cheese, but their market is smaller and more contained than the chefs and shops of my big city. It was to be a quick foray into the farmers' markets of the South and a peek at a place without the well-established dairying of Wisconsin or the Northeast. It turns out that cheese in the South is about one main theme: the weather. Quite simply, the weather changes everything.

The winter of 2007–2008 in New York was pitiful. We had snow, sort of, twice. But I am a solid product of the Northeast, and the seasons, if increasingly in theory rather than in reality, are the backdrop against which I understand food: it doesn't grow in the winter. Animals must be herded inside. It's cold, dead, and frozen, and the red barns with which I am so familiar are a necessity as much as a pleasantry of the landscape. The most obvious (and increasingly disturbing) juxtaposition to my cyclical environment is the year-round heat of central California, where cows, in particular, are annually misted and shaded, inside, to keep them comfortable. This bothers me, because I can't help but wonder what those cows are doing there in the first place. Of course, the Pacific Northwest has mellow, damp fog that makes for a milder climate, but it's a place I'm less intimately acquainted with, so I tend to forget it's there when I think of the Big Picture of Cheese. In my head, I default to seasons (spring, summer, fall, winter) and arid heat. I overlook the in between.

There aren't actually that many cheesemakers in the South, and when they band together in a formal organization, they define themselves as Cheesemakers of the Southeast, a massive area that includes Virginia, Alabama, Georgia, Kentucky, Florida, the Carolinas. In one afternoon's drive I shot up 1,400 feet in elevation, racing the tight curves of the Blue Ridge Mountains, where Confederate flags and busted truck hulls could be found aplenty, and in that single day felt as if I'd been in two or three worlds. Hardly one cohesive region. But a few consistencies emerged, different from anywhere I've been. The most significant was the weather, and the dandy result, for both seasonal and year-round cheesemakers, was this little miracle: Grass. Grass. Grass.

Pasture is the new buzzword in food. Pastured pork. Grass-fed beef. Cage-free, omnivorous, grub-busting chickens and their eggs. And of course, grass-fed milk. Let me lay out the primary problem with pasture so you're not surprised: if you eat food that is pasture-based, it will not be consistent. I do not mean it will be bad sometimes and good sometimes (though it might). What I mean is, it will not be the same each time. I am used to eating food that always tastes the same. It has taken several generations and many billions of dollars to produce food that is exactly the same, every time you eat it. Every Perdue chicken breast, at every store in America, every time I have ever eaten it, tastes the same. It was only a few years ago that I began to eat anything *but* Perdue chicken breast. And let me tell you, I was shocked by how *flavorful* pastured chicken can be. Not taste from the pesto I spread on it or the lemon I squeezed over it or the tomato I stewed it in. The chicken had its own chickeny intensity. The second time I tried, it was a little meatier, like the dark meat on the Thanksgiving turkey. The time after that it was soft, mild, and a bit sweet. I wasn't sure if I liked that. I had expected chicken to be a blank palette of chewy protein onto which I could layer flavor.

Then I drank pastured milk. Then I drank pastured raw milk. You know what that's like? It's like smelling mown grass and licking sweet-cream ice cream. If you don't know the taste of grass from chewing a sun-fattened blade, perhaps you've crunched raw asparagus and know the watery chomp of cucumber and freshly washed lettuce that is free of dirt but still smacks of earth when you bite into the crunchy, juicy ribs of the leaf. That's what grass-fed milk is like. It's all those things, in your milk (which is, of course, full fat, so it's lush and creamy, and ideally really, really cold). The first time I drank pastured raw milk I had that instant-healthy feeling I get when I go to Life Thyme Market on Sixth Avenue and the rasta guy crushes me an amazing mixed juice of whatever veggies he's got around. It tastes alive. Perhaps a better way to say it is that you can taste a connection to the land. The food tastes of an animal, of a food source.

You can count on the fact that pastured will be different from what you are used to. The beef is leaner yet meatier, the dairy is grassier, the eggs are simply better. They're shockingly orange and so eggy and rich and wonderful. I once had a scrambled duck egg for breakfast that looked like mandarin oranges puréed and dumped onto my plate.

But back to North Carolina. It's difficult to talk generally, overarchingly about the character of "cheese" because the end product is so closely tied to the animal from which it comes. The milk of goats, cows, and sheep tastes different, and then, through cheesemaking techniques and aging, a producer can conjure up a dozen different cheeses from the milk of one animal. The South doesn't have a storied history of dairy farms, but it abounds with goats, though Steve Tate at Goat Lady Dairy confirmed many of my biased northern suspicions about goats in the South. In my meanderings I saw a dozen or so yards with plucky, twitchy goats flowing over small hills and dilapidated sofas. He warned me that these absurdly pastoral scenes belied the blatant abuse of goats left to wander with no food or water. Goats' reputed willingness to eat anything from weeds to tin cans isn't, in fact, true. Steve was quick to point out that many starve from disregard. The trendy, foodie perception of goats as clever little milk machines, charming and naughty players on the American cheese scene, is challenged down South, where goats reflect the poverty of people who can't afford cows. Goats were not traditionally perceived as neat or progressive; they were the thing that Grandma stewed up when there was nothing else to eat. Cheesemakers who've chosen to milk goats mentioned the challenge of getting people to try the cheese in the first place. Many folks remember the pungent pee smell of a billy goat's skin a little too well and assume the cheese will carry a similar reek.

Goats figure prominently in small American cheese operations because people have found, again and again since that first wave of cheese explorers in the early 1980s, that you can begin a "backyard" operation of sorts, with relative ease, if you're milking goats. They're small, their milk is plentiful, and fresh goat cheese can be made and sold in a matter of days. Cash flow is always key here. But in the South, at least on the Carolina/Virginia border where I was hanging out, the buying public has a greater resistance to the bounty of the goat. It was against this established goat prejudice that I noticed another phenomenon. Cows. But on a much different scale than the one to which I'm accustomed.

Cows dotted fields on nearly every back road, though it was the fuzzy forms of black-and-brown beef cattle that were most common. There were no barns. I saw one silo in four days. The cows wandered in small packs, snuffling through the early-spring growth, their babies nearly hidden under weedy yellow stalks of I-know-not-what. Historically, the area was not prosperous. Today, it's still relatively poor, and that wild feeling I got as I drove was due in no small part to these roving cattle. I learned later that more than a few people make their living off these herds, turning the cows out onto the open land to graze for two or three years until they're large enough to be slaughtered for beef. Beef cows were everywhere, with their preternaturally wide heads, looking like softer, larger pit bulls as they munched or lay with blocky legs folded neatly under their hulking weight.

The outcome of southern weather is that it's just temperate enough from late fall to early spring that animals can be pastured year-round. As I talked to various locals, I realized the profound impact of mild weather. Actually, Rick Feete at Meadow Creek Dairy succinctly summed it up for me: it means that cheesemakers with animals on pasture, unlike those who are reliant on barns to house their animals, can be in the business of making milk instead of in the business of moving shit. That's exactly how he said it, and he meant shit as in manure, not just shit as in random farm-related stuff to be hauled hither and yon.

A farmstead operation means the responsibility of feeding, breeding, tending, and milking animals, plus the responsibility of making, aging, marketing, and selling cheese. The cheesemakers I visited function similarly to their beef cattle counterparts, though their preference in breed is Jersey, the fawn-colored, dewy-eyed cows known for their small size and incredibly fatty milk. The cows were all outside, so the labor of animal husbandry became one of milking and pasture rotation (a new field for grazing after each milking). Certainly, fence repair, calving, milk parlor maintenance, and a million other things figured into the daily landscape, but Rick's point was well illustrated: with cows out on grass, cheesemakers can exert most of their effort on milking and cheesemaking rather than bringing feed into a barn and moving poop out of it. With the moderate climate in this part of the United States, where winter snows are a rarity and dry, punishing summers an anomaly (though everyone mentioned the drought of 2007 as a nearly crippling phenomenon that challenged the natural balance in this part of the world), cows can be out all year.

Plenty of cheesemakers equip themselves to gather food, by either growing or buying, and invest money, hours, and machinery to keep their barns clean and their cows healthy. So what's the impact of pasture? Plenty. Pasture impacts everything from the nutritional makeup of the milk to the flavor of the cheese to the size and scale on which cheesemakers can (and must) function. Many cheesemakers I know who aren't in the South turn their animals out when grass is available, but winter seriously compromises this opportunity. Certainly, not all pastured cheesemakers are confined to the Southeast, but it was here that I had the *aha!* moment.

Remember, the very reason I'd come in the first place was because many of these producers are too small to send their cheese to New York. The pasture commitment is part of the reason. The model of rotational grazing looks to New Zealand, where cows are turned out to graze on a fresh field of grass after every milking. That means, conservatively, that a cheesemaker needs an acre per cow. The cost of land is the most obvious barrier to growing this system ad infinitum, but a more practical one is distance. With twice-daily milkings, cows have to walk to and from the milking parlor. Part of the health benefit (for the cow) of pastured dairying is exercise, but beyond a certain point the cows burn so much energy walking that their milk production dwindles to unusable lows for the cheesemaker. Thus pasture-based milking is limited in the size to which it can grow.

The two halves of Rick's summation: not needing to move in feed means that farms rely on the sun's energy and local flora to feed their cows, which, in turn, produce nutritionally superior milk, higher in beta-carotene and CLA (conjugated linoleic acid, which has been shown to reduce the risk of cancer) than grain-fed or even dried-grass (hay or silage)-fed cows. The other half—moving shit out—means that cows produce manure in the fields through which they graze, returning nutrients to the soil and providing a natural fertilizer that keeps the ground rich and the grasses diverse for future feedings. It is a neatly confined, cyclical, self-perpetuating system, though one inherently limited in scope: smaller herds of cows and cheesemakers who tend to produce solely for their local or regional market.

This interests me for a couple of reasons. The first is that we're in the middle of an agricultural crisis, born of several generations where bigger yields have been prioritized over flavor, quality, and health (environmental, animal, and human). We're also in the middle of a natural resource crisis in which fuel costs have increased by 30 percent in the past year. Trucking in hay from miles away or trucking manure out for disposal is becoming more difficult and expensive than ever. The smaller, pastured operations of the South, selling to a limited, regional market, represent an increasingly necessary and sustainable model for cheesemaking in America.

But what about the cheese? One of the first tips I tell students is that you can begin to identify a cheese just by looking at it. One of the first signposts is the color of the paste. A deep, rich, buttercup yellow cheese is, almost certainly, not just a cow milk cheese but a *grass-fed* cow milk cheese. That's the higher level of beta-carotene, right there in the wedge for you to see.

As for the flavor? I won't say grass-fed cheese tastes

Why Does My Cheese Look Jaundiced?

One of the neat tricks I teach in classes is how to begin to identify cheese by looking at it. Before you smell it, and certainly before you pop a chunk into your mouth, how can you guess what it might be? And therefore what it might taste like? The color of a cheese's interior paste can be a big cue. If a cheese is a deep buttercup yellow, you can be fairly certain that it is cow milk. But even more, you can comfortably assume that it is the product of grass-fed cow milk. The beta-carotene in lush forage, sprouting from nutrient-rich soil, is fat-soluble and passes through a cow straight into her milk. The resulting cheese is richly yellow, anywhere from straw to nearly bourbon-colored in intensity. This is helpful for several reasons:

- If you're avoiding cow milk, go no further.
- If you're looking for the most vitamin- and nutrient-packed milk, grass-fed is best.
- If you're looking for the soul of a place (the French call it terroir), you must seek animals that are eating the forage of a place.

Grass-fed milk is bound to be inconsistent in flavor and texture. It will not be the same every time. That's why you want to try it, ideally, repeatedly over several months. The milk, and the cheese made from it, will change as the plants, flowers, rain, and sun shift.

better, because it doesn't, necessarily. A good cheesemaker can make good cheese with any milk. But grass-fed milk does capture the essence of a place with greater specificity than any other. The very essence of the soil, the nutrients and minerals, the wild yeasts and airborne bacteria that grace each blade of grass are transported through an animal's milk and flavor the cheese made from it. And the milk changes with the seasons. The superiority or, perhaps more accurately, the inimitability of pasture is well recognized by Europeans, who go so far as to classify summer cheeses fueled by Alpine forage with different names from their wintertime counterparts (Beaufort d'Alpage, for example). Cheesemakers committed to pasture are choosing to limit their production. They may not produce all year, depending on their location. Or they may siphon some of their milk to other outlets should the weather shift and the need for supplemental feed arise.

In limiting their size, they are also choosing what I increasingly regard as self-sufficiency: the ability to feed and milk their animals and maintain a cheesemaking operation with minimal reliance on the catastrophically expensive (and increasingly destructive) tools of modern-day agriculture such as diesel, trucks, and pesticides.

Ultimately, though, these American cheesemakers resonate so strongly with me for the simplest, even the most romantic, reason: because they are feeding animals the diet that evolution intended. When you put the proper fuel into the machine, you will get the proper output. By that I mean milk, but also waste. Or is it? Because if cows are field-bound, manure begins to look less like waste than like a powerful elixir for better raw material.

Some Grain with Your Grass?

All but the most extreme dairies using a pastured approach still feed some grain to animals, especially cows. The strain of milking is great, and without supplemental grain, cows do not get the nutrition necessary to support their bodies and a generous milk supply. I do not, in fact, know any cheesemakers who exclusively grass-feed their animals, though supplemental feed is minimal, usually in the range of eight to ten pounds per cow per day.

NOTES ON AMERICA'S GRASS-FED CHEESES

➤ MEADOW CREEK DAIRY
GALAX, VIRGINIA

Meadow Creek is one of the primary reasons I headed South in the first place. I'll lay out my biases again: I love soft, melting, sunny-rinded, stinky, meaty cheeses. They are my beloved treasures, and I could eat them every day and never tire of them. Meadow Creek's **Grayson** is one of my preferred. The closest "well-known" comparison would be Italian Taleggio, but Grayson is so much better. Whereas Taleggio has a slightly sticky, drooping texture, a bit Laughing Cow–ish, and a mild, salty, bready taste, Grayson is rustic and far more complex. Its minimum two-month aging and more assertive pressing mean the paste is compact and elastic and the flavor expands and unfolds throughout the season, powered by the farm's pasture. Toward the end of the cheesemaking season, each bite is wheaty and autumnal, like rye and brown bread, the gluey washed-rind grainy with salt crystals, and I imagine the cows plucking up reedy, weedy stalks that have persevered in the growing chill, long after tender spring grasses have shriveled and died.

Not only do I love stinky cheese, I love the allure of small American farms. The characters are better than any I could invent. Cue my arrival in the desolate, slightly decrepit valley of Meadow Creek Dairy. An ancient farmhouse, which looks either haunted or as though it might fall down any minute, sits across the dirt road and past the creek, a few hundred yards from the wide-windowed cheesemaking room/residence being constructed above. For now, Helen and Rick Feete, the couple who own the farm, are in a mobile home. Not long after I arrived, standing around kind of awkwardly because I'd just plopped into these people's work and lives, I perused the newspaper clippings pinned to the wall, which appeared to be from 1991. One showed Rick with the kind of seriously burly, mountain-man beard one acquires after several months away from the razor. The Rick standing alongside me was rail thin, very tall, and leathery brown, with hard hands and a remarkably bare chin. "Nice beard," I mentioned.

"Oh, right. I had that for twenty-five years. I told Helen when she bought me a tractor I would shave it off. Hey, Helen, wanna show Liz the tractor you got me?" Turns out Rick had

gone clean-cut only a week earlier. Helen, with her strawberry-blond halo of frizz, pointed out the new machine through a glass pane. To further compound my social discomfort, I asked their son-in-law Dan where he had grown up, as I had a nagging feeling we'd gone to high school together. He looked so familiar. Dan blinked and said, "I'm from Russia." That would be strike two on my aesthetic and cultural observations on the extended Feete family.

Wanting to raise kids and spend time together, Rick and Helen pursued farming, and dairying in particular, as the career of choice. So in the early 1980s, they began working at a traditional confinement dairy. In 1988, they decided to break off on their own but found the cost of a confinement operation to be prohibitive. There is a lot of necessary equipment, feed to buy for the animals, and waste to move out. A few treatises on New Zealand–style rotational grazing—cows out on grass—promised a model that was attainable.

What I love so much about this is the fact that, in the beginning, the decision of confinement versus pasture was one of pragmatism. Ultimately, it promised to be easier, more affordable, and more sustainable *to dairy the way that cows were built to be fed and milked.* The confinement dairy model is preferable only for an enormous operation with the capital and will to run in a mechanized fashion. Helen and Rick's realization is similar to that of many family farms I know: the way it's been done historically is actually more attainable. Meadow Creek has been profitable for twenty years, though making cheese for only ten. For the first ten years they sold all their milk to a very large regional cooperative that pooled many farms' milk and sold it for drinking. In the second ten years, all the milk not used for cheese has gone to the same co-op. The Feetes get no credit for their cows' pastured diet, nor any bonuses for an organic-minded, sustainable farm. They've been profitable without receiving a premium price for their milk.

The environmental sustainability extends to this rocky, craggy corner of Galax, Virginia. Rotationally grazed cows eat the grass and return its nutritive value to the land in the form of steaming cow patties; the cows fertilize the earth that sustains them. Bringing in hay from the outside sucks all the value from one farmer's land and dumps it (with all its potentially foreign plant matter) onto the cheesemaker's plot. Meadow Creek is designed to feed itself, though not without serious effort on Rick's part to reseed and develop the pastures, one acre at a time.

Though the animals and land could handle this model of systematic, year-round dairying, the people behind it could not. After six years of milking, every day, twice a day, Helen and Rick decided to go seasonal. No grass meant no milking, which meant the cows were dried off in December, spent three months resting and recuperating, gave birth, and began being milked again in mid-March. Hence, there was a fallow period for all involved.

At year ten cheesemaking was added to augment, rather than replace, milk sales. The farm's herd grew a bit, but the idea was to transform the finest of the grass-fed raw milk to cheese. That allowed the seasonal transitions, and all the inconsistencies of fat and protein in the milk, to go to the milk co-op. Only the prime spring, summer, and fall milk went into cheese. That balance between milk and cheese has tipped steadily in favor of the cheese. In 2008, 40 to 50 percent of the annual yield of eighty milkers went into cheese, with a goal of 60,000 pounds of cheese. That's *twice* what it was in 2006. Even as the balance tips, the milk half of the equation remains critical. Meadow Creek has a consistent outlet for its milk at any and all times and can choose to make cheese only when the raw material is up to par.

All of Meadow Creek's cheeses are raw. In its part of the United States, pasteurizing one cheese means agency pressure to pasteurize all cheeses. There isn't much history, and Meadow Creek is the biggest cheesemaker in the state. Although the laws on the books prohibit raw-milk cheeses, Helen and Rick have had remarkable success working with their local health inspectors and educating them on the reality of cheese and bacteria. Rick looked at me very matter-of-factly and reminded me that washed-rind cheeses are washed for the express purpose of growing bacteria. They're aged in a cave at 95 percent humidity and washed once a week. As he said, "These are dirty cheeses."

I'll rephrase it in a less alarmist way: these are not sterile cheeses. But no cheese is sterile. Incomparably clean milk, which Meadow Creek's unquestionably is, is not free of bacteria. This can be tricky for small cheesemakers whose local inspectors have been trained to think that safety equals sterility.

This education extends to the general market as well. Meadow Creek was an anomaly among the other farmers' market–driven cheesemakers I met in the South. Ninety-eight percent of Meadow Creek's cheese is sold wholesale, packed into boxes, and shipped off to New York and beyond. The Feetes have found that the hot, moist summertime weather, when the markets are in full swing, is particularly problematic for the style of cheese they make. That and the fact that most

Clean Versus Sterile

I do not use the antibacterial hand gel that dissolves when you rub your palms together. Even when I travel to teeming third-world places, I prefer hand wipes to hand gel. Ever since a doctor friend pointed out, "Great. Use the hand gel, and now you're covered with millions of dead bacteria. Wouldn't you rather wash them off your hands?" Ew. Yes, I guess I would. In my mind, hand gel is sterile but hand washing is clean. There's a lot of life in life. Infinite numbers and ranges of microorganisms that we can't see, smell, or taste are part of life. Bacteria are part of life. Our intestines are lined with them, and every spoonful of yogurt dumps thousands of bugs into one's system. These bacteria are not just normal, they're critically beneficial. A healthy gut, like any healthy system, is a system in balance.

That's important when you think about milk. Fresh, healthy, unpasteurized milk is teeming with bacteria—cheese too, and every other food you eat, to boot. The push for "clean" food should not be confused with a desire to make our food a blank slate of sterility. To sterilize food, it must be aggressively heated or irradiated (the process of exposing food to ionizing radiation, which has the effect of disabling the DNA of microorganisms, viruses, bacteria, or insects; it's exposing food to radiation, but in doses that are designed to kill microorganisms without having any effect on the food itself), killing potentially harmful pathogens in, on, and around it and, frankly, destroying a lot of nutritional value and flavor in the process. Bacteria, molds, and yeasts are not inherently bad. Pathogens that result from sick animals, unsanitary milking or cheesemaking conditions, or careless milk handling are. Many of these potentially harmful bugs are naturally occurring and omnipresent. They are safe, however, because they are kept in check in a healthy creature. It is easy to take milk, kill everything in it, and reintroduce the stuff you might want (and hope you don't get anything unexpected). It is much harder (and I'm suggesting better) to create a system in which animals are able to produce healthy, clean, balanced, nutritionally rich, and flavorful milk and work with this unique substance to make a unique product.

local consumers think their cheese is like a rank dead thing. Helen and Rick have not found their immediate vicinity to be an enthusiastic market. So though Goat Lady Dairy has worked to reeducate folks about what goat cheese can be, Helen and Rick have holed up on the farm and sent their cheese out into the wide world.

They've also begun playing mad scientist with their cows, buying bull semen from classic breeds of French mountain cow, such as Tarentaise, Abondance, and Montbéliarde, and cross-breeding their herd of Jerseys. This is in an effort to produce more balanced milk, with comparable amounts of fat and protein, instead of milk that's skewed to typical Jersey richness. That and the fact that they wish to modify the easily burstable fat molecules Jerseys are known for. And you thought it was just about making some tasty cheese?

Meadow Creek does that as well. In addition to its lush,

gutsy Grayson, there's a cheese called **Mountaineer**, but I'll focus on what I love. Grayson's paste is deep golden yellow, thick, and drooping, and contrasts like a bad pair of trainers with the damp, tacky, electric orange rind that encases the whole blocky square. The *B. linen*-y exterior sticks to the finger pads, and for several hours, you smell a combo of moist, crumpled socks and fatty pork sausage. Inside, the luscious paste is plump as a burlesque girl, and all that supple fat carries an intense, burly flavor. There's a ton of jerky, bacony intensity, but the bite is held together by vegetal, grassy austerity. It's rustic, impeccably balanced, and though you're not supposed to take "good" cheese and melt it, Grayson relaxes into an unctuous pool of neon yellow glory ooze, the flavor somewhere between ballpark peanuts and coarse pâté.

➤ SWEET GRASS DAIRY
THOMASVILLE, GEORGIA

Sweet Grass is actually several companies operating together as a milk-making, cheesemaking machine fueled by the power of grass. It started as an idea in the minds of two young parents, partners in an award-winning dairy in northern Florida. That dairy had nothing to do with grass: the awards were won for the high volumes of milk the herd of 1,100 milking Holsteins cranked out during their average life span of two to three years. A confinement operation, the cows lived on concrete and lived off silage and grain. Though their milk was abundant, their foot problems were as well, and though the operation was profitable, Desiree and Al Wehner imagined there must be a better way.

Al was the western New York descendant of German dairy farmers; Desiree had no farming background but really loved the animals. In 1993, they decided to break off from their partners and take their 50 percent equity in cows, cull it down to the very best animals, and move north. They found cheap land in Georgia—rolling, lush grass with nary a barn in sight—and turned their Holsteins out onto Green Hill. The cows apparently had no idea what to do. The desire—the ability—to graze on grass had been bred out of them, and the amount of moving, walking, and digestion required proved to be more than the cows could handle. The Wehners sold their herd and replaced it with another dirt-cheap buy: Jersey cows. No one wanted the little cows that gave smaller amounts of fatty milk. They were a good bargain.

I think it's fair to say that when the Wehners made the move from conventional to pastured dairying after hearing a lecture about the New Zealand rotational approach, their primary reaction was feasibility. I don't doubt that healthier cows, longer lives, and environmental sustainability were appealing, too, but the real kicker of grazing cows is that the whole approach is cheap. Sweet Grass was profitable from the first year. Minimum overhead offset the need for maximum milk yields. There were no combine machines to grow and chop silage (fermented hay or corn stalks to feed indoor animals). No feed-mixing wagons or need to put up feed. No fuel to run tractors. The dirt-cheap farmers became self-described dirt farmers. Al Wehner's primary responsibility is to grow the soil. Rotate the cows, maintain and enrich the mineral content, establish the cycle of dung beetles and earthworms to recycle manure and grow more grass.

In addition to the 340-acre Green Hill plot, the couple bought a second parcel of 140 acres in 1996, in a better school district for their three kids. It was a wooded, brushy patch with only 20 acres of pasture that Desiree realized, after her cheese-making crash course at Cal Poly, was ideal for goats. So, in 2000, the original Green Hill expanded to include Sweet Grass Dairy: cheesemaking operation plus goat herd. Desiree had been making cheese in the kitchen for years. To test the sincerity of her own interest in cheese, she made a batch every day for a year, aging the wheels in old refrigerators on the porch. Still going strong after twelve months, she sought a business license, which was issued at the end of 2000.

By 2002, it became clear that Desiree needed to slow down, and the happy coincidence of her son-in-law's misery in Atlanta and his desire to be around food meant that he moved down to learn the cheese. Their oldest child, Jessica, remained in Atlanta and began ferreting out the local chefs. She, it seemed, had no small gift for sales and marketing. And he, it seemed, was a damn good cheesemaker. In 2005, Jessica and Jeremy Little bought Sweet Grass Dairy: the cheesemaking operation and the goats.

In 1996, Al and Desiree had begun another pastured dairy on 340 acres called Grassy Flats. Having sold Sweet Grass Dairy, they focused their attention on their five hundred cows and expanded their milking operation. Only 8 percent of the milk of Green Hill's five hundred cows goes into cheese. The rest, and all of the milk from Grassy Flats, is sold to a fluid milk cooperative. Jessica and Jeremy buy the milk not from her parents but from the fluid milk cooperative, which long ago cinched a contract for 100 percent of the family's milk.

When Desiree was making cheese at Sweet Grass, she cycled through a portfolio of twenty-plus styles. These days, Jeremy has narrowed it down to about ten, both cow and goat milk choices that impress me for their delicacy and nuance. **Green Hill** is the one we carry at Murray's and the one I know best. An homage to the original plot from which the milk hails, it's a fantastically well executed, sweet little morsel of buttery goodness. See the difference shape makes? Cowgirl Creamery's Mt. Tam looks like a White Castle slider. Sweet Grass Green Hill is like the patty alone. The difference is that the fluffy white rind can break down the interior paste to gooey perfection far more easily in the flat patty than it can in the entire two inches of the burger/bun. That means that Green Hill is sandy dappled like Mt. Tam, with a completely benign aroma. It has very little smell at all. I'm guessing that means rich, slathery insides with no ammonia or bitter flavor.

It's all a matter of surface area. If the cheese is relatively thin and flat (think Brie), the molds covering the outside can break down fat and protein much more quickly than they can with a fatter cylinder of cheese. The trade-off with the tall pieces is that by the time total breakdown has occurred and you're scooping up whippy insides, the molded rind has become too dominant. Not an issue with Green Hill. The rind is thin and mild, not snappy and bitter the way so many rinds can be. There's still a high note of acidity, a tart, cultured taste to what is otherwise a mouthful of mild, buttery richness.

What's lacking? The intense, fungal, mushroomy soul I love. But I don't think that's the intention here. It's like good cultured butter meets smearable approachability. It's luscious. It's mild. It's really easy to like. Plus, it's loaded with beta-carotene from the pastured cows, so you don't have to go eat carrots to get your vitamins. Other cow choices I like are **Thomasville Tomme**, a raw, semisoft hunk with a thin, dry, natural rind. It's very straightforward, with the slightest fruity undertone and a creamy, pliable bite. The new one Jeremy just sent me is **Asher Blue**, named for the Littles' second son. I got many warnings not to talk about it because the production is so limited, but I can't help mentioning it. It's an unusual style, rinded, dense, and dry, more like Jasper Hill Farm's Bayley Hazen Blue. The blue veining is fierce and deep, with powdery, dusty pockets and what my boss Rob calls "worms"—when the puncture points (made to let in oxygen and develop interior blueing) fill with mold in a textured string, which he hates but I kind of like. The cheese smells like deeply browned, buttered toast, and the mold itself is fudgy and earthy. I hope Sweet Grass will make more in the coming years, because it could be one of the greats.

As for the herd of goats that live at Sweet Grass Dairy, their milk is transformed into several offerings. They are delicate, and the mold-ripened cheeses like **Georgia Pecan Chevre** and **Lumiere** grow a thick, droopy crust in nanoseconds if they get too warm. This makes shipping a tricky thing, and nearly ensures that the cheese you find farther away from Georgia will likely suffer from that unfortunate ripening where the moist, slightly flaky insides veritably squirt out of the heavy, hanging rind. Both are younger styles, both are pasteurized, and the two capture the terroir—the flavor—of this herd's milk. Sweet Grass goat milk tastes more than I'm used to, full, herbaceous, and garlicky, like the loopy green garlic shoots known as scapes. One of my colleagues likened it to licking wet goat. Not in a nice way. But all of the women who were tasting it with me appreciated its complexity beyond the normal "grassy," "lemony," or "zesty" notes. It's been suggested that men and women detect different flavors. Perhaps we do.

Lumiere, not to be confused with the animated dancing candlestick from *Beauty and the Beast,* is a beautiful, limp, ashed rind, incredibly blue, its snow white interior cut by a line of ash. All that green, scapey, mellow flavor is like walking into a hothouse full of steamy plants. Georgia Pecan Chevre is coated in ground pecans under its bloomy white rind and when it gets the proper dose of salt tastes like a bite of pecan pie, without the sugar. A note of regional pronunciation from my southern colleague Jason: it's pronounced "pi-CAN," not "PEE-can." The latter refers to the wide-mouthed vessel you take on long car rides.

➤ UPLANDS CHEESE COMPANY
DODGEVILLE, WISCONSIN

Uplands is most often associated with Mike Gingrich, the guy who makes the incredible cheese. But Uplands is in fact a close partnership between Mike (and his wife, Carol) and the couple who manage the land and the cows: Dan Patenaude and his wife, Jeanne. There are few cheesemaking operations in America where the land/animal manager is more crucial than this one.

Uplands is known for its vigilant commitment to pastured cows. The farm milks seasonally, when there are grass, herbs, flowers, and forage in this hilly, ridged area of southwestern Wisconsin. The milk is seasonal, and the cheese is made from the finest milk of the season. While the cows are fed about eight pounds of grain each day to maintain essential nutrition, supplemental feed is kept in strict proportion to pasture, which makes up 75 to 80 percent of the animals' diet. In times of excessive heat and drought, the cows must be fed more than five pounds of hay per day to make up for lost forage, and cheese-making ceases. Whatever fluid milk does not go into cheese (about one third of the total yield in 2008) is sold to a local organic milk cooperative for a premium price.

Although the Gingrich/Patenaude partnership dates back to 1994, the families owned separate plots of land and were conventional dairy farmers in the late 1970s and early '80s. It was Dan who turned his cows out to pasture early in the 1980s, an incredibly progressive and unusual thing at the time. The two men decided this approach to grass made enormous sense but could sustain the families only on a larger scale. Together in 1994, they bought a 300-acre plot high along the ridgeline, with steep hills and enormous open vistas, and went into seasonal grass-based dairying. On a blowsy blue fall afternoon, I marveled at the cows, those enormous, solid creatures, making their way up and down the slopes, onto a new patch of field after each milking. The thing about Wisconsin is that there is a lot of snow, and if you're going to milk only when the cows are on grass, you're not going milk for much of the year. By 1997, it became clear that the value of grass feeding and the challenge of the limited production could not support two families selling to the fluid milk industry. Even the organic co-ops didn't pay enough to live on. Cheese, however, was a different story. Cheese wasn't the original intention, but Mike and Dan realized that the flavor profile of their fleeting, blade-fueled milk might make good, even exceptional, cheese. Plus, moving the cows outside meant there wasn't enough work to keep the two men busy full-time. It seemed that Mike was destined to become the Cheese Guy.

To this day, Uplands makes a single cheese. It took five years of preparation before a single crumb was produced. For the second half of the 1990s, the partners prepared to become cheesemakers and land tenders. The soil was seeded and groomed to improve the variety and content of its yield. They began with a herd of the standard black-and-white Holstein cows—the only kind, Mike mentioned, that you could buy in bulk—and carefully began to cross-breed the Holsteins for the first five years with Jerseys, Brown Swiss, and Ayrshires. Then came the genetics of the French breeds: Normandy, Tarentaise, and Abondance cows, followed, finally, by New Zealand Friesians and Jerseys. All these years I thought Mike was playing genetic engineer, carefully cultivating his cows to deliver superior fat, protein, and flavor characteristics. When I asked him what he was looking for in mixing all these cows together, his decidedly practical answer was: fertility. A grass-based operation requires the cows to get pregnant at the same time, three months after the birth of their last calf in early spring, so they can be milked throughout the summer and early fall and then "dried off" (not milked) during the winter. Then more calves, more milk, more grass, and the cycle begins anew. A cow that doesn't get knocked up when you want her to is a cow that's unproductive for an entire milking season.

After three years of preparation, including tons of cheese research and recipe testing, the first wheels of **Pleasant Ridge Reserve** were made in 2000. The milk was carefully transported to a nearby cheese plant, where Mike rented space one day a week because his parcel of land had grass, cows, a barn, and little else. Incredibly, the cheese was recognized as the best in America a mere year after it was made, named "Best in Show" by the American Cheese Society in 2001. As demand climbed and the feasibility of remote cheesemaking became harder, the partners invested in an on-site cheesemaking room and aging cave in 2004. Despite the difficulties of the new space and equipment, the cheese won "Best in Show" a second time in 2005. In 2008, another addition was made to the aging caves, giving Uplands the potential to hit its theoretical maximum production: 100,000 pounds of cheese a year, assuming the weather cooperates and there is ample grass to feed the herd.

Pleasant Ridge Reserve is a mercurial thing. It's available after four months of aging, but the best wheels are held back to nine, twelve, or even fourteen months, when their flavors deepen into a million fleeting nuances that roll over you long after the last bit of cheese is eaten. The prairie grasses of Uplands' land change throughout the grazing season, influencing the herbaceous, wheaty, or fruity undertones of the cheese. Within all these variables, the cheese is always exquisite. I am not inclined toward hard cheeses in general or Alpine cheeses in particular, like the Beaufort or Comté that guided Uplands' recipe. Yet Pleasant Ridge Reserve strikes me anew each time I taste it. It is miraculously consistent in its appeal.

It's amazing for me to taste cheese in groups for the difference not between good and bad cheese but between good cheese and exceptional cheese. As the last of this batch of six I am tasting, the first thing that pops about Pleasant Ridge Reserve is the infinite variety of texture, even within a small subsection like hard cheese! There is no indication that Pleasant Ridge Reserve is composed of what were once separate curd bits. There is no graininess, no chunky break, no mealy residue as in so many (even very tasty) pressed cheeses. Instead, it's like perfectly cooked filet mignon: the slightest bit of resistance before your teeth sink into rich, succulent flesh.

It's worth waiting at least nine months, but ideally twelve, to get the best of what this cheese can be. There's a lot of savory to the flavor—onions caramelized with painful sloth over a barely flickering flame, breaking down into sweet skeins thanks to a few spoonfuls of beef stock. Hovering over the whole thing is a dank, dried fruitiness, like dates without the numbing sugar. Pleasant Ridge may well be the finest cheese made in America. It is certainly one of the finest, and I would argue that the intense and laborious management of the land and cautious, careful selection of wheels for aging are the two biggest reasons why.

LITTLE CHEESE

ON A RANDOM TUESDAY NIGHT IN MARCH, I FIND MYSELF standing in a hot, crowded little shop on Capitol Square in Madison, Wisconsin. My eyes have that itchy, bleary scrape each time I blink, and when I try to socialize my brow twitches, my lips pulling into a tweaky grimace. I'm really tired. I want to go back to my hotel room or out to a small, quiet table where I can wipe away an entire day's worth of cheese tasting with some bitter greens and puri- fied water. Instead, I take one of every crunchy, eggy, cheesy delight that's passed under my nose. A breaded ball full of thick, béchamelly fondue. A miniquiche for one, though it's four inches in diameter with a butter-packed shell that disintegrates as I brush against the fluted edge. A young hipster offers me a tartlet with the perilous crust, this time filled with brackish black wild mushrooms. I reach for one, hoping for the earthy, fungal lull of hen of the woods, and then decline because I do not need to eat a bite of Every Single Thing. I waver, and he points out that they're hot. Now. No matter. I decide to get one on his return loop and then spend the next ten minutes craning my neck for the mushroom boy. When he ambles back to my corner, I see his empty tray and grease-flecked napkin. I figure a glass of wine might ease my forced smile and inane questions, but it just drives me to another poor choice—poor for my digestive system, but generally delicious, which is to slurp down a six-ouncer of Brenda Jensen's brand-new yogurt when it's passed my way. I can never say no to the gelatinous, panna cotta jiggle of fatty sheep milk, and though this is her first batch, served in ugly plastic cups that say "Catalina" in royal blue (apparently she bought the cups from a nearby yogurt plant), it is silky, slippery, and delicious. I almost forget I'm not hungry.

When the ragtag crowd forms an oval and begins introductions (they start with name and favorite dairy product), I almost forget that I'm beat. I simply can't turn down an evening with the Cheese Underground. There are established cheesemakers I know, fledging farmers I've met, and cheese legends I've only heard of. But as introductions heat up, the stories get good. One tells, quite earnestly, of accidentally growing staph on a batch of cheese that failed to acidify quickly enough, retained too much moisture, and "pissed whey all over the cave for the next month." I'm reminded of the celebrity Ashton Kutcher's unfortunate thirtieth birthday party, at which the guests were exposed to staph by a restaurant worker and received the following T-shirt apology in the mail the following week: "I WENT TO ASHTON'S BIRTHDAY AND ALL I GOT WAS STAPH." I'm thinking this cheesemaker might offer a similar recompense to his friends, who apparently experienced some intestinal . . . interruption.

Next up is a moppish older woman leaning heavily on her cane. She points out that her presence at this cheese tasting is ill timed. She milks goats, and in midwinter they're all still pregnant. There is no milk. Plus she has only twelve goats. Plus she had a knee operation, so she hasn't really made any cheese in five months, anyway. Still, she passes around wedges of an aged cheese made the previous fall and Cryovac'd so she'd have edible, durable cheese to sell while she went under the knife. The stuff is moist and pliable with the calm, even sweetness of good aged goat cheese. It's soothing, with a hazelnutty edge that I love in this style. It's no wonder: she's been playing with goat cheese for twenty years.

Then there's the inimitable Mary Falk. This woman is the biggest ballbuster ever. She's bursting with energy, constantly swiping her voluminous, wild gray hair out of her face with weathered hands that sport seven different chunky rings, talking a mile a minute, with a smart-ass remark for everyone. She's best known for making a raw-milk "product" aged for less than sixty days and selling it at the St. Paul (Minnesota) Farmers Market as Fish Bait. Of course, raw-milk "products" aged for less than sixty days are illegal only for human consumption. And Fish Bait, obviously, is meant only to catch fish. Apparently there were shoppers aplenty in St. Paul who wanted to hit the lakes the summer Fish Bait began and every year since. Mary stood up to discuss a recent ADD grant she and her husband, Dave, were recently awarded. In my foggy-trying-to-be-funny-for-the-cheesemakers state, I yell out, "ADD? What's that stand for, Mary?" Turns out she wasn't, for once, joking.

ADD stands for Agriculture Development and Diversity. I recover with a modest "That would give me ADD, too." Whew. Saved. They all titter, and I save face in front of the cool, the small, the elusive: the tiny American cheesemaker.

As important as the established cheesemakers are, the folks who embody the romance of eat-local, cook-regional, gather-in-groovy-hippie-conferences to talk cheese (in other words, the teeny cheesemakers) are still the sexiest. They're the ones Florence Fabricant ferrets out for her weekly column in *The New York Times'* Dining In/Dining Out, the ones chefs ask about first, the ones I stumbled upon the summer I rented a house on Penobscot Bay, Maine. These obscure cheesemakers are the equivalent of a roadside tamale lady during the Los Cabos getaway or the discovery my parents made road-tripping through central California in the early 1970s. They arrived at a friend's home in the dark dinner hours, proudly hauling a dusty cardboard box overflowing with artichokes. Apparently everyone looked up from their fourth drink long enough to observe, "Oh. You found Castroville."

Little cheesemakers are one facet of the Food Find. Over the years, my Finds have included the blueberry pie lady from a Maine summer, who sells her drippy, clumpy, butter-crusted treasures still in the Pyrex and trusts you'll bring the dish back; the ancient Italian woman in Emilia-Romagna who, with gestures and pidgin exchanges alone, led me into the back room of her open-air restaurant, warm and moist from the low-lying Parma fog, and showed me the curing Culatello di Zibello (literally, pig's ass cheek) she had strewn in porky abandon over my hand-rolled egg pasta a few minutes earlier; and the Bun Cha on Hang Manh Street in Hanoi, where a bowl of crusty, astringent hibachi-cooked pork was offered up beside sweet, cool broth and sticky, tangled rice noodles for me to dip, and slurp, and liberally sprinkle with the watery crunch of sprouts and feathery cilantro fronds.

The racy thrill of the Find is addictive—these obscure food makers who strike you as delightful, charming geniuses, perhaps because they are, or, more likely, because they're a fixture of a life into which you have briefly, fortuitously stumbled. It is their utter normalcy in a place to which you do not belong that makes them sparkle so brightly. And their spread! My God! On an August Saturday in Belfast, Maine, when the sky is cerulean, the pine trees are straight, and the air whiffs of harbor, boat rope, and lobster shells; the sun is bright but the air is cool, maybe even broken-cotton-sweatshirt cool, and your belly is sated with a cup of coffee and that slab of pie you ate in a rocking chair, hearing the buoys slap in the bay, your lap covered with an old quilt . . . on *that* Saturday, when you find the local goat cheese, lined up in knobby little rounds, some dusted with dried rosemary from the cheesemaker's garden, and the cheesemaker nods at you from the flatbed of his pick-up truck . . . *that* goat cheese will be the most perfect cheese you have ever eaten. It will be an impeccable balance of moist squish and delicate, acidic crumble. You will feel it smear under the pressure of your tongue into mouth-watery, lemony, sun-warmed-herby crumbs. It will be an epiphany, and you will laugh out loud and call your friend or mother or lover over and point to each imperfectly shaped lump, trying to decide which one. Which one do you want to buy? And what bread to spread it on? And which wine to savor? And soon, by 8:15 in the morning, that modest nugget of yesterday's milk will have planned your entire day. *That* is the power of the small, local cheesemaker.

I've had a few of those mornings, in a few towns in America, and they usually happen when I find, by perseverance or sheer dumb luck, the local farmers' market. Farmers' markets make me think of the Amish. Raymond Fisher, Mark Stoltzfus and dozens of other Amish producers have consistent consumers for their cheese, regardless of its quality. In this sense, though their closed community limits their exposure to new cheese, the Amish are virtually guaranteed customers, regardless of the cheeses' flavor. Their Amish neighbors are hardly driving to the local supermarket to pick up a fine wedge of Dutch Gouda or comparing Raymond's Swiss to the cave-aged Gruyère they enjoyed on their last ski retreat. The cheese the Amish make is the cheese that's known, and locals aren't expecting anything different. Now, "English" visitors to Amish country are another story. They're more likely to find the cheddar bitter in comparison to the block one they buy at home or find the Swiss kind of bland compared to the one used on fancy urban panini, but the acquisition of these cheeses, even if they're mediocre, becomes a wonderful adventure. To buy a hand-wrapped piece of cheese directly from a small Amish boy in suspenders—or, even better, to put a few wadded-up singles in the narrow slit of an honor box and steal away with a small bottle of raw milk or cream. *That* is an experience. The taste of the cheese becomes part of remembering how you discovered it in the first place.

The farmers' market is the same way. I'm not saying to expect that the cheese or meat or produce should or will be subpar, but the margin of error is considerably more generous than mine can be when I'm deciding what cheeses to buy for Murray's. In the late 1990s, Murray's used to carry a small selection of not-very-good American cheeses. We wanted to support these fledgling producers, even if their cheese wasn't as tasty as those we were importing from Europe. Nowadays, there is simply no need to make this choice. There are so many, and so many excellent, American cheeses that a cheese like Raymond's wouldn't stand a chance outside the ramblings of Pennsylvania suburbanites. To survive, and certainly to flourish, in the current market, a cheese can be many things: unique, with a good story, filling a void, or hitting a price point. But above all, it must taste good, and indeed, it must taste better than the twenty-five other American cheeses I got samples of this week or last week or last month.

The farmers' market is blessedly more elastic. My local market is in Grand Army Plaza, Brooklyn. The offerings in April are limited, yet I manage to buy eggs, bread, kale, a giant unwieldy spray of forsythia, and a few wrinkled, slightly mushy offerings hanging on from last fall: apples, and a butternut squash. I *want* to buy things, as I do every week. I love wandering from stall to stall, fingering the bruised veggies, sipping a cup of cider, imagining who is possibly going to purchase the giant vacuum-sealed package that contains a beef heart or the smaller, squishier package that contains two lamb hearts. It's romantic and fun, you can smell and touch everything, and all the booths are manned by old, grizzled guys with big beer guts or waifish, angular girls with many piercings and woven hemp hats. It's great. And for cheesemakers, it's forgiving, in a few ways.

For cheesemakers whose production is teeny tiny, or even

medium tiny, everything made can be sold at a farmers' market. And a premium price can be asked. Many is the time we call Mark Gillman at Cato Corner Farm and wheedle, needle, beg for just a little more **Hooligan** or **Bridgid's Abbey**. But who can blame the guy when he cuts us off? He can sell a bit more to Murray's at a discounted wholesale price, or he can take a fuller load to the Greenmarket and siphon it off, a $6 quarter pound at a time. And next week, when he doesn't have any Hooligan because it needs another wash or because the *B. linens* in his aging room have gone haywire, no one at the Greenmarket rides his tail. People might be disappointed, of course, but they buy something else, leave happy, and come again next week. Meanwhile, stores and restaurants will call Mark every day, worriedly checking when the **Hooligan** will be back. That's the way it goes. We pay a lower price and we want it all the time, except when we don't want it. Market shoppers are there for an experience, to eat more seasonally, more locally. If anything, inconsistent supply is part of the charm.

Perhaps even more significant than their flexibility on availability and price, patrons of the market are inevitably choosing from a smaller pool of cheeses. Even at the largest and most influential farmers' markets, such as those in Ann Arbor, Ithaca, Madison, New York City, San Francisco, and Santa Monica, how many cheeses can there possibly be? Twenty? Maybe thirty? It's never going to be a one-stop shop, as leading retailers are expected to be. A good, solid cheese is going to fly in these markets, while it might languish and die behind the counter of a cheese shop or certainly a supermarket. This opportunity of the farmers' market has led me to mentally categorize cheese samples in a new way: the technically-proficient-very-straightforward-but-otherwise-lacking-in-wow-factor cheeses. For me, at Murray's, I have to choose. How many fresh goat cheeses can we justify? Well: if one is a small round, another is briefly aged, a third is sold in bulk loaves, a fourth is so creamy it arrives in a cup, the fifth is made for only three months a year, a sixth is dusted with crushed chervil, and a seventh is remarkably inexpensive compared to the first six, the answer is seven. At that moment I can justify carrying seven fresh American goat cheeses, because they are just different enough that we can promote them to the proper consumers. But if we're talking apples to apples—or more likely, bulk goat loaves to bulk goat loaves—then I will carry only one. It will be the one that is least chalky, with no gritty residue, with a fresh, milky smack and racy, citrus finish, at the best price I can find, preferably from within two hundred miles, and made as recently as I can get it. The producer from California simply doesn't stand a chance, nor does the producer who can only, maybe, on a good week guarantee me thirty pounds of loaves. I want it from nearby, I want it made for me every week, and I need scalable supply. So I'll taste the loaf from California and let the cheesemaker know how we think it measures against all the other fresh ones we've tasted, but in the end I will never buy that cheese. It is a technically-proficient-very-straightforward-but-otherwise-lacking-in-wow-factor cheese. Plus it violates other criteria I have laid out.

As American cheeses have gotten exponentially better and the samples that arrive through Murray's back door have improved by leaps and bounds, it has become harder and harder to pick which to buy. The major criteria used to be "Is it edible?" Seriously. There were so many ass-kickingly bitter, thick, chewy, tough-rinded, weepy, droopy, sour-tasting monstrosities that when we got a tasty one, or even an unoffensive one, we were gung ho to bring that bad boy in. Now, an American cheese needs to be superlative. Bloomy-rinded specimens of any milk type are at an immediate advantage because there are still so few good ones from which to choose. Which style is suffering from greatest overexposure? Semisoft cow milk cheese and block cheddar. Now, those are *perfect* farmers' market cheeses. Most of the time I taste them and pause in appreciation for what the Italians would call a magnificent "table cheese." Table cheeses aren't sexy, glam, or exotic. They're not "washed-rind" or "bloomy-rind" or moldripened of any sort. They're an easy point of entry, familiar, tending to be two to six months in age. They are firm but creamy and tender undertooth, earthy, buttery, and approachable. They are the cheeses you nosh without thinking, because they are pleasing in their grassy, vaguely nutty, edging-towardbuttermilky way. And they're precisely the cheeses you find on some paint-chipped old farm table in whatever small town you're driving through and think, as you buy a wedge for lunch, along with a glug of beer or wine and a handful of cherries, "This is heaven."

So for whatever road trip lies in your destiny—or, if you're like me, for whatever walk begins each Saturday's food shopping—here's to the finds of America's farmers' markets: from tiny and obscure to straightforward, old-fashioned, good eating.

NOTES FROM AMERICA'S
FARMERS' MARKETS

➤ ANCIENT HERITAGE DAIRY
SCIO, OREGON

It's still not entirely clear to me how Ancient Heritage Dairy took shape in this world. It seems an oddly ambiguous, shifting evolution that began with Paul Obringer's job transfer from Boston to Portland, Oregon. His wife, Kathy, described their arrival in Portland as a kind of homecoming and settling into the place they were made to be in, though they'd found it by accident. That was about 1993, and a few years later their young son was tested for allergies and found to be unable to drink cow or goat milk (at least pasteurized; later they discovered he could handle raw goat), and highly sensitive to diesel and gasoline fumes. Precisely the things one finds in the city. Portland is pretty tame compared to Manhattan, but it became clear that moving away from development would be ideal. They bought eighty acres of clear-cut land and inadvertently grew their equity in the land by developing pastures and building fences. They had goats for their boys' drinking milk, and all of their children took a shine to animals and 4H. Sheep came first, but their daughter's love of cows led to the purchase of a few of those. They homeschooled their children, primarily to encourage these kinds of interests; Kathy mentioned that if it were up her she wouldn't have chosen dairy cattle, but then "We're not just doing this for me."

As for animals, well, you just learn one day at a time, apparently. Paul's previous job in publishing sales and marketing made him great with people and promotion (sales and marketing being one of the hardest things for small cheesemakers to tackle), and Kathy's training as an artist made the science of cheesemaking tricky but the creativity of invention really enjoyable. She'd been making yogurt for the family and playing around with cheese, but the initial plan was to freeze sheep milk for retail, targeting kids with allergies like their sons had. Then they realized they'd need a *lot* of sheep.

In 2005, ten years after their initial move to the country, the family relocated to their current plot an hour south of Portland, between the Cascade and Coastal Mountains, and began cheesemaking in earnest. Their flock is currently sixty big, and Kathy talks about growth, but not beyond a hundred or so sheep. The birthing (aka lambing) and milk flow begin in early March and continue until October, when the animals can graze on pasture, leaving Ancient Heritage with the same challenge of seasonality that all sheep dairies have: no milk in the winter. The first winter they borrowed cow milk from a neighboring organic farm. It had become abundantly clear that they couldn't make it through the winter without another job or extra income, so they tried blending cow milk into their reserves of frozen sheep milk from the summer and making mixed-milk cheese. Turns out it worked, and many of their customers at the farmers' markets actually preferred it. The following spring they bought some Ayrshire cows for the dairy.

My favorite of its cheeses (and I've not tasted all of them)

Ancient Heritage at Market

These days, half of Ancient Heritage's annual production of 18,500 pounds is sold at two farmers' markets: the seasonal Portland Market, which runs on Saturdays from March until Christmas, and the year-round Hillsdale Farmers' Market. The other half is sold to small, regional stores (and a bit to Murray's, all the way in New York!).

is the **Adelle**. Think big fat gumdrop blanketed in a wrinkled white rind, edged around the top and bottom with an ochre perimeter that comes with time plus moisture plus *P. candidum*. Not necessarily a bad thing. Do not fear a white rind shaded with yellow. I fear a bright white, utterly impassive rind, because it suggests mold that has been sprayed on, rather than coaxed organically through labor-intensive aging. It's a shortcut used by big industrial producers, like flocking a Christmas tree with fake snow. And it makes for Bright. White. Bland. Chewy. Totally. Shelf-stable. Cheese. No thanks.

I'm kind of entranced with the smell of the Adelle, because it has a bit of rubber-raft, petrol funk and is a little garlicky. The rind has a wrinkled, brainy appearance that means more than one kind of mold. I like many-molded cheeses. They often have a depth and complexity, with each strain doing its part to make something really excellent. Inside, pasteurized cow and sheep milk have been blended and aged into a cool flaky cheesecake. If I didn't know the cheese was made of sheep and cow milk, I might even guess goat thanks to that tart, mouth-watery taste. Then again, it's dense and rich, with the obvious lanolin heft of the woolly milker.

I've said it before, and I'll say it again: it's hard to make a good bloomy rind, and American producers haven't been doing it for very long. There's often separation between the inside and the outside, a bitter taste, and a chewy, snappy texture, instead of the mushroomy yielding skin I crave. Adelle is holding up this go-round, but there's a telltale crevice snaking around the cheese, a little gap where the cheesecake has gone gooey and the rind sits like a slightly ill-fitting jacket. No matter. It tastes of leather, and proper salting gives each bite the body to handle that earthen sheath. The seasonal counterpart of Adelle, made of pure sheep milk, is **Valentine**, named after Val, a favorite ewe. There's also a raw-milk, aged recipe for a firmer cheese that's a cross between Tomme de Brebis and Vermont Shepherd. The pure sheep version is **Scio Heritage**, and the milder, nutty mixed-milk is **Hannah Bridge Heritage**. In the summer there's sheep milk **Scio Feta**.

➤ BLEU MONT DAIRY
BLUE MOUNDS, WISCONSIN

My first trip to Wisconsin took me to lots of producers with deep, well-established roots and storied factories in big open fields of green. When our van pulled down a long, gnarled dirt drive past a bunch of solar panels and lurched to a halt in front of a low, isolated house, I got a jittery "cheese-find" feeling. This place was cool, in a remarkably imprecise hippie way. I had no idea if the cheese would be edible, but it had the guts of a good story. The house is the home of Willi Lehner and his partner Qui'tas, who picked up the moniker during her time on a reservation in New Mexico. Awesome. All signs continue pointing to intriguing cheese folks. *The New York Times'* kind of American cheesemaker, rather than the historically important but otherwise boring kind. Willi's parents were Swiss, and his brother is the cheesemaker for precisely one of those boring historical jobs, making, it must be noted, the best Havarti I've had in America. I can't imagine that Willi is anything other than the black sheep of the family. In his twenties he paid for European travel by working on an Alp, making cheese in an open copper kettle, skimming cream off the vat every morning to make cultured butter, and returning to the mountain whenever he was low on funds.

Once home, he began traditional Wisconsin cheesemaking of the block sort, got bored, and started "playing around." With a particular interest in cloth-wrapped ("bandaged") cheddar, he took off for the United Kingdom, visiting sixteen producers throughout England, Ireland, and Scotland. Most profound was the idea that a tiny cheesemaker, making 500 pounds a day, could produce four distinctive types of cheese from a single vat.

Now Willi does the same. He and Qui'tas have no cows, choosing instead to buy milk from area farms, focusing on organic and pasture-based milk where possible. Willi makes cheese at other people's plants, muscling in with his pickup truck full of milk and hopping on the cheesemaking line at odd hours to crank out cheddars, washed-rinds, and Gouda types. He also built two groovy subterranean caves for aging the cheese, one for washed-rinds and the other for natural

rinds and cheddars. They're still relatively empty in their new-
ness, the walls painted a warm terra-cotta hue with big smiling
suns for decoration. It's the Southwest by way of Somerset.

Sitting on a stool in Willi's open kitchen, drinking creamy,
rich brown ale, I carefully tasted each cheese he fed us. The
first, and unequivocally the best, was an **eighteen-month cheddar**, formerly bandaged, now scraped clean for the noshing. It
smelled of macaroni and cheese, but then there was a great
burst of sweet. Fudgy little nuggets lodged in my teeth, melting and smearing into a perfect balance of cheesy-savory-bread-
crumby-toffee. I wanted to eat and eat and eat. The **two-year**
was still swaddled in its dusty, cheese-mitey bandage. The
presence of cheese mites as a natural and balanced aspect of
the cheese aging process can be detected by a heady, honeyed
aroma. The cheese (even the room!) will smell of mead, and
this sweetness permeates the cheese. Willi's cheddars had it in
spades. The dense, crumbling hunks were surprisingly moist,
punctuated with white specks of delightful, crystallized
crunch.

Then there's the **organic bandaged cheddar**, or, as Willi
calls it, the Halloween Cheese, because it was made on October 31, 2007. With eight months of age on it, the flavor is dark
and masculine. I immediately piped up that it reminded me of
meat, tasting dried sausagey. Willi looked at me and said, "That's
an interesting way to describe it." Which translates to "Girl,
you're nuts. It doesn't taste like meat." But no matter. To me it
does. There are a lot of celery and cave smells near the rind. For
this one, Willi bought milk from Mike Gingrich at Uplands
Cheese Company. In addition to being organic, the cheddar
is raw milk. The high acidity makes for typical cheddar

Cloth Binding and Cheese Mites and Crystals, Oh My!

Cheese can have weird and foreign-looking things in and on it that affect aging, flavor, and texture. Cloth binding is generally fine-mesh cotton cheesecloth that is wrapped around a wheel and brushed with melted lard. This creates the foundation and food to support the microorganisms that will colonize the cheeses' exterior and, over time, create a semipermeable rind that allows moisture to evaporate but protects the interior paste from excessive drying and undesirable invasive molds. Cheese mites (*Tyrophagus casei*) measure from 0.39 to 0.7 millimeters in length and live a brief fifteen to eighteen days, preferring warmer, moist environments such as cheese caves. The mites burrow into the rind of the cheese, leaving behind a thin gray powder made up of (don't freak!) their shedded skin (dander), themselves, and their excrement. They cause cheese to have a sweet floral aroma and a powdery, crumbling rind. Crystals are the white grains speckling the interior paste of aged cheeses, generally around nine months and up, that crunch under tooth. They are crystallized peptides—little bits of protein chain bound to minerals such as calcium. The snipping of protein chains is part of the anaerobic ripening of cheese and is affected by moisture and enzyme activity.

sharpness, but that porky lull balances the heady, husky flavor.

The last cheese Willi busted out is going down in my top ten new favorites. It's made only a few times a year, and its name, **Earth Schmear**, is an allusion to its cheesemaking process. Inspired by cheesemakers he visited in Ireland and their emphasis on the terroir of a region, Willi came home and had an epiphany. He was gardening, hands in the dirt, and realized that soil was where his local microbes lived. So he dug up a clump, poured water over it, and after a day filtered the brew and used it to wipe down naked wheels of cheese that had been twice dry-salted. His schmear of earth water introduced local microbes, which proceeded to grow on the rind. The one-pound wheels are barely orange, just brushed apricot on the outside. The cheese starts as Havarti and acidifies for twenty-four to forty-eight hours, which means a rich, buttery beginning and a cheesecakey tang from the acidification. Just the slightest bit of runny under the rind, and the interior is all tart and flaky. It tastes like loamy garden, sea salt, butter, and sour cream cake. It's amazing. At four weeks old, it's also pasteurized, which proves you can have a brilliant cheese even if it's not raw milk.

➤ BLUE LEDGE FARM
SALISBURY, VERMONT

In the summer of 2007, after getting really lost and driving forty miles in the wrong direction, I found my way to the home/farm of Greg Bernhardt and Hannah Sessions. I was so late that Greg was feeding their daughter dinner and getting ready to jet off to the movies, leaving me to wander behind Hannah as she milked goats, and I feigned nonchalance as her two-year-old son kept toddling off in wellies and a diaper. Hannah was amazingly self-possessed juggling her child, her animals, her farm, and what would eventually be her cheese. Barely thirty, she and Greg took on a dilapidated cow dairy with the intention of transforming it for goats. It took two years, and they began cheese production in 2002.

Hannah is tall and blond, with the wholesome appeal of the best J. Crew models, but far more ripped from lugging hay bales and cheese curd and whatever else needs to be moved. She was so at home, moving rhythmically up and down the line of goat udders, chatting with a total stranger who had arrived at the least opportune time. I asked her how they had come to be here, making cheese, with no farming background, and her blasé response ran along the lines of "I just really like physical work." I hear that a lot from American cheesemakers who've taken up this incredibly heavy and difficult mantle for no obvious reason that I can relate to. Again and again, people say, "I want to work with my hands. I hate to sit still. I love the animals." In talking to dozens of cheesemakers, I thought I would find some cosmic explanation for choosing the relentless schedule, the incredibly long hours, and the ceaseless physicality of cheesemaking. But everyone answers like Hannah did, as if it were the most obvious thing in the world. They do it because they love it. And in many cases they can't imagine doing anything else.

Intensity and dedication, however, do not a great cheesemaker make. When I first tasted Blue Ledge's cheese, around 2005, I was thrilled to see some goat cheeses that bucked the usual style. Not just fresh chèvre or goat cheddar but a clever little bloomy rind and a hearty washed-rind, **Riley's Coat,** named after their dog (turns out Riley's fur was the same burnished red as *B. linens,* the stinky bacteria that grows atop washed-rind cheeses). But in the beginning, their cheese varied wildly. Sometimes it was good, but other times it wasn't.

You could taste, from the beginning, that Blue Ledge's milk was different. Although the small bloomy **Crottina** was pasteurized, all of its cheeses smacked of the earth. It has an incredibly diverse bit of land, with open field but also woody nooks and the damp, sinking bogs of wetlands. The complexity was apparent in the paste of the cheeses, but the rinds often ran roughshod over the fantastically nuanced flavor.

Because Blue Ledge is seasonal, we carry its cheese at Murray's only during the spring and summer months. In 2008, our first batch arrived in late April. Before that, the rind of the Crottina looked to have grown too quickly, into a thick chew that separated from the insides, so the core of each little piece lay under a tent of its own skin. The flavor used to be astringent and a tad soapy. In 2008, it was different. I sat down to taste and noticed that the rind had narrowed considerably. It was a thin, slightly papery dusting, holding tight to the dry, packed interior clay of goat cheese. It smelled complex, a little peaty even, but fresh and milky. I struggled to articulate what had changed with Crottina and finally wrote:

> *Can we say "Most Improved"? The rind is so much better. Thin, and the flavor pops. It's got a good dose of salt and it's SO rich. There's some little piquant wa-hoo in the background.*

Blue Ledge Farm at Market

Along with Champlain Valley Creamery and Twig Farm, Hannah and Greg sell their cheese at the Middlebury Farmers' Market. They can also be found at the Rutland County Farmers' Market, Tuesdays and Saturdays, from May to October. Located in Depot Park in downtown Rutland, the market may be seasonal, but the months it's open, farmers are selling rain or shine. Only 10 percent of Blue Ledge's cheese is sold directly to retailers like Murray's, so a summer foray up north is your best bet.

That's all I managed to attribute to the cheese: "wa-hoo." I was at a loss to describe what looked and tasted like a completely new cheese. Goat cheeses are often zingy and fresh, but what's mind-blowing about Crottina is the incredible richness it retains. It was a high/low flavor balance: tart yet buttery. Grassy yet earthy. The rind was as delicious as the interior, though muted, and its texture was gossamer.

Blue Ledge Farm has been making cheese for six years. It has branched out to buy milk from other goat farms so it can expand its production. It has added raw-milk cheeses. In such a short time it has embraced a lot of change. But what interests me is that, in six years, it's gone from making well-intentioned but inconsistent and often flawed cheese to making exceptional cheese. The speed of its development boggles me. Many producers take six years just to settle in and regularly produce cheese at all. Seven years ago I could count on one hand the American cheesemakers who were producing something I'd want to eat because it was objectively delicious. Hannah and Greg, along with so many others, are undeniable proof that cheesemakers are catching on, and catching up, at warp speed.

➤ CAPRIOLE GOAT CHEESE
GREENVILLE, INDIANA

"Four days ago it all started. Goats started squirting out every-where. Country living is wonderful. When it rains, you can't get on the Internet." So began my most recent phone call with Judy Schad. It's been a while since we've seen one another, but she remains an elegant, classy southern lady whose involve-ment in goats and curd never ceases to amaze me. She looks and sounds as if she should be a politician's wife, yet she spends a fair share of her days tromping around in rubber boots with her arms buried up to the elbow in warm goat milk. I bet she wears good lipstick even then. Judy holds a special place in my heart because it was one of her cheeses that, back in 2000, turned my wavering intrigue into decisive action and led me to throw my "normal" job out the window and plunge into cheese.

Judy might be considered a member of the second genera-tion of American cheesemakers who began producing with the French in mind and personal pleasure close at hand. Capriole cheese began in 1988, but it was in 1976 that Judy got the farm bug. She and her husband, an equally genteel lawyer, lived in a "gorgeous Tudor house" in Louisville, but Judy had a hard-working mother and a frugal Dutch grandmother. As her friends joined the country club, her reaction was "What are you all thinking?" Outside of her immediate Louisville enclave

The Beginning of the Plunge

Sometime after my first failed attempt at a cheese job with Steve Jenkins, and after Christmas at Eli's and some months into my legitimate corporate job, my then-boyfriend called me to say he had made us two dinner reservations. One was for a respectable 7 P.M. tasting menu, and the other, which he thought I might like, was at 9:45. I remember walking near Wall Street and saying, "There is only one restaurant in all of New York that I would wait until 9:45 to eat at." That restaurant was the newly opened Artisanal, helmed by Picholine's Terrance Brennan. Cheese was its thing, first, second, and foremost. We skipped out on the 7 P.M. at Eleven Madison Park, having only drinks and appetizers, before scuttling up to that weird, deserted space just south and east of Grand Central. Artisanal is deafeningly loud, a bustling brasserie with a halfhearted attempt at a retail cheese counter in the back. I recall two things: (1) We ate only cheese, bread, wine, and green salad for dinner. It was my first of many such meals. (2) We ordered a wonderfully wizened round of cheese like a golf ball, covered in a slightly powdery rind, sheathed in ash, moist and flaky underneath. That night, it was truly the most delicious thing I had ever eaten. The cheese was bright yet stony. It tasted ancient, all clay and minerals, but at the same time my mouth watered like that of a chronically underfed student. I loved it so deeply. It embodied everything mysterious, exciting, and awesome about cheese. I even bought one to take home. It was Judy Schad's Wabash Cannonball, and it was the cheese that resurrected all the reasons why I'd become interested in cheese in the first place. A few months later, I called Murray's for my "informational interview."

a back-to-the-land spirit fluttered. It all seemed so spontaneous, so organic. So Judy got the farm and got one of every animal to go on it, except horses because they weren't nearly productive enough and pigs because that was one step into eastern Kentucky that Judy couldn't take. So there she was, on her farm, with some goats, which she likens to excessive summer tomatoes. You have to use them, can them, jar them, or, in the case of goats, make cheese with their milk.

So that's what Judy started doing. In the early 1990s, she traveled to France under the tutelage of the French cheese ager (*affineur*) Chantal Plasse. Along with fellow American Cheese Society member Mary Keehn from Cypress Grove, Judy visited Aix-en-Provence, where she found countless goat tommes—larger-format cheeses with natural rinds built of layers of ambient mold that grow from the surrounding air. In the Loire she was yanked off the street to judge a goat cheese competition and fell hard for what she calls the "sweet, musty little thing." Not a fan of Brie and Camembert, Judy didn't aspire to make white-coated, bloomy-rinded cheese. It was the funk of the washed-rinds and the sticky, almondy *Geotrichum* mold she loved.

Back in the United States, as early as the mid-1990s, Capriole cheese was landing in New York City. I found it there in 2000. But New York holds no special appeal to Judy Schad. I believe the words she used were "I don't care if New York buys my cheese." Meaning: she would rather sell it, face-to-face with consumers, at one of the four farmers' markets she now frequents. Twenty years ago there were no farmers' markets. Louisville, Kentucky, now has seventeen, but in 1988 there were none. A cheesemaker in that neck of the country had no choice *but* to sell nationally. These days, it's a pleasantly

Capriole at Market

Judy Schad may be focused on her local market, but she works the crossroads that her backyard represents. Capriole cheeses can be found in farmers' markets in three states: Indiana, Kentucky, and Illinois. Look for them at the Bloomington Community Farmers' Market located at 401 North Morton Street in Bloomington, in Showers Common next to City Hall. It runs on Saturdays from May to October. There's also the May-to-October Saturday Broad Ripple Market in Indianapolis, located in the parking lot behind Broad Ripple High School. In Kentucky? It's the Bardstown Road Market in Louisville, on Bardstown Road next to Deer Park in the parking lot of the Presbyterian church. That runs Saturdays, April through December. Chicago's year-round Green City Market, held on Wednesdays in Lincoln Park, offers a more urban experience, albeit one that often includes famous chefs making seasonal recipes with Judy's cheese. Just as all the other farmers' markets are winding down, the Indy Winter Farmers' Market begins on Saturdays in mid-November at 2442 North Central Avenue (southwest corner at 25th and Central Avenue).

different story. The opportunity to sell at a local market means that cheesemakers starting today have it easier. One of the biggest challenges of moving cheese around the United States is that the country is so damn big. Farms beginning today enjoy the immediate markets that have only recently come to Capriole—the chance for a "small-minded person," as Judy describes herself, to sell in her own backyard.

I share Judy's opinion that America's cheese market is, pardon the bad pun, ripe with opportunity for cheesemakers to become increasingly local, so tiny producers can support themselves in their immediate vicinity. Judy's operation isn't that tiny—she milks five hundred goats on her 80 acres—but in comparison to Cypress Grove or Vermont Butter and Cheese Company she's limited. The sadness for me is less access to all of her cheeses, and to the cheeses of comparably localized cheesemakers. For you, it's a unique chance to eat exceptional cheese next time you're in Indiana, Kentucky, or Smalltown, U.S.A.

The Capriole cheese that did me in was **Wabash Cannonball**. It is still a lumpy little ball, irregular in its dips and edges like the first Christmas cookies formed by small and inexperienced hands. Beneath the damp white coat the cheese is covered in ash, creating a grayish haze that gives way to a stark, characteristically white goaty interior. Tasting Judy's cheeses recently, I was struck by their tenuously wonderful texture. So many cheeses suffer from gluey weight or grainy residue, but Capriole's are moist yet light and melting on the tongue. There's a little shop in Camden, Maine, that sells perfect fudge that sits momentarily in your mouth, apparently dense and impenetrable, and then slides away into wisps. Judy's cheeses do the same. The younger, pasteurized styles like Wabash Cannonball and **Piper's Pyramid** are notable for their creamy, cloudlike whirl. Piper's is dusted with paprika, its rusty face breaking down a thick cream line and creating a masculine, leathery finish that tastes bigger than the fleeting tartness I expect.

When Capriole makes a larger-format, aged wheel, it is always raw milk. Stink lover that I am, the mustardy yellow **Mont St. Francis** is one of my preferred. It reminds me of the obscure washed rinds of Portugal, smelling of olives and something musty and tasting barny. If I didn't know, I might guess it to be sheep milk. Again, that mastery of texture is apparent, but in firmer styles it translates into an incredibly fatty chew. Named for a nearby monastery, Mont St. Francis is beefy and full, and I've had it just over the border from Capriole at a friend's Kentucky wedding. Not surprisingly, it balanced the smooth, woody, alcoholic heat of barrel-aged bourbon just perfectly. For summertime fragrance, **Juliana**, dusted in herbes de Provence and pepper, reminds me of another sheep treasure, the Corsican round Brin d'Amour. It's not as oozing and squashy, but it offers a satisfyingly toothsome bite beneath the aromatics of rosemary, marjoram, basil, bay, thyme, and the barest echo of lavender. Capriole is one of the few American producers experimenting (and mastering) aged goat cheeses, and many remind me of the great tommes of eastern France.

> ➤ **CATO CORNER FARM**
> *COLCHESTER, CONNECTICUT*

If Cypress Grove's Mary Keehn is of the opinion that a cheese-maker should make one thing and make it well, Elizabeth MacAlister and Mark Gillman of Cato Corner Farm believe that to triumph at the farmers' market, you'd better have something for everyone. Folks come to grocery shop, and, at least in New York City, the market system in which Cato Corner participates, folks want lots and lots of choices. Some like it mild,

Cato Corner at Market

The New York City farmers' market, which in fact encompasses dozens of different locations in all five boroughs, is officially called Greenmarket. Cato Corner participates in three Greenmarkets: the flagship market in Union Square, where it can be found on Saturdays throughout the year, as well as two Brooklyn outposts: Grand Army Plaza in Park Slope and the Dekalb Avenue market in Fort Greene. Both locations are open on Saturdays all year round.

some like it runny, some want cheddar, others crave adventure. Cato Corner is feeding Manhattan and Brooklyn, with multiple Greenmarket locations. That's a lot of wants to address.

Incredibly, they are all filled by the milk of forty cows, tended by Elizabeth and transformed by her son, Mark, just outside Hartford. Like a growing number of dairies its size, Cato Corner rotationally grazes its Brown Swiss and Jersey cows on pasture from May to November, turning the herd onto a new crop of grass after each milking. All of Cato Corner's cheeses are raw milk, and they range in age from sixty days to a year.

You can see the seasonal changes in the cheese. The flavor varies throughout the year, but where I really catch variation is in the texture. Winter milk is fueled by dried hay and grain, when the cows are indoors, protected from inclement New England weather. This dried fodder, compared to summer green grass, means more fat in the cow milk. More fat means gut-bustingly creamy cheeses. On average, the percentage of fat in the milk climbs from 3.9% in summer to 5% in winter! **Hooligan**, one of my favorites from Cato Corner, sometimes bulges to the point of splitting during the winter, the thin washed rind unable to contain the gush of liquescent insides that drip and ooze out. I visited its booth at the market in March, and my only note on Hooligan was "makes me think of the rolls that bulge over your waistband. Like biting a baby's upper thigh."

The feel of this cheese, full of winter fat, is one of superlative indulgence. Come late spring and summer, the cheeses firm up; they are austere as their flavors grow truer to grass, and each bite requires a bit more chew, offers a bit more resistance. By the end of grass season, the cheese is firm and speckled with irregular holes, "eyes," that look as if some witch has pricked it with a jagged lance. You can still see the basket weave imprinted on the pale apricot rind, marks from the plastic mats the cheese rests on as it ages for sixty days, though it evokes the more romantic wooden weave of baskets that ancient farmers used to drain their cheese.

Hooligan was one of the very first American cheeses on my radar in the summer of 2002, and one that figured prominently in my research about the complexities and confusions of American cheese names. The main problem I was seeing then, and one that still challenges those of us selling this cheese, is that cheesemakers differentiate themselves from crappy mass-produced "American" cheese with the name of their unique farm and the poetics of a wily, sarcastic, or regionalized cheese name. From the consumer's point of view, it's never obvious what you're getting.

Though "Cato Corner Hooligan" doesn't promise the buyer anything, it captures the spirit of a dirty boy who will flip you the bird without a second's warning. And Hooligan is a flip-you-the-bird kind of cheese. It's stinky and sticky, and in 1997, when the farm began, this style of cheese was not widely known, let alone desired, by most shoppers. It has all the funk and obscenity of good French monastery cheeses like Livarot. I loved Hooligan, loved the salty lick from the outside and the smell I can only describe as cat-butty. I have cats, and I love them, but they do stick their butts in your face sometimes. At the very center, when the cheese isn't perfectly ripe, you get a breath of yogurt, and surrounding it is the plush, meaty flesh of the cheese. I loved that I could go buy it directly from the cheesemaker at the farmers' market, and Mark, with his incredibly tall, lanky frame, translucent skin, and shock of red hair and beard, seemed like some kind of wondrous, elongated cheese gnome. I felt I had found something special and excitedly brought it back to the counter of Murray's, proud of what I'd discovered and thinking we could sell it at the store.

I was sorely rebuffed. Everyone on the counter circa 2002 had a dozen reasons why my idea was crap: it was too expensive, it wasn't good, it was good only that day but not other days, nobody wanted that, we had so many great French cheeses, it would languish in the case, and so on and so on. In the beginning Hooligan *was* inconsistent, and back then it was a lot more expensive than the European cheeses (oh, back in the day when the euro cost 80 cents!), but I just remember it being funky and delicious and feeling as if it were some marvelous secret.

It's still the only Cato Corner cheese we carry at Murray's

with any regularity, mainly because the supplies are limited and most goes to the farmers' market. Why sell to a store at a lower price when you can sell out direct to consumers at a higher price? When I'm wandering the market, I graze through their many selections. There are ten (!) core choices and then variations on those as the cheese is aged for additional periods of time. There are semisoft, buttery, mild table cheeses, good for noshing (**Bridgid's Abbey, Dutch Farmstead**), a range of pungent stinkers that I have a soft spot for (Hooligan, **Despearado, Drunken Hooligan, Drunk Monk, Fromage d'O'Cow**), occasionally a cheddar (**Jeremy River**), a cow milk interpretation of Manchego (**Womanchego**), firmer, nuttier specimens (**Bloomsday, Vivace**), some blues (**Black Ledge Blue** and **Misty Morning**), and on and on.

For thoughtless satisfaction, I'll take Dutch Farmstead over Bridgid's Abbey for its total buttery yum. It's really straightforward, the interior moist and heavy and begging to be heated into a butterfatty pool without a whiff of sharpness or intensity. Limp. Bridgid's Abbey is more complex and tangier, with a yogurty bite. The washed-rinds are all amazing, variations on Hooligan washed in pear mash and eau-de-vie for golden, mushy fall fruit roundness (Despearado) or nutty and wheaty doused with Willimantic Brewing Company's brown ale (Drunk Monk). Fromage d'O'Cow is simply a larger, flatter wheel, Hooligan's big brother, but the size variation delivers a firmer, richer texture and intensely savory notes, like slow-roasted, oil-drenched garlic.

Cato Corner captures savory notes really well, and Black Ledge Blue, though it looks mold-dappled and kind of funky on the outside, is dense and smooth inside, without the typical wet crumble and excessive salt of so many blues, American or otherwise. The overwhelming impression is one of spoonfuls of crunchy, meaty bits, carefully scraped from the bottom of a well-used cast iron pan. Cato Corner's cheeses can be found in shops across New England and even a few nationally, certainly in New York, at many restaurant tables, and relatively easily online, but its focus and commitment are firmly on its customers at the farmers' market. They will deny their cheese to the retailers first, the restaurants second, but never to the people who come shop face-to-face in New York every week.

➤ CHAMPLAIN VALLEY CREAMERY
VERGENNES, VERMONT

Champlain Valley Creamery is, for me, synonymous with a single word: Yoder. Yoder is Carlton Yoder to you, and he's the cheesemaker and owner of CVC. Yoder turned up at Murray's in 2005 with the simplest of things but absolutely impossible to find: old-fashioned **cream cheese** without any kind of crap in it to stabilize, preserve, or otherwise gum the whole thing up. Cream cheese is really just a fresh cultured cheese that's allowed to acidify very slowly, turning in the course of a night from milk into a thick pudding that is scooped from the vat, hand-salted, and packed into little plastic tubs. Here's the thing about real cream cheese: it has flavor. It's not the Philadelphia you know—it's much thicker (like the difference between Greek-style yogurt and regular yogurt) and considerably tangier. I was so excited when Yoder showed up that we took the cheese over to the New York institution Russ & Daughters, where the smoked salmon, sturgeon, trout, and three dozen other fishes are sliced by hand for that essential New York Sunday breakfast of bagels and lox. We showed up, waving this amazing, organic cream cheese as thick as spackle, and Mark Federman, the owner, took one taste and told me there was no way he would buy the cream cheese—because it had way too much flavor. It wasn't what people expected from cream cheese. Correct! Because for the last fifty years we've all been tricked with junky gummy milk spread masquerading as cream cheese.

Open a tub of Yoder's goods, and you can see that the cream cheese isn't really white. The plastic container is white. The cream cheese is the color of wedding cake icing. I hadn't tasted it in a while, so I opened one up and began to eat it straight off the knife. If mozzarella were made spreadable, it would taste like this. The knife makes a quiet ripping sound when you dig a chunk out, and it's flakier than any cream cheese you've had before. Much milder than sour cream, the cheese itself tastes like completely clean, rich, grassy milk. It's a softer, sweeter taste than yogurt. It's just really delicious.

Yoder is also making a triple crème called **Champlain Triple**. He warned me that my sample was young, but at two weeks I thought it was perfect. In fact, I got the distinct impression that with many more days the horsey-leathery notes of the rind would devolve into bitterness, with a whiff of dirty stable. It's much fluffier than, say, Cowgirl Creamery Mt. Tam, and I like the earthen edge. Some of my favorite French triple crèmes have it, and they're a lot more interesting than the typical butter and salt of industrial triples.

All of Yoder's milk is pasteurized (it has to be for this fresh stuff that's never more than two weeks old) and certified

> ### Champlain Valley Creamery
> ### at Market
>
> If you're lucky, you'll find Yoder at the Middlebury Farmers'
> Market, held each Wednesday and Saturday at Marble Works by
> the Falls. The market is seasonal and open from May to October.
> Yoder is usually there with his wife, Moira, and their ridiculously
> plump, bouncy daughter, Little Yoder, aka Lila.

organic, from a single dairy in nearby Bridport milking Brown
Swiss, Holstein, and Jersey cows.

➤ ESTRELLA FAMILY CREAMERY
MONTESANO, WASHINGTON

Estrella is a cult thing. I wish I could say I've visited the farm,
but I haven't. I would like to report a deep and intimate knowledge of its cheese, but it's hard to find beyond the Pacific
Northwest. In truth, I e-mailed Kelli Estrella with breath held
and fingers crossed that she would send me even a few tiny
samples to taste. She did, very pleasantly, after several weeks.

Although its herd of cows and goats is milked twice daily
and cheese is sometimes made as frequently, the quantities are
small. The selection, however, is vast. There were eighteen
cheeses at last count. There is something unusual about this
family. In 2001, the Estrellas moved to their current 180-acre
property, looked around their dining room table with their
three children, and saw abundant food. There were empty

Estrella Family Creamery at Market

On Saturdays, Estrella Family Creamery cheese can be found in Seattle's University District Farmers' Market. It's the city's oldest and largest farmers-only market, founded in 1993 and operating annually with more than fifty participating Washington State farmers. On Sundays, look to the year-round Ballard Avenue Market. EFC can also be found in small area shops—if you're lucky.

seats. So they went out and adopted three children from Liberia. They now raise these six clever, curious, beautiful kids on the farm, where everyone shares the work of animal tending, milking, and cheesemaking.

Estrella Family Creamery is a grass-based dairy, with temperate enough weather that the animals can forage year-round on organically managed pastures, and the cheeses are all made from raw milk. That's true for many cheesemakers, though. So why is its cheese so magnificently different? When I have traveled in France, to the kinds of farms everyone imagines but few of which actually exist, the cheese tastes like its place. In Provence, a herd of Rove goats, the country's first domesticated breed, with their enormous curving brown horns, plucked through dry, dusty summer fields and stood on their hind legs to peel leaves from the drooping summer trees. There, the cheese was dusky with sarriette, the milk smelling of fresh-stripped bark. Up on the ancient volcanic plateau of Auvergne,

Salers cows ambled through fogged-out green pastures, their hollow, eerie cowbells clanging across the land. The cheese was moist and dank, smelling of the packed soil room where the wheels aged, the sour cheddary paste balanced by ashy minerality. It was like eating the air, the water, the soul of the place.

Estrella cheese does the same thing. It's superlative: complex and "old world" in a way that's hard to articulate. It feels ancient, connected to the earth in a profound and unequivocal way. With eighteen choices, I'm not going to love every single cheese, but truly, there aren't any bad ones. **Brewleggio** is a raw cow variant on Taleggio: plumper, pocked with holes, and sporting a rind that looks dappled in mildew but so much better and more interesting. All that interior air makes a mouthful like biting a squashy down pillow. It feels pleasing. The flavor is fruitier, milk-fatty and lush. **Jalapeno Buttery** is a trimilk mix of cow, goat, and sheep, a creamy, semisoft table cheese laced with chunks of fresh jalapeno. I don't know a single cheesemaker who uses fresh pepper. Everyone uses canned or jarred peppers. The heat of fresh peppers is totally absent. Until you bite down on one. Then it's insanely jalapeno spicy. When I tasted it I wrote, "Milky, fresh . . . Really hot!!! Shit!!!" There's the charmingly named **Weebles**, modeled after a Balkan Provolone/kashkaval into the classic gourd shape. You know the song: "Weebles wobble, but they won't fall down!" Weebles were those egg-shaped children's toys that bopped right and left but never tipped over. This cheese will tip over, because it's shaped like a pear. It's also smoked over alderwood and aged for four months. That choice of wood makes the creamy, semifirm paste smoky but extremely delicate, like smoldering birch bark.

Bleu Mont Dairy and Fantôme Farm at Market

The Dane County Farmers' Market on the square in Madison, Wisconsin, is the nation's largest, with an average of 30,000 to 40,000 visitors each week. The market is open on Saturdays and Wednesdays, April through November. Farmers are outdoors around Capitol Square in the summer, and indoors from November to April.

Two of my favorites reminded me of the elusive French goat cheese Chevrotin des Aravis, made in the Chaîne des Aravis in the mountainous Savoie. We can't import it anymore because it's illegal, but it's such a pristine, seductive cheese. Estrella's **Red Darla** may lead to expletives. I wasn't the only one who started cursing, and I was tasting with five coworkers. The smallish wheels are plump, shiny, and bulging, the rind washed in red wine though the fruity, tannic implications are reduced to a dank, stewy brew that punctuates the eggy paste within.

Caldwell Crik Chevrette, blended from cow and goat milk and named for the on-property creek, is another washed-rind, with higher tang from the goat milk and a funky, meatier lull than Red Darla's, more akin to a good mold-ripened crespone. A little bit petrolly, even. **Grisdale Goat** is all straw, sweet, aged goat milk and nut skin, and then there are **Sublime, Valentina, Gaupier, Old Apple Tree Tomme, Montesano**, and on, and on.

➤ FANTÔME FARM
RIDGEWAY, WISCONSIN

Anne Topham and Judy Borree have been making goat cheese since 1984 and sell everything they produce from their ten to twelve goats at Dane County. They make some of the best-aged mold-ripened goat cheeses I've had in the United States, and though they are all pasteurized, there is an incredible depth of flavor. The cheese smacks of the land. Their fresh **chèvre** is buttery with sour cream acidity and is whipped when salt is added, making the texture incredibly airy and fluffy. What's interesting is that Anne uses cultures traditionally used for butter and buttermilk production. The acidification is an incredibly slow eighteen to twenty hours, which brings out the distinctive flavors of butter, unusual for a goat cheese. There are ashed and aged styles. I was recently able to taste **Fleurie Noir** in both fresh and aged versions. The cheese is deeply impressive. The salting in the fresh is perfect, and the thick, dusty molded rind of the aged smells of grass and soil.

➤ GOAT LADY DAIRY
CLIMAX, NORTH CAROLINA

My spring of 2008 began at the communal table of Goat Lady Dairy, with Steve Tate, his wife and son, my old cheese friend Tia, my new cider-making friend Diane Flynt, and Steve's sister Ginnie, who bought this 200-acre homestead as a hobby farm in 1984. We had verdant boughs of asparagus, snapped from the side garden, and warm homemade bread slathered with orange-yolked clots of egg salad courtesy of the green-speckled hens a dozen

Goat Lady Dairy at Market

Goat Lady Dairy can be found at the Greensboro Farmers' Curb Market and the Piedmont Triad Farmers' Market. The origins of the Curb Market date to 1874, making it one of the oldest markets in North Carolina. The market is open year-round on Saturdays, in the old National Guard Armory building in Greensboro. The Piedmont Triad market is open on Saturday and Sunday, year-round, in Colfax, North Carolina.

yards away. And cheese. Sometimes you eat a meal that puts the pieces of your soul back together. I didn't want to leave.

Goat Lady (that's Ginnie the name refers to) began as part of the second wave of new American cheesemakers. These are the pleasure seekers, inspired by the delicate and mysterious cheeses of France. These days, 20 percent of the farm's income comes from its nifty Farm Dinner program, where forty-six guests pay to eat dinner or Sunday brunch on the farm, made from the meat, produce, eggs, and cheese produced on-site. The other 80 percent comes from farmers' market sales of cheese, made from the milk of their 130 Alpine, Nubian, and Saanen goats.

Over lunch, Steve told me a story about visiting cheese-makers in the Italian Alps. His group wanted to know how these young Italian men had learned to make cheese. Apparently the translator went back and forth trying to communicate this most baffling question. In the end, the inquiry was abandoned. The answer, it seems, was that the ability to make cheese simply was. Like tying your shoes. These Italian men had no recollection of learning, because cheese was simply what they did. Americans, including Steve, don't have that luxury of inheritance. He figured it out as he went, taking over from Ginnie when increasingly scientific methods became necessary. "Too much technology can ruin the handmade," warned Steve, "but you need just enough to keep it consistent." Remember, this is a man who was (and still is) fighting the popular North Carolina assumption that goat cheese is all pissy and terrible. In the case of Steve's cheese this is not in fact the case; his offerings are nearly as restorative as lunch at the Goat Lady farm table. My notes from that gracious afternoon:

Sandy Creek looks exactly like a mini Humboldt Fog (see Cypress Grove, page 192). At about six ounces it, too, is pasteurized, with a lovely, thin, manageable bloomy rind and drier, slightly pasty texture. Good salt. Taste the grapevine. Steve just says—the way the ash attracts that blue flavor. Clay. Pasteurized.

Providence is kinda like Italian Taleggio but drier curd, more acidity. Less retained moisture in the finished product. Brined for 24 hours. Washed 1x week. Raw milk. Doesn't taste like a washed-rind. It's got the salt of a washed-rind but the smooth sweetness of aged goat milk. Like Garrotxa. A milky sweetness, like chewy caramels. Curd is cooked for 5 minutes, to 90–95 degrees. Pressing is done only by flipping. Maybe a tad too much salt? My teeth sink in. Creamy. Grape on the finish.

Smoky Mountain Round: Little nugget of fresh goat. Moister than Up in Smoke. Wet and smooth.

*Churned in the mixer? No—hand-salted. Doesn't have
that tiny, nearly grainy curd most freshies do. Very smoky.
It's all you taste, but I don't mind. Texture like delicate
custard. Light light, smearable.*

Goat Lady also makes pasteurized **fresh chèvre,** spreadable, in nine flavors, which is churned in a mixer to salt it, as well as **Camembert, crottin, feta, marinated chèvre,** and aged **Grey's Chapel**.

➤ TWIG FARM
WEST CORNWALL, VERMONT

My drive to Twig Farm in early summer was one of many visits undertaken to answer the question "How and why do people become cheesemakers?" Twig is three people: the cheesemaker and goat herder, Michael Lee; the marketing/business maven, at-home consultant, and wife of Michael, Emily Sunderman; and their rambunctious, goat-chasing son, Carter. Their driveway is easy to miss, and I drove past it three times before turning down a leafy, shadowed dirt road that wound its way to a sleek, modern, L-shaped building made of smooth, bright green metal. I would be lying to say I wasn't a tiny bit disappointed. Where was the farm? The porch? The rolling fields? What was this new, shiny thing in the middle of the woods? What were the woods doing there, anyway? Didn't animals graze in rolling fields of lush green grass?

I know well enough to know that the answer is: It depends on the animal. When I visited a goat cheesemaker in Provence some summers ago, I followed his goats down blowsy, dusty dirt roads, out of the beating summer sun, and into scraggly, maze-like paths that ran through heat-baked brush. Every few feet a goat would stop, hop up on its hind legs, its hooves propped against a tree trunk, and delicately, efficiently, and effortlessly strip leaves from branches. Twig's goats are no different.

After lunch on the shaded cement slab that runs between the house and the milking parlor (Emily served sandwiches made with their own **Goat Tomme**, and I was shocked that the thick, nubbly gray rind had been left intact; between bread, with garnish, it was chewy and woodsy, like pine nuts and ferny milk, awesome and delicious), I followed Michael to retrieve the goats for milking. He offered me a cup of fresh, frothy goat milk, and I obligingly took a big swig while he watched, encouragingly. "What does it taste like?" came the excited inquiry. And I thought. Well, it tastes like goat milk, which is like foamy, pulverized, powdery goat cheese but warm, and liquid. It was unusual, even for me, and a little weird.

Michael's smile drooped as he took a sip, and then came the immediate correction: "Don't you taste it? Oh yeah, they got into a lot of bark today." See? Even my palate needs refinement. Goats like bark and twigs, sticks and strips, herbs, flowers, leaves, and bits, nuts when they can get them, although too many or the wrong kind can be poisonous; they'll munch grass but prefer to pick and sort while their twitchy stub tails wiggle like short, furry rattlesnakes.

The Lees left Boston to follow Michael's dream of cheesemaking (after buying and selling it at the retailer Formaggio Kitchen), and returned to Emily's ancestral land (her dad's property is adjacent) to give it a go. Emily is the kind of woman I wish I lived closer to so we might be friends, and even in the country she keeps one foot planted in the niceties of urban living. She telecommutes, and her home office (and their home in general) manages to be comfortable but incredibly cool, filled with enormous, glorious paintings by Michael, Emily's musical instruments, floods of sunny light, books, and neat little kid toys.

Michael's philosophy on cheese is not dissimilar to that of Mateo Kehler, the young cheesemaker turned ager who now distributes Twig's cheese outside New England. None of Twig Farm's cheeses is pasteurized. Why, Michael asks, would I go to such great lengths to make exceptional milk, only to pasteurize it? The cheese, in other words, is merely a humble vehicle for that lathery, barky milk. The herd is small, twenty-five goats. Michael makes a range of cheeses, though only seasonally, because the milk flows from March to November, and the requisite sixty aging days means spring-through-Christmas availability.

Especially for such a new cheesemaker (Twig started in 2004), the cheese is excellent. A big part of the appeal for me is that there are a million fresh chèvres but a mere handful of aged goats with rinds, and an even smaller subsection of rinds that are thick and aromatic, smelling of earth and forage. Twig's cheeses are surprisingly French in character, although unlike most French cheeses that come quickly to mind. They are of the earth, of the patch of land surrounding Michael and Emily's slick green home.

The first I tasted was Goat Tomme, and I was delighted because it reminded me of the greatest version of one of Spain's greatest cheeses, Garrotxa, the one produced by the farm called La Bauma, which I visited in the summer of 2003. The rind has the velvety fuzz of reindeer antlers, but gray and slightly damp. Inside, the semisoft, bone-colored paste is chewy and moist. As goat cheese ages, the acidic tang mellows and the sweetness isn't like that of buttery rich Brie types. No, it's soft,

Twig Farm at Market

As if the draw of Yoder alone weren't enough to get you to Middlebury, Michael, Emily, and Carter spend summer Saturdays selling from the back of a pickup. They are also distributed to the country's best small cheese shops by the Cellars at Jasper Hill.

and woodsy. There's something piney about it, pine-nutty, all green, wet branches after you swallow the first crumbling bite. Goat Tomme hangs in that delicate balance between rustic, earthy, and refined. The Lees blend their own raw milk with that of goats from Dan Robertshaw's neighboring farm in Bridport. I know of few cheeses like it and relish every chance I get to gnaw away. The placidly named **Square Cheese** is not dissimilar, though square rather than cylindrical in shape. It's actually tied in cloth, which is knotted atop the cheese, its weight pressing into the center and contorting the whole thing into a deformed, gray, furry Hershey's Kiss. Unlike Goat Tomme, the milk is exclusively Twig's, making the cheese a true farmstead.

Soft Wheel (aka **Washed Rind Wheel**) calls it like it is. It's soft. It's washed-rind. It's raw goat, occasionally cut with Joe Severy's cow milk when supplies are running low. The wheels are tangerine-colored and sticky, pungent and lush, with a squidgy, pudgy layer under the rind. The perfect dose of salt, meaty, but again tempered by the sweetness of woody, aged goat milk. Each little bite is succulent and sags slightly at the edges, with an eternal finish of hazelnuts and grass.

THE ROGUE CHEESEMAKERS AND THE FUTURE OF AMERICAN CHEESE

A CHAPTER ABOUT ROGUE CHEESEMAKERS BEGAN AS A NIFTY play on words. It wasn't immediately clear where to put my notes on Rogue Creamery. Its origins and Vella connection might make it a "factory" cheesemaker. But its commitment to entirely handmade cheese didn't fit with the other factory producers. Then there were the restaurants that line up every winter to clean Murray's out of Rogue River Blue. Perhaps Rogue belonged in the chapter with chefs. Then there's the commitment to pastured animals. Rogue has a lot in common with the producers from Down South. What about associating them with grass? In fitting everywhere, Rogue Creamery seemed to fit nowhere, as do many American cheesemakers in this book who are pioneering or loved by chefs: a natural-rinded sheep cheese, but also a grass-based dairy. A cheddar that's sold primarily at the farmers' market. Classifying these complex cheeses by one trend, one mission, one identity is nearly impossible. So perhaps a catchall chapter for the rogue cheesemakers was the answer. Everyone I couldn't neatly compartmentalize in one chapter or another would wind up rogue. That was the initial idea, anyway.

Over the past year, I've realized that the rogue cheesemakers are something else entirely. They can't be rogue if their multidimensional farm or cheese so closely resembles the multidimensionality of many American cheesemakers. No, the rogue cheesemakers are the pioneers of the Next Generation of American cheese. They are, in 2009, what the goat ladies were in 1982: a small group that will shape and determine the next thirty years of American cheesemaking. Each has, in kind, latched onto an essential element of cheese: what animals eat, how cheese is aged and distributed, and the expanding markets for artisan American cheesemakers. Spread out across the country, of varying sizes, with disparate goals, the rogue cheesemakers are my first inkling of the future of American cheese.

GRASS: ESSENTIAL FOOD FOR SUSTAINABLE CHEESE

➤ EDELWEISS GRAZIERS COOPERATIVE
MONTICELLO, WISCONSIN

In 1993, two families in southern Wisconsin decided to change their farming methods. Rather than maintain a confinement operation, growing feed outside to bring to cows inside, they broke with their neighbors (and many of the traditions they had been raised with) and undertook an intensive rotational grazing approach to feed their cows grass. What they saw was animals with fewer health problems, improved pastures, less soil erosion, declining fuel use, and a changing flavor profile in their milk. The Master Cheesemakers of the sister companies Edelweiss Creamery and Maple Leaf Cheese agreed to try a batch of cheese with this milk alone, and together in 2006 they formed the Edelweiss Graziers Cooperative. Since then, three more families have joined the cooperative and committed to the following standards:

- The cows' intake must be a minimum of 60 percent grass.
- Each farm must provide a minimum of 1.5 acres per cow.
- No silage (fermented hay, corn, etc.) may be fed to the cows.
- Fencing must be moved every twelve hours so the cows are on fresh pasture.

Because the weather in Wisconsin allows grazing only from April to December, the members of the Graziers Cooperative dry off their cows (stop milking) for the fall and winter months or continue milking, with the cows inside eating hay and grain, and sell their milk for conventional cheesemaking.

I first learned of the Graziers Cooperative when I visited Maple Leaf in the fall of 2007. Jeff Wideman, Maple Leaf's Master Cheesemaker, mentioned that the five farmers in the cooperative believed they had healthier animals, not just from their pastured diet but from the walking they do to and from the milking parlor twice each day. He threw out that comment, and I prepared for him to tell me why these farmers were kind of delusional and why their animals weren't, in fact, any healthier than anyone else's. Cynically, I always expect old-timers to be suspicious of newfangled trends in milk, dairy, and cheese. But sometimes I'm reminded that the old-timers recall when *everyone* did it this way. And Jeff said, "It's true. If you look at their vet bills, they're much lower than everyone else's."

Lower vet bills are but one illustration of the increased economic value all the co-op members are experiencing with their grass-based approach. The Holstroms, the fourth family to join the Graziers, turned to pasture not for idealistic reasons but because the cost of raising crops to feed their herd was crushing the viability of their farm. Although many of the Graziers milk only from April to October, the reduction in overhead, equipment, and feed, combined with the animals' excellent health, makes this method of farming more profitable.

There are plenty of cheesemakers in America practicing a grass-based approach, but the Graziers represent an exceptional commitment on the part of an otherwise traditional Wisconsin cheesemaking factory. Graziers' milk is being made into cheddar and Gouda, as well as some of the larger, traditional wheels of Emmenthaler that Edelweiss is known for. The partnership between factory and dairy is strong—critical, in this case, to add value to the milk of these farms. But the Graziers are demonstrating that small, grass-based dairies (member Tim Pauli has twenty-seven cows) can be more profitable than larger conventional ones; that such farms can preserve and even improve the land on which they operate; and that the milk, and thus the cheese, they yield can be higher in vitamin A, beta-carotene, and conjugated linoleic acid (CLA). Edelweiss has acknowledged the increased value of this milk and understands that it can be marketed and sold as a premium product. In the summer of 2008, as gas tipped $4.50 a gallon and the price of corn and soybeans had climbed by 80 percent in the previous year, I could only hope that dairy farmers struggling to pay their bills embrace the methods that have sustained farms for hundreds of years: family-sized operations feeding their warm-weather herd on grass and locally produced hay and forage through the winter. And that the cheesemakers with resources to buy, transform, and market this milk in the form of delicious cheese get on board the vital importance of grass. It's a premium product, and it will garner a premium price.

AGING AND DISTRIBUTION: THE CRITICAL CHALLENGE OF GETTING GOOD CHEESE TO MARKET

➤ THE CELLARS AT JASPER HILL
GREENSBORO, VERMONT

When Jasper Hill was getting started, Mateo Kehler constantly reminded me of the challenge of cheese—after it was made. I would have thought that postmake was the easy part: the farming, the cleaning, the animals, the recipes, even the bookkeeping, those seemed challenging. But the cheese aging? That was a simple, straightforward matter of turning, patting, washing, brushing, and cleaning. Time-consuming, yes. But straightforward. Practically speaking, however, time is what cheesemakers lack. They can't skip milking, cheesemaking, vet visits, sales calls, boxing and shipping of product. But they can skip thrice-weekly turns and pats of the cheese and instead do it only once. They can cut those corners, but the ultimate quality of the cheese suffers.

The concept of the Cellars grew from these restrictive realities for the small cheesemaker. But there were also the demand by and interest of the large cheesemakers. You may recall that the neighboring Cabot Creamery wished to make a traditional, clothbound wheel of cheddar but had nowhere to put such a thing. Vermont Shepherd had been unable to handle the maintenance of such a project for precisely the reasons listed above. It was too small to do everything. And so, looking to the *affinage* models of England and France, Jasper Hill Farm undertook the construction of an 18,000-square-foot aging facility, known as the Cellars at Jasper Hill. The first of its kind in the United States, its purpose is to allow farmers and cheesemakers to focus on their craft (cheese, and in some cases animals) while turning the aging, marketing, and sales over to someone who can do it properly.

The potential for the Cellars' model is precisely its egalitarian selection. In fact, the whole balance rests on bigger cheeses from bigger producers, whose greater name recognition can capture a national market. There is virtually unlimited opportunity for better versions of the everyday cheeses Americans know from the supermarket: cheddar, Colby, Gouda, and the like. In partnering with cheesemakers and aging their wheels to a finer final flavor, the Cellars at Jasper Hill can begin to meet the insatiable market demand for good (but familiar) cheese. Along the way, smaller farmhouse cheese-makers can ride that demand to better cheese of their own *and* easier distribution.

One of the greatest challenges small American producers face is national distribution. Hundreds of cheesemakers, each making a handful of products, do not hit the critical mass necessary to move pallets of cheese by truck. Most rely on specialized couriers like FedEx and UPS to transport ten pounds here or forty pounds there. The result is exceedingly high transportation costs attached to a cheese that might begin its life at ten or twelve dollars a pound in the first place. Small American cheesemakers are hobbled by their inability to get product to market affordably. Larger producers, meanwhile, are continually searching for the next great cheese that will boost sales, improve brand awareness, and generally grow the value of their companies, at a time when the country is asking, with more and more insistence, for (in Mary Keehn's words) "something real." A better-crafted cheese, made with higher-quality milk, represents a far greater long-term value than another block cheddar with wasabi powder, salsa and lime, or whatever flavor a commodity producer can conjure up. In other words, small cheesemakers need the volume and distribution system of big guys, and factory cheesemakers need the cachet, craft, and flavor represented by the little guys. The Cellars at Jasper Hill is the first vehicle to enable this symbiosis.

At day's end, the Cellars offer partnership and Jasper Hill's stellar reputation as cheesemaker (and media darling) to producers of all sizes across the state of Vermont. It's an incredibly exciting model of centralized aging and distribution, one that can, in the coming decades, be regionally duplicated across America.

ABROAD: THE NEXT FRONTIER
FOR AMERICAN CHEESE

The export of American cheese is nothing new. As the world's largest milk supplier and the producer of more than 25 percent of the world's cheese, much of what this country makes is sent elsewhere. More than 64,000 tons, in fact. The very systems of dairying that I condemn, and the commodity machines that produce 10 million pounds of cheese a day, are feeding a world market. America's modern "efficiencies," such as year-round milk production, quick-freezing technologies, processed, emulsified cheese, and cheese powder are exported to nearly every country in the world.

The world's concept of American cheese has been limited to those commodified efficiencies. America makes the world's supply of dairy-originated junk. The idea that anyone would want, heck, that America even *made* cheese that could sit alongside English, Italian, or French offerings on a market counter was unheard of. Until 2003. That year, Rogue Creamery's Rogue River Blue won Best Blue Cheese at the World Cheese Championship in London. It beat the best of Stilton, Gorgonzola, and Roquefort, and quietly, a bit of interest blossomed. The first who inquired was Randolph Hodgson, the owner of the famed London retailer and exporter Neal's Yard Dairy. Then came stirrings from Whole Foods, as it prepared to open its first overseas outpost on Kensington High Street. No artisan American cheese had been exported, and, to further complicate matters, no raw-milk American cheese had ever been exported. The language for the export of raw-milk cheese did not exist, and Rogue found that adding a single sentence, a brief provision, to the FDA's approved export forms was a process that would take three to five years. With no real order, only insinuated interest, Rogue lacked the muscle to initiate governmental change. In October 2004, Neal's Yard Dairy placed a formal order for one hundred wheels of Rogue River Blue, and Rogue began the labyrinthian negotiations with the FDA, FSA (Food Safety Administration), and USDA to gain permission for the export of its raw-milk blue.

The availability of Rogue's cheese is limited, even here in the States. So why, I asked David Gremmels, would it even want to ship its cheese to London? It couldn't even meet the demand at home. David acknowledged that it was a boon for their brand to sit alongside the best cheese in the world at Neal's Yard Dairy and other overseas retailers, but even more so, that modifying U.S. export regulations would secure the future of American raw-milk cheese. "It's not just Rogue River, it's the greater group of farmstead and artisan raw-milk cheese we were advocating export for." Alloting some of its precious Rogue River Blue allowed them to "put its best foot forward."

With little forward motion by 2006, Whole Foods' global cheese buyer, Cathy Strange, threw the muscle of her global reach and sales volume into the project and organized a reception for, among others, the head of the FDA for Great Britain. Rogue pulled in the support of its senator, governor, and congressmen to advocate for the regulatory change. And in October 2007 it was approved. Randolph's hundred wheels arrived in England just after New Year's, in January 2008. In addition to the British market, Rogue is now exporting to Canada and to Japan, which, despite a lack of dairy in its traditional cuisine, has a growing and aggressive interest in fine cheese. Rogue's goal for 2009 is to export the first consolidated pallet of American farmstead and artisan raw-milk cheeses, not just its own but that of other producers. It seems a probable outcome as Uplands Cheese Company has also begun the laborious paperwork for export privileges, and expects to expand its market to the United Kingdom in the summer of 2009.

I remember a time, less than ten years ago, when New York City was the emerging market for this misunderstood food that everyone had heard of but nobody really knew: "American cheese." Now I can see the time when American cheese will mean something beyond a processed abomination. It will come from a diverse range of healthy animals, not just cows, that eat from the land. It will not taste the same every time, because it will be made by hundreds of cheesemakers, all striving for their own balanced minerality, fruity complexity, or milky sharpness. It will be lauded as good for you because it is a simple, unprocessed food made from a mere three ingredients. It will not be viewed as the fuel of heart attacks and obesity, because it is real food and our bodies know how to break it down and use it efficiently long after we've savored a bite of something that tastes truly excellent. It will be available in varying shapes and sizes at local markets and national chains. It will be sought by countries that recognize the United States as a producer of traditional food, not just cheap food and lots of it. It will change the landscape, because people will know that they can support their families and still operate on a human scale.

Several years ago, my mother asked me why I would spend so much of my money on food when I could spend so much less. I remember this aching incredulity because I couldn't begin to imagine how she could ask such a thing. My answer was simple: I buy the best food I can because I put it inside my body no fewer than six times a day. I can't imagine *anything* more important to demand the best of than food. Luckily for me—and for us—there are thousands of simple, miraculous cheeses being made all across this country, and a small wedge can be bought by anyone. One day, all our kitchens will be stocked with local cheeses instead of chips, and I really believe that day isn't so far off. This is the future of American cheese.

APPENDIX
COMMON MILKING BREEDS

Cows

Cows are enormous milk producers, weighing up to 1,500 pounds and requiring vast areas of open space to graze and masticate. Their milk cycle lasts three hundred days, and at peak lactation a cow produces up to 120 pounds (or 60 pints) of milk each day. Despite the characterization of milk as white, cow's milk has a yellowish cast from the beta-carotene in a grass-based diet. The exception to this is Ayrshire cows' milk, which is pure white regardless of the cows' diet.

> *Abondance:* The famed French mountain cheese Abondance takes its name from this breed of golden brown cow with white head, belly, and legs whose milk is also used for the Haute-Savoie cheeses Beaufort, Reblochon, and Tomme des Bauges. American producers have begun cross-breeding their herds with Abondance

stock, as the animals are known for their ability to with-stand extreme temperature variations, making them ideal for grass-based operations. They are also especially fertile.

Ayrshire: Ayrshires came to the United States in 1822 from the county of Ayr in Scotland. Their color varies from light to deep cherry red, mahogany, brown, or a combination of these colors with white. Some are all white. Ayrshire milk has a moderate level of butterfat and a relatively high protein content. The Ayrshire is unique because it was bred for cheesemaking rather than butter production. In butter production, the goal is fast separation of cream from milk for easy skimming. Ayrshires' milk, on the other hand, is naturally homogenized; the fat remains suspended throughout the milk, and there is less chance of rancidity as the fats break down in aging wheels of cheese. A mature Ayrshire can weigh up to 1,200 pounds.

Brown Swiss: Brown Swiss is one of the oldest dairy breeds in the world. It came to the United States from Switzerland in 1869 and ranges in color from light to dark brown. Brown Swiss have the best fat-to-protein ratio for cheese-making of any dairy breed. For this reason, Brown Swiss producers regularly produce more cheese for their milk than cheesemakers with other breeds. Brown Swiss milk is extremely high in protein, and the cows are prized for their ability to adapt easily to a variety of different climates.

Dutch Belted: The "belt" is a band of white that wraps around the cow's midsection, balanced by a black head and trunk. The breed descends from the belted cattle of Switzerland and Austria and was established in the Netherlands in the seventeenth century. First imported in 1838 to the United States, they were exhibited as a rare and aristocratic breed by the circus man P. T. Barnum, who later found them to be great milkers on his New York farm. The breed is known for its grazing ability and efficient conversion of grass to milk. Of moderate size (somewhere between Holsteins and Jerseys), Dutch Belteds give milk of 3.5 to 5.5 percent butterfat, with unusually small fat globules, making the milk naturally homogenized and superb for cheesemaking.

Guernsey: Guernseys came to the United States in 1831 from the English Channel isle of Guernsey, off the coast of France. Their color is a shade of fawn with white markings, and they weigh 1,150 pounds when mature. Guernseys are known for producing high-butterfat, high-protein milk of a distinctive golden color, indicative of a high concentration of beta-carotene. Guernseys are known for their ease of calving and ability to produce milk efficiently from less feed, making them excellent grazers ideal for pasture-based milk production.

Holstein: Thanks to the breed's flexibility, productivity, and economical milk production, the Holstein is now the most common breed of dairy cattle around the world. In the United States, Holsteins constitute 90 percent of the 10 million dairy cow population. The Holstein's most outstanding characteristic is its combination of a high volume of milk production at an acceptable milk fat percentage. Typical Holstein milk is 3 to 4 percent milk fat.

Jersey: Originating not in the state of New Jersey but on the English Channel isle of Jersey, these relatively small (900 pounds), fawn-colored cows are the smallest of all dairy cows. They make up for their small size by producing milk with a higher protein and fat content than that of other breeds.

Montbéliarde: Another French Alpine breed, with distinctive red-and-white pied markings and short horns.

Montbéliardes are relatively new, and the name was first used in 1872 at a French agricultural competition. Their milk is especially well suited to cheesemaking, with high concentrations of kappa casein, which maximize milk yield. Although their yields are lower than Holsteins', the two are increasingly crossbred to introduce the Montbéliardes' longevity and fertility. They also have lower somatic cell counts and are less inclined to suffer from mastitis, a particularly valuable characteristic for large confinement dairy operations.

Tarentaise: The final in the triumvirate of French Alpine breeds, the Tarentaise originates in the area of Haute-Savoie and is a major contributor to the milk of Beaufort cheese. Tarentaise have adapted to the climbing necessary at 8,000 feet and are robust and well muscled as a result. This is a primary reason why they are also used for beef production. From a cheesemaking perspective, it is their production efficiency and easy calving that make them ideally suited to outdoor, pastured dairying.

Sheep

An average 150-pound ewe produces four and a half pounds of milk each day in a lactation cycle of five to seven months. Though sheep yield far less milk than cows and goats, their milk contains 10 percent less water and with its higher fat and protein content yields two and a half times as much cheese as that of its dairy sisters. Though the prevalence of dairy sheep in the United States has steadily increased in the past decade, there are far fewer sheep than goats, or certainly cows, in this country. This belies the long history of sheep as dairy animals that were, in fact, milked before cows. The international sheep dairy industry is concentrated in Europe, especially around the Mediterranean, though there are concentrations of sheep dairying in Eastern Europe and Israel. Sheep, like goats, are known for their ability to survive and thrive in marginal climates, as they do not require large fields of grass and are better able to climb comfortably in high, rocky terrain.

>*Dorset:* The Dorset is purportedly a mix between a Spanish and English sheep and can be found throughout England. It first arrived in the United States via Oregon in 1860. The sheep are all white and have strong, coarse wool. Dorset ewes weigh from 150 to 200 pounds, and rams weigh from 225 to 275 pounds. The ewes are good mothers and generous milkers and can give birth even when "out of season."

>*East Friesian:* The East Friesian originates from northern Germany and Holland. It is known for its white woolly body, bald face and legs, and "rat tail." The East Friesian produces the most milk per lactation of any sheep breed: 1,000 to 1,300 pints per lactation period. At 6 to 7 percent milk fat, East Friesians also boast the fattiest milk of any breed. The animals can grow to 150 pounds, and though they are excellent milkers, they do not thrive under mass herding conditions and cannot adapt well to particularly harsh environments.

>*Lacaune:* The signature dairy breed of southern France, Lacaunes are the milkers responsible for the famed blue Roquefort. Lacaunes give milk of high fat and protein content, though their production per lactation cycle tops out around 325 pounds. They do, however, thrive in groups, making them ideal for herding and dairying.

>*Trade Lake:* Although Mary and Dave Falk have not started an official Trade Lake registry for their unique sheep, their flock of three hundred constitutes a singular breed. After twenty generations of breeding, the Trade Lake genotype is set, and the flock has been bred for optimal grazing ability and hardy stock. The Trade Lake sheep

began with four maternal breeds: Dorset Horn, Romney Marsh, Clun Forest, and Finn, all of which thrive on pasture. In 1994 some East Friesian stock was introduced, but this was crossed out after three years, when the resulting lambs yielded lower-butterfat milk and did not perform as well on a grass diet. As of 2009, the percentage of East Friesian stock in the genome does not exceed 12 percent.

Goats

An average mature dairy goat female weighs 150 pounds and can produce six to eight pounds of milk per day. Goat milk is often made into lightly aged styles of cheese that have a fresh, tangy taste. Goats breed in the fall and give birth during the winter into early spring, from about January to March. Like cows, they lactate for about ten months. They go out to pasture at the start of spring, which is why some of the best spring and summer cheeses are fresh goat milk cheeses, with supremely grassy flavor characteristics. Goat's milk has no beta-carotene, as the animals convert beta-carotene into vitamin A, leaving their milk a pure, snowy white. Many breeds of goats best suited for milking originated in the Middle East and were brought to Europe by various nomadic groups such as the Saracens. The five major breeds of dairy goats in the United States are the Alpine, La-Mancha, Nubian, Saanen, and Toggenburg.

Alpine: Originating in the Alps, these goats were brought to the United States from France, where they had been selected over Swiss breeds for their uniformity, size, and milk production. These are hardy, adaptable animals that thrive in varying climates while maintaining good health and excellent production. Alpines range in color from pure white to shades of fawn, gray, brown, black, red, or buff to piebald or various combinations. The French Alpine is a larger and rangier goat and varies more in size than do the Swiss breeds. Mature females weigh around 135 pounds, males around 170 pounds.

LaMancha: LaMancha is a relatively new breed developed in California from Spanish Murciana origin with Swiss and Nubian crossings. They are known for excellent adaptability and good winter milk production. Their milk fat content is high, and they are able to produce milk even under stressful conditions. They have straight noses and short hair and appear to have no external ear. In fact, they may have either a "gopher" ear, with a maximum length of one inch (but generally nonexistent) with little or no cartilage; or an "elf" ear, with a maximum length of two inches and an upward- or downward-facing end.

Nubian: Anglo-Nubians were developed in England by crossing British goats with bucks of African and Indian origin. The Anglo-Nubian produces meat, milk, and hide. It is not a heavy milk producer but has a high average butterfat content of 4 to 5 percent. The Anglo-Nubian breeding season is much longer than that of Swiss breeds, so it is possible to produce milk year-round. Well suited to hot conditions, the Anglo-Nubian has been used in grading-up programs in many tropical countries to increase the milk and meat production of local breeds. The original goats imported from Africa, Arabia, and India were long-legged, hardy goats that bred well with British dairy goats. The Nubian is the most popular goat in the United States. It's also the cutest, with long, floppy ears.

Saanen: The largest breed of dairy goat, Saanen bucks can weigh more than 200 pounds, and both bucks and does are easily spotted for their bright white color. They are prolific milkers, and their milk can be as rich as Jersey cows'. The breed originated in Switzerland but is now found across Europe and the United States.

Toggenburg: The Toggenburg is a Swiss dairy goat from the Toggenburg Valley of Switzerland at Obertoggenburg.

It is credited with being the oldest known dairy goat breed. This breed is medium size, sturdy, vigorous, and alert in appearance. Slightly smaller than the other Alpine breeds, the does typically weigh 120 pounds. Toggenburgs perform best in cooler conditions. They are noted for their high milk production, which has an average fat content of 3.7 percent.

INDEX